Carnegie Commission on Higher Education
Sponsored Research Studies

THE UNIVERSITY AS AN ORGANIZATION
James A. Perkins (ed.)

NEW DIRECTIONS IN LEGAL EDUCATION
Herbert L. Packer and Thomas Ehrlich

WHERE COLLEGES ARE AND WHO ATTENDS:
EFFECTS OF ACCESSIBILITY ON COLLEGE
ATTENDANCE
*C. Arnold Anderson, Mary Jean Bowman,
and Vincent Tinto*

THE EMERGING TECHNOLOGY:
INSTRUCTIONAL USES OF THE COMPUTER
IN HIGHER EDUCATION
Roger E. Levien

A STATISTICAL PORTRAIT
OF HIGHER EDUCATION
Seymour E. Harris

THE HOME OF SCIENCE:
THE ROLE OF THE UNIVERSITY
Dael Wolfle

EDUCATION AND EVANGELISM:
A PROFILE OF PROTESTANT COLLEGES
C. Robert Pace

PROFESSIONAL EDUCATION:
SOME NEW DIRECTIONS
Edgar H. Schein

THE NONPROFIT RESEARCH INSTITUTE:
ITS ORIGIN, OPERATION, PROBLEMS, AND
PROSPECTS
Harold Orlans

THE INVISIBLE COLLEGES:
A PROFILE OF SMALL, PRIVATE COLLEGES
WITH LIMITED RESOURCES
Alexander W. Astin and Calvin B. T. Lee

AMERICAN HIGHER EDUCATION:
DIRECTIONS OLD AND NEW
Joseph Ben-David

A DEGREE AND WHAT ELSE?:
CORRELATES AND CONSEQUENCES OF A
COLLEGE EDUCATION
*Stephen B. Withey, Jo Anne Coble, Gerald
Gurin, John P. Robinson, Burkhard Strumpel,
Elizabeth Keogh Taylor, and Arthur C. Wolfe*

THE MULTICAMPUS UNIVERSITY:
A STUDY OF ACADEMIC GOVERNANCE
Eugene C. Lee and Frank M. Bowen

INSTITUTIONS IN TRANSITION:
A PROFILE OF CHANGE IN HIGHER
EDUCATION
(INCORPORATING THE 1970 STATISTICAL
REPORT)
Harold L. Hodgkinson

EFFICIENCY IN LIBERAL EDUCATION:
A STUDY OF COMPARATIVE INSTRUCTIONAL
COSTS FOR DIFFERENT WAYS OF ORGANIZ-
ING TEACHING-LEARNING IN A LIBERAL ARTS
COLLEGE
Howard R. Bowen and Gordon K. Douglass

CREDIT FOR COLLEGE:
PUBLIC POLICY FOR STUDENT LOANS
Robert W. Hartman

MODELS AND MAVERICKS:
A PROFILE OF PRIVATE LIBERAL ARTS
COLLEGES
Morris T. Keeton

BETWEEN TWO WORLDS:
A PROFILE OF NEGRO HIGHER EDUCATION
Frank Bowles and Frank A. DeCosta

MENTAL ABILITY AND HIGHER EDUCATIONAL
ATTAINMENT IN THE 20TH CENTURY
Paul Taubman and Terence Wales

AMERICAN COLLEGE AND UNIVERSITY
ENROLLMENT TRENDS IN 1971
Richard E. Peterson

MAY 1970:
THE CAMPUS AFTERMATH OF CAMBODIA
AND KENT STATE
Richard E. Peterson and John A. Bilorusky

PAPERS ON EFFICIENCY IN THE
MANAGEMENT OF HIGHER EDUCATION
Alexander M. Mood, Colin Bell, Lawrence
Bogard, Helen Brownlee, and Joseph McCloskey

The following reprints are available from the Carnegie Commission on Higher Education, 1947 Center Street, Berkeley, California 94704.

ACCELERATED PROGRAMS OF MEDICAL EDUCATION, by Mark S. Blumberg, reprinted from JOURNAL OF MEDICAL EDUCATION, vol. 46, no. 8, August 1971.*

SCIENTIFIC MANPOWER FOR 1970–1985, by Allan M. Cartter, reprinted from SCIENCE, vol. 172, no. 3979, pp. 132–140, April 9, 1971.

A NEW METHOD OF MEASURING STATES' HIGHER EDUCATION BURDEN, by Neil Timm, reprinted from THE JOURNAL OF HIGHER EDUCATION, vol. 42, no. 1, pp. 27–33, January 1971.*

REGENT WATCHING, by Earl F. Cheit, reprinted from AGB REPORTS, vol. 13, no. 6, pp. 4–13, March 1971.

COLLEGE GENERATIONS—FROM THE 1930s TO THE 1960s, by Seymour M. Lipset and Everett C. Ladd, Jr., reprinted from THE PUBLIC INTEREST, no. 25, Summer 1971.

AMERICAN SOCIAL SCIENTISTS AND THE GROWTH OF CAMPUS POLITICAL ACTIVISM IN THE 1960s, by Everett C. Ladd, Jr., and Seymour M. Lipset, reprinted from SOCIAL SCIENCES INFORMATION, vol. 10, no. 2, April 1971.

THE POLITICS OF AMERICAN POLITICAL SCIENTISTS, by Everett C. Ladd, Jr., and Seymour M. Lipset, reprinted from PS, vol. 4, no. 2, Spring 1971.*

THE DIVIDED PROFESSORIATE, by Seymour M. Lipset and Everett C. Ladd, Jr., reprinted from CHANGE, vol. 3, no. 3, pp. 54–60, May 1971.*

JEWISH ACADEMICS IN THE UNITED STATES: THEIR ACHIEVEMENTS, CULTURE AND POLITICS, by Seymour M. Lipset and Everett C. Ladd, Jr., reprinted from AMERICAN JEWISH YEAR BOOK, 1971.

THE UNHOLY ALLIANCE AGAINST THE CAMPUS, by Kenneth Keniston and Michael Lerner, reprinted from NEW YORK TIMES MAGAZINE, November 8, 1970 .

PRECARIOUS PROFESSORS: NEW PATTERNS OF REPRESENTATION, by Joseph W. Garbarino, reprinted from INDUSTRIAL RELATIONS, vol. 10, no. 1, February 1971.*

. . . AND WHAT PROFESSORS THINK: ABOUT STUDENT PROTEST AND MANNERS, MORALS, POLITICS, AND CHAOS ON THE CAMPUS, *by Seymour Martin Lipset and Everett C. Ladd, Jr., reprinted from* PSYCHOLOGY TODAY, *November 1970.**

DEMAND AND SUPPLY IN U.S. HIGHER EDUCATION: A PROGRESS REPORT, *by Roy Radner and Leonard S. Miller, reprinted from* AMERICAN ECONOMIC REVIEW, *May 1970.**

RESOURCES FOR HIGHER EDUCATION: AN ECONOMIST'S VIEW, *by Theodore W. Schultz, reprinted from* JOURNAL OF POLITICAL ECONOMY, *vol. 76, no. 3, University of Chicago, May/ June 1968.**

INDUSTRIAL RELATIONS AND UNIVERSITY RELATIONS, *by Clark Kerr, reprinted from* PROCEEDINGS OF THE 21ST ANNUAL WINTER MEETING OF THE INDUSTRIAL RELATIONS RESEARCH ASSOCIATION, *pp. 15–25.**

NEW CHALLENGES TO THE COLLEGE AND UNIVERSITY, *by Clark Kerr, reprinted from Kermit Gordon (ed.),* AGENDA FOR THE NATION, *The Brookings Institution, Washington, D.C., 1968.* *

PRESIDENTIAL DISCONTENT, *by Clark Kerr, reprinted from David C. Nichols (ed.),* PERSPECTIVES ON CAMPUS TENSIONS: PAPERS PREPARED FOR THE SPECIAL COMMITTEE ON CAMPUS TENSIONS, *American Council on Education, Washington, D.C., September 1970.**

STUDENT PROTEST—AN INSTITUTIONAL AND NATIONAL PROFILE, *by Harold Hodgkinson, reprinted from* THE RECORD, *vol. 71, no. 4, May 1970.**

WHAT'S BUGGING THE STUDENTS?, *by Kenneth Keniston, reprinted from* EDUCATIONAL RECORD, *American Council on Education, Washington, D.C., Spring 1970.**

THE POLITICS OF ACADEMIA, *by Seymour Martin Lipset, reprinted from David C. Nichols (ed.),* PERSPECTIVES ON CAMPUS TENSIONS: PAPERS PREPARED FOR THE SPECIAL COMMITTEE ON CAMPUS TENSIONS, *American Council on Education, Washington, D.C., September 1970.**

INTERNATIONAL PROGRAMS OF U.S. COLLEGES AND UNIVERSITIES: PRIORITIES FOR THE SEVENTIES, *by James A. Perkins, reprinted by permission of the International Council for Educational Development, Occasional Paper no. 1, July 1971.*

FACULTY UNIONISM: FROM THEORY TO PRACTICE, *by Joseph W. Garbarino, reprinted from* INDUSTRIAL RELATIONS, *vol. 11, no. 1, pp. 1–17, February 1972.*

MORE FOR LESS: HIGHER EDUCATION'S NEW PRIORITY, *by Virginia B. Smith, reprinted from* UNIVERSAL HIGHER EDUCATION: COSTS AND BENEFITS, *American Council on Education, Washington, D.C., 1971.*

ACADEMIA AND POLITICS IN AMERICA, by Seymour M. Lipset, reprinted from Thomas J. Nossiter (ed.), IMAGINATION AND PRECISION IN THE SOCIAL SCIENCES, pp. 211–289, Faber and Faber, London, 1972.

POLITICS OF ACADEMIC NATURAL SCIENTISTS AND ENGINEERS, by Everett C. Ladd, Jr., and Seymour M. Lipset, reprinted from SCIENCE, vol. 176, no. 4039, pp. 1091–1100, June 9, 1972.

THE INTELLECTUAL AS CRITIC AND REBEL: WITH SPECIAL REFERENCE TO THE UNITED STATES AND THE SOVIET UNION, by Seymour M. Lipset and Richard B. Dobson, reprinted from DAEDALUS, vol. 101, no. 3, pp. 137–198, Summer 1972.

*The Commission's stock of this reprint has been exhausted.

The University as an Organization

The University as an Organization

edited by James A. Perkins

Chairman of the Board
International Council for
Educational Development

A Report for
The Carnegie Commission on Higher Education

MC GRAW HILL BOOK COMPANY

New York   St. Louis   San Francisco   Düsseldorf
London   Sydney   Toronto   Mexico   Panama
Johannesburg   Kuala Lumpur   Montreal
New Delhi   Rio de Janeiro   Singapore

The Carnegie Commission on Higher Education,
1947 Center Street, Berkeley, California 94704,
has sponsored preparation of this report as a
part of a continuing effort to obtain and present
significant information for public discussion.
The views expressed are those of the authors.

Library of Congress Cataloging in Publication Data
Perkins, James Alfred, date
The university as an organization.

A report for the Carnegie Commission on Higher
Education.
Includes bibliographical references.
1.   Universities and colleges—Administration.
2.   Management.   I.   Carnegie Commission on Higher
Education.   II.   Title
LB2341.P43   378.73   72-8336
ISBN 0-07-010053-5

   3456789MAMM798765

Contents

xi

Contributors

James A. Perkins
Chairman of the Board
International Council for
Educational Development

E. D. Duryea
Professor, Department of Higher
Education
State University of New York at
Buffalo

John D. Millett
Vice-President and Director
Management Division
Academy for Educational
Development

Irwin T. Sanders
Chairman
Department of Sociology
Boston University

Barbara B. Burn
Director of International Programs
University of Massachusetts,
Amherst

Ralph M. Besse
Partner
Squire, Sanders, & Dempsey,
Attorneys, Cleveland

Stephen K. Bailey
Chairman, Policy Institute
Syracuse University Research
Corporation

W. McNeil Lowry
Vice-President
Division of Humanities and the
Arts
The Ford Foundation

John J. Corson
Chairman
Fry Consultants, Inc.

Lyman A. Glenny
Director
Center for Research and
Development in Higher
Education
University of California, Berkeley

Thomas K. Dalglish
Postgraduate Researcher
Center for Research and
Development in Higher
Education
University of California, Berkeley

Samuel B. Gould
Chancellor Emeritus, State
University of New York
President, Institute for Educational
Development

Morton A. Rauh
Vice-President Emeritus
Antioch College

Foreword

One of the best ways to appreciate the uniqueness of American universities as organizations is to compare them with other kinds of organizations and institutions. By understanding how universities are different from other enterprises—by understanding what they are *not*—we sharpen our comprehension of what they actually are. The contributions to this multiperspective analysis of university organizations effectively promote that kind of understanding.

As the various chapters show, it is easy to be misled by superficial similarities and shared characteristics. Because universities, like many other kinds of institutions, require prudent management to conserve limited resources, it might be concluded that they should be operated according to business models. Because universities must respond to large and diffuse constituencies, one might suppose that governmental bureaus might be trustworthy models. Because they promote investigation and scholarship, they share missions of foundations. Beyond the similarities, however, there are significant differences. A few of the universities' unique characteristics particularly worth noting are:

1 They are unique in the way that they combine basic missions—instruction and the advancement of scholarly exploration—with an imposing array of other services and activities required by our society.

2 They are organizationally unique because no one has absolute authority within the organization. Presidents and faculty members operate in overlapping spheres of power and influence. New spheres of influence—overlapping the others—are now being occupied by students.

3 Ultimate authority for public and private institutions alike resides in governing boards whose membership comes from society at large or represents some other externally oriented constituency.

4 Universities tend to encompass for many of their members not only the work-associated aspects of their lives but the social and recreational aspects of their lives as well.

5 The outputs of universities are largely unmeasurable—their effectiveness cannot be assessed easily.

6 Although, legally, they are created by society, they stand quite apart from society in many ways. They are shielded to a considerable extent from external interference with the teaching and learning processes that take place within them; they are withdrawn from society by a tradition—that may be faltering—of disengagement from social and political activism.

By understanding such unique characteristics of universities as organizations, one can see why the merits of often-heard proposals that universities should adopt the practices and procedures characteristic of institutions that existed in an earlier time, in other lands, and for other missions are open to question. While some of the strategies and methods of business might be employed by universities with some benefit, the two enterprises respond to different motivations and reward systems. Although both universities and government bureaus desire autonomy—and run similar risks in its abuse—they are accountable to different kinds of authority and constituencies for the use of that autonomy. Although universities can borrow techniques and devices from other types of organizations, they can rarely do so without significant alteration. And there is no reliable model for university organization that surpasses the model set by the best universities themselves. Universities are clearly a genus apart.

As the authors of the various chapters in this volume demonstrate, universities are not only unique as a class of organizations but have within them distinctive subclasses. The American university is outlined here as unique not only as a result of discontinuities and branching in the mainline history of universities generally during the many centuries of their existence, but also as a result of the needs and aspirations of the people of a particular nation. Then, within American universities, there is still further diversity. While the similarities of individual universities compared with one another are numerous and obvious, careful investigation soon makes clear that differences also exist, and that they are often sufficiently profound to prevent easy transference of management techniques and organizational structures from one university institution to another. The reality is very complex.

The Carnegie Commission on Higher Education is grateful to all the authors of the chapters in this book for their valuable analyses and observations. For the planning and editing of the studies, we were very fortunate to enlist the talents and experience of James A. Perkins. As a former foundation executive, government official, and university president with wide acquaintances with business and education leaders throughout the world, he has firsthand knowledge of all the subjects touched upon in this most interesting book.

Clark Kerr
Chairman
Carnegie Commission
on Higher Education

December 1972

Introduction

The purpose of this volume is to bring fresh perspectives to a topic that may already be suffering from overkill. Yet, despite all that has been written about the university in recent years, few understand the nature and purposes of its organization. For this reason, among others, we chose to approach the study of the organization of the university obliquely, to expose facets of its structure from a variety of vantage points. Each section and each chapter of this book, therefore, comes at the topic from a different angle.

First, in Part 1, we trace the historical evolution of the university and its relationship with society and government. A contrasting and perhaps unique treatment of the topic is introduced in Part 2 of the book: comparisons of the university with alternative forms of organization in the business corporation, the government bureau, and the large foundation. Part 3 deals with the internal structure of the university, with particular attention to the board of trustees. Finally, in Part 4 we briefly examine some institutional developments that may be in store for the university.

Throughout we have tried to hold the line of discussion to the university as an institution rather than as a functioning organism, though obviously these subjects are ultimately inseparable. We have also tried our best to stay away from the intriguing topics of university politics and governance, in the hope that by restricting the breadth of our inquiry we might increase its depth. Finally, with the exception of one chapter dealing with universities abroad, the book focuses primarily on university organization in the United States.

These chapters have been written by those thoroughly experienced in university affairs. The list of authors includes persons from the spheres of government, business, university administration, faculty, and educational systems. No attempt was made to reduce these chapters to an identical mold, for to have done so might have been at the cost of some of the free-swinging creativity which, we think, readers may identify as the style of this particular work.

We do not pretend that this volume is the last word—or even the next to last word—on university organization. We hope that, at the least, it will provide new insights and remove some of the blocks to an understanding of the university.

I am indebted to the associate editors of this volume, Irwin T. Sanders and Barbara Baird Israel, and to the staff of the International Council for Educational Development for their help in preparing the manuscript—particularly Joan Mowery, Margie Sifuentes, and Dianne Ramsteck. And finally, I must express my deep gratitude to the Carnegie Commission on Higher Education for making this volume possible.

James A. Perkins

*The University
as an Organization*

Part One
Perspectives

1. Organization and Functions of the University

by James A. Perkins

The organization of the university is usually described in simple terms: a board of trustees, which receives a charter from the state, appoints a president to administer, and approves a faculty to teach and to select the students to learn. The board, the faculty, the administration, and the students together make up the academic community which embraces a familiar triumvirate of functions — teaching, research, and public service.

But such simplicity is deceptive. Organizationally the university is, in fact, one of the most complex structures in modern society; it is also increasingly archaic. It is complex because its formal structure does not describe either actual power or responsibilities; it is archaic because the functions it must perform are not and cannot be discharged through the formal structure provided in its charter.

The predicament of university organization has arisen in part because of its conflicting missions. Further, the university is asked not only to perform conflicting missions but also to perform them within the framework of an organizational design appropriate to its earliest mission — that of teaching or the transmission of knowledge. The newer functions of research, public service and, most recently, the achievement of an ideal democratic community within the university have organizational requirements that are significantly different from those necessary for teaching.

The evolution of university structures is treated in depth in later chapters, but a brief look at the origins of the university as a teaching institution is in order.

THE MISSION OF TEACHING In the Middle Ages, as the search for knowledge moved from the monastery and church to secular institutions, the university came into its own. The twelfth and thirteenth centuries saw the founding

3

of one after another of the most illustrious centers of learning—
Paris, Cambridge, Oxford, Bologna, and Salamanca among them.
Designed as places for the convenient interaction of master and
scholar, these teaching institutions generated the main features of
the university as we know it today.

From the beginning it was recognized that the university must
establish a delicate balance of independence and dependence with
the society, secular or religious, that created it. The need for independence was grounded on the demonstrable need to examine
orthodoxies if the learning process was not to be strangled by con-
striction of the field of inquiry. At the same time it was recognized
that church and state had fundamental interests in the university—
mainly the training of new elites—that demanded a loose monitoring of the whole exercise.

This early need to establish quasi independence took various
institutional forms: in Bologna, a union of students; in Paris, a
union of professors; and many centuries later, lay boards of trustees
or regents. Sometimes the guarantee of independence was a hollow
one. But generally, it was early recognized that autonomy required
the support of institutional arrangements, and these arrangements
became the cardinal piece in the organizational design.

Whatever the ruling body, it needed an agent or administrator.
In the early university there was little to administer. A presiding
officer could be recruited from the faculty on a rotating basis and
he became the rector or chancellor, while the minor bookkeeping
could be handled by a clerk. To paraphrase an observation on other
offices, it could be said that the rector reigned but did not rule,
the king's or bishop's agent ruled but did not reign, while the clerk
neither ruled nor reigned.

As the numbers of students increased, as the university center
or campus became established as a permanent fixture, as endowments had to be invested and property taken care of, the tasks of
administration and consequently the burdens of administrators
increased. Sometimes the circumstances were disguised by administrators buried in church headquarters or ministries of education. But visible or invisible, the requirements of administration
grew, while the institutions of administration tried to keep pace.
They never quite did—nor have they yet.

Just as the growth of the apparatus of the university led to a
growth of administration, so, too, the growth of faculty and curric-

ulum led to faculty organization and cohesion. While money and property became the province of the administration, courses and degrees became the responsibility of the faculty. The result was two kinds of de facto organization within the university, both controlled by the state or a body chartered by the state. When property, funds, libraries, and endowments became critical features of the university, faculty and administrative assignments became closely related. As long as the central and almost exclusive mission was teaching, the need for administration was so slight that conflict between faculty and administration rarely arose.

Governing authority, faculty, and administration — all appeared in primitive form in the earliest universities. The organization of studies underwent a similar development. The growth of knowledge required division of material. Subject matter was originally broken into the trivium — grammar, logic, and rhetoric — and the quadrivium — arithmetic, music, geometry, and astronomy. From these simple beginnings, subject matter divided and subdivided as specialization became the order of the day, with a consequent proliferation of lectures and courses. These, in turn, required organizations competent to contain and define their scope; thus colleges and departments arose as the administrative subdivisions necessary to take care of the new academic subdivisions.

The necessity to present knowledge in logical sequence led to progressive sets of lectures, and these required an established meeting place where teacher and student could come together over an extended period of time. Hence the origin of the classroom, with courses of study and series of lectures as the central activities around which a simple administrative apparatus was built.

In the medieval university, learning was not, however, confined to the classroom. Close connections between teacher and student were thought to be essential to the learning enterprise; the desire to reinforce these led to the establishment of residences where living and learning went hand in hand. Though of less importance on the Continent,[1] the residential college became the pivot of university instruction at Oxford and Cambridge and is still a basic part of the British university system. These forerunners of our

---

[1] It is interesting to speculate on the cause of this difference in the development of collegiate structure. It may well have been the fact that Oxford and Cambridge were in small towns while Paris, Bologna, and Salamanca were in established cities.

present-day residential colleges, like other features of the medieval institution, had as their raison d'être the promotion of the teaching-learning enterprise.

By the opening of the sixteenth century, the general structure of the university as a teaching institution had been substantially established, including the main organizational features that are still in evidence today. To reiterate, these structures were developed in response to the prime function of teaching. In order to deal with a body of expanding knowledge, the teaching enterprise required continuity, a fixed meeting place, close connections between master and scholar, independence from church and state, and a minimal administrative apparatus that could support these needs. At this point we turn to the beginnings of organizational dislocation in the evolution of the university.

THE MISSION OF RESEARCH
One of the roots of the university's organizational difficulties today is the conflict arising from its assumption, primarily during the nineteenth century, of a new mission—research.

Before the nineteenth century, a primary rationale for scholarship or research was its impact on teaching. Private study, reflection, and writing were almost always viewed as vital ingredients in preparing the teacher for his job—in keeping his mind sharp, his lectures fresh, his students intellectually alert. Scholarly effort outside the classroom was therefore considered a necessary adjunct to teaching. During all these centuries, however, such scholarship was regarded as an individual pursuit rather than an institutional one. Consequently, the university made only minimal provisions for its support. This was all to change. Gradually, scholarly attention turned from the transmission of known truths to a search for new knowledge. This shift in the scholar's concerns gave rise to an enterprise that followed its own dynamic laws of growth. By the end of the nineteenth century it was clear that research had become an end in itself, regardless of its impact on teaching. It was also clear that the research mission had gained equal footing with the teaching mission in the university. But in the process organizational problems of great complexity arose. It was still assumed (it is even today by some) that teaching and research were closely connected and that consequently their organizational requirements could be easily accommodated. But as research became an end in itself, its connection to teaching eroded.

Today teaching and research are missions with distinctive styles and different, often contradictory, requirements for organizational structure. The differences are important. In research, ideas become more important than people, the laboratory and the library more important than the faculty meeting, and external funding more important than the internal budget allocation. The judgment of peers in one's field of specialization, rather than the progress of the student, becomes the critical measure of performance.

The ascendance of research also brought about a different view of undergraduate and graduate instruction. To a research man, the more mature student is the more useful. A freshman in an introductory course is not likely to interest the research professor working on newly discovered papers about gunpowder factories in Paris in the early eighteenth century. To such a professor the student becomes interesting as he involves himself either in learning the techniques of scholarly research or in working as an assistant to the professor. For these purposes, the senior is better than the freshman, the graduate student better than the senior, the post-doctoral student better than all those still laboring for degrees.

The teacher-student relationship was not the only one to be affected by the new emphasis on research: equally transformed was the relationship between members of the faculty.

Scholarship is, generally speaking, an individual enterprise, and even large-scale research activity that involves a number of persons usually centers around the direction of one person. The working associations of the scholar are therefore with assistants and co-workers on his research project rather than with faculty who happen to teach in the same department or at the same institution. Nor is the scholar dependent on the judgments of his institutional colleagues concerning his research. Imagine a distinguished professor submitting a draft manuscript to a departmental meeting for criticism! Rather, he presents his work to those in his field who can pass competent judgment, and these specialists are for the most part scattered over the academic landscape.

As a consequence of the research scholar's changing horizons, the traditional instruments for conducting university business—the departmental meeting and the faculty assembly—have been seriously undermined. The research professor now goes to faculty meetings only in times of university crisis, and he goes to departmental meetings primarily to ensure that he gets a teaching schedule that does not interfere with his research activity. These former focal points of faculty unity must now operate with members pursuing disparate goals.

New Administrative Structures

More important than the negative effects it has had on existing structures is the fact that the research enterprise has produced significant organizational requirements of its own.

When libraries and laboratories, the first needs of the researcher, were relatively small and primitive, they could operate under the existing administrative structure. As their size and expense grew, and as the staff to man them became a substantial segment of the university community, centralized management became a necessity. Yet the notion that these adjuncts of research require completely different skills from those necessary in a teaching enterprise, a different style of management, and different controls has gained only grudging acceptance. Even today, universities with very large libraries and complex laboratories operate on the assumption that these can be maintained and managed by members of the faculty, either individually or collectively.

The push of technology and the interest of government and other outside agencies vastly accelerated the research enterprise. In earlier days, time off was considered the essential, and sometimes the sole, prerequisite to scholarship—and this the university could provide in the sabbatical year and the three-month summer vacation. But as the search for knowledge broadened and deepened, travel and therefore travel funds, laboratories and therefore equipment funds, assistants and therefore funds for assistants—all these and more became necessary to the research enterprise. And these the university could provide in only limited amounts. Thus the research scholar had to look elsewhere, to the associations or committees that work closely with money-dispensing agencies—foundations, industry, and government. As we have already noted, the network of associations necessary to the scholar's research activities is structured by the problem, not the institution.

As the dimensions of research activity increased, the growth of new structure outside the formal and traditional university patterns was inevitable. First, the research entrepreneur needs protection from distractions—from, for example, a heavy schedule of undergraduate instruction. The research effort also requires administrative devices that can cut across departmental and even collegiate levels to bring together those interested in similar problems. Finally, the research enterprise requires, or at least seems to require, its own budget and the freedom to manage, independently, funds received from outside agencies. The answer to these needs has come in the form of institutes, agencies, and councils — all of which have proliferated in recent years.

These new structures have, for the most part, escaped the direct control of departments and collegiate faculties. They deal directly with top university administration for space and personnel and with outside sources for funds and, when necessary, political backing. Clearly the department could have only a minimal role in activities organized on such a scale. It might intervene if it believed the research enterprise would take too many of its key people away from the campus on research activity elsewhere. But when there has been conflict over research activities between a department and its members, the traditional departmental apparatus has been fairly useless in resolving it; the final decisions, therefore, have often escalated up to the office of the president.

Just as the departmental apparatus is hobbled in dealing with research activities, so too is the university as a whole limited when it must digest decisions on research programs and funding that have been worked out on a regional or national scale, outside the university. As yet the university has made no significant organizational changes to deal with these kinds of decisions.[2]

At best it has tried to minimize damage to teaching programs and campus design. At worst it has, without participating in the basic decision itself, accepted decisions that adversely affect its activities. This disjunction between campus organization and national or supracampus programming decisions has been one of the forces leading away from the ideas of individual autonomous campuses and toward that of systems of institutions at state, regional, or national levels. Multicampus systems can deal much more effectively than can individual institutions with large-scale programs: systems can allocate resources between campuses, make decisions about where high-cost specialities can best be located, and undertake the large-scale planning required for new facilities.

---

[2] Any university president who has ever faced the question of accepting a $10 million synchrotron when his campus has been designated as the appropriate site for such a major project, and when both capital and operating costs are guaranteed for years to come, can know how little use there is in the existing administrative apparatus. Even though such a matter has campuswide implications, it would rarely be raised, let alone discussed, at a campuswide faculty meeting.

In summary, the growth of research activities has both undermined traditional organizational structures, such as the department, and created new structures that are frequently in competition with existing ones. The traditional pattern of organization that we have inherited from the Middle Ages—faculty-oriented with administration providing the minimal coordination necessary to keep faculty in some kind of marching order—no longer answers the complex needs of the modern university. And the lack of any overall organizational doctrine to embrace both the teaching and research functions has seriously weakened the organizational spine of the university. Administrative inventions to remedy this are still in their infancy.

THE MISSION OF SERVICE TO SOCIETY The assumption of a third large function—that of public service— has added one more dimension to the university's organizational agony. For if the traditional structure is largely irrelevant to the research function, it is antithetical to servicing the needs of society.

In the general sense, of course, the university has always provided a service to society by its production of scholars, teachers, and presumably a more educated citizenry. In the United States, however, particularly since the beginnings of land-grant colleges a century ago, institutions of higher education have been called upon to perform more direct service to society. The agricultural programs of the land-grant colleges, which blended teaching, research, and service to the agricultural community, are often cited as examples of how successfully the university can perform in relation to the private entrepreneur and state and federal governments. But the pressures on the university today to perform public service are more complex and divisive.

There are two complications in the university's assumption of this function. First, public service requires institutionwide commitment. But such commitment is difficult to arrive at given the decentralized structure of the university. Moreover, neither teaching nor scholarship operates happily or effectively when it must respond to a commitment made by the institution as a whole.

A vivid illustration of the difficulties may be seen in the university's acceptance of government-sponsored research projects in the fifties and sixties. The institution's commitment to such projects was felt, in the recent years of anguish over United States government policies, to be unsupportable by many in the university community. (Obviously, when there is little agreement in society as a whole about its purposes and priorities, the university's dilemma in undertaking public service is further complicated.) But the organizational problem is clearly that neither the department nor the research institute is equipped to deal with public service activities; faculty are no longer running the show. The contractual commitment of the university to public service can be entered into only by the administration—generally by the president. Yet the success of such projects requires faculty support and, at the least, the tacit acceptance of such commitment by the rest of the university community.

The second serious problem is the contradiction between being of service to the public and maintaining the autonomy of the institution (including academic freedom for the individual professor). Serving the public involves public judgment about how well the service is performed. But the imposition of standards set outside the university goes counter to the concept of the university as an autonomous institution that sets its own standards, free from societal pressure. Similarly, this imposition is contrary to the tradition of the autonomy of the faculty member within the classroom.

With respect to the teaching process, society has come to accept the idea that it should provide funds but permit the university to determine how those funds are used. In general, the same is true of the public's attitude toward research. In both cases, the public does not feel confident to pass judgment, not only because the content is beyond its capacity but also because measurements of success are so difficult to establish. But with respect to public service, measurable, practical results are expected. While the test of utility with respect to teaching is postponable and with respect to research a matter of faith, when public service is undertaken, the university is expected to produce constructive guidance for society. The difference in these expectations produces a different view about the relationship between the university providing the service and the society that both asks and pays for the service.

To the extent that university performance is measured by nonuniversity institutions, its autonomy is compromised. Of course government—particularly state government—has always had the right, and indeed has acted on the right, to measure the success of the institutions it supports. State governments have often advanced or withheld funds based upon such judgments, although in most cases this has happened to individual programs and projects rather than to institutions as a whole. It would be easy to exaggerate the extent to which autonomy has been compromised by the public service function, but the university has entered into a partnership with society that calls for different premises from those that supported the teaching and research functions.

THE MISSION OF CREATING AN IDEAL DEMOCRATIC COMMUNITY

In recent years a fourth function has been added to those of teaching, research, and public service—namely, that of achieving an ideal democratic community within the institution. This new mission stems from the notion that the policies of the universities must conform to the social aspirations of its members and that its very style and organization must conform to the idea of a democratic society. Legitimate authority, according to this view, does not and cannot come from trustees as corporate owners. It can come only from the expressed wishes of the constituent members of the campus—faculty, students, and staff. Thus, decisions made by officials without community participation may be legally correct but democratically corrupt.

To the extent that the university has assumed this new mission, drastic changes have been required in its overall functioning and therefore in its organic structure. The student is demanding a say in the process by which decisions are made within the university, all the way from the departmental level up to the president's office. The academic process is now viewed as one in which teacher and learner are equally involved, both in the selection of topics and in the manner in which those topics can be taught. As students insist on the right to participate at the point where decisions are made about the content of their instruction, they are focusing on the department. So now the departmental meeting, which was designed for decisions about teaching, and which became irrelevant for the research function and even destructive for the public service function, has come full circle and is the embarrassed object of unexpected student attention.

The notion of an ideal democratic community runs afoul of any number of traditional concepts of university organization. Among these are the idea of faculty as a body whose independence, collectively and individually, is guaranteed by academic freedom; and the idea that the chief executive officer, the president, may properly be appointed by a body not elected by the local community.

It is hardly surprising in this context that universitywide structures have begun to emerge in which faculty, students, and administration all participate. Some even include members of boards of trustees. While these organizations have been truly responsive to the concept of the ideal democratic community, they clearly complicate the business of university management. And, although most of them were set up as advisory bodies, many are beginning to acquire large powers.

The significance of these new structures is, of course, that they in fact do what they were designed to do—cut across the traditional organizational forms that handle the other three major functions of the university—teaching, research, and public service. The emergence of a universitywide organization with representation from its constituent parts has begun to raise important questions about where power really resides. Have the department and college faculties lost out to the universitywide structure? In its preoccupation with gaining the capacity to make legitimate decisions, has the community lost the capacity to make decisions at all?

The universitywide organization has also changed the role and mission of the president and very probably will change the way in which he is elected. If the organization is a response to the idea of an ideal democratic community, then the president must be elected by such an organization or at least the constituency that it represents. Although the formal power to appoint the president resides in most instances in a board of trustees, it may be difficult for the trustees to resist the claim of a nominee promoted by the universitywide body, particularly if that body has representation from the trustees on it.

Finally there is the impact on the idea of the board of trustees itself. As later chapters will be devoted exclusively to this topic,[3] it is relevant at this point to note only that as the board of trustees has moved from an external body representing the public interest to an internal coordinating body with representation from faculty and students, conflict with a universitywide body with somewhat similar representation is bound to arise.

CONCLUSIONS Perhaps a case has now been made to suggest that a new look at university organization is overdue. New functions have been assumed that have conflicting organizational requirements. These

[3] See Chaps. 11, 12, and 13.

the university has tried to handle within an organizational structure designed essentially for the promotion of instruction.

Before recommendations for organizational change can be made, we must back up several steps and look at the university from different perspectives. The chapters in this book are designed and written for this purpose. But the reader must remember that we are preoccupied not with the pathology of the university but rather with fresh insight that may lead to useful prescription.

2. Evolution of University Organization

by E. D. Duryea

It has become customary in histories of American higher education to begin with a description of medieval origins. In general, there is good basis for looking back to those distant and turbulent days. The idea of a university itself as a formal, organized institution is a medieval innovation, which contrasts to the Greek schools and to the rudimentary organizational precedents in ancient Alexandria and in the Byzantine and Arabian cultures. The medieval universities instituted the use of many contemporary titles such as *dean, provost, rector,* and *proctor.* They initiated the idea of formal courses and of the curriculum leading to the baccalaureate and the master's and doctor's degrees. Our commencements are graced annually by the color and distinction of medieval garb. Fascinating anecdotes confirm that student violence has early precedents.

The point is, of course, that complex institutions such as universities do not appear full-blown at a particular point in time. They evolve through that complicated process by which men and cultures mingle over a history fraught with traditions and happenstance. Contemporary Western culture itself originated in the centuries that followed the "dark ages," and the university has served as one of the major institutions by which this culture has been transmitted over the years.

Within this context, certain aspects of the university's organization do have some important medieval precedents. Other aspects of its organization reflect the more direct influence of the English colleges of the sixteenth and seventeenth centuries. A history of American colleges and universities must be written also with due recognition of that educational revolution which took place in this country during the four decades following the Civil War. As Laurence R. Veysey (1965, p. 2) comments in his detailed interpretation of that era, "The American university of 1900 was all but unrecognizable in comparison to the colleges of 1860." The contemporary system of higher education dominated by the large, multifunctional university stands as a heritage of those years. Organizationally as well as educationally, its form and function were set by the time of the First World War. Its history during this century is primarily a chronicle of expansion and consolidation.

Reflecting these major historical influences, the following analysis examines the evolution of university organization from three major perspectives. The first deals with (1) the origins and use of the corporate form by which authority was granted to lay governing boards and (2) how their legal control has been modified by alumni and faculty influences that go back well into the nineteenth century. The second views the origins and expansion of the organizational structure of universities, an evolution epitomized by the comment that the old-time college president has all but disappeared behind a bureaucracy of academic and administrative offices and councils. In this sense the transition from the small, struggling colleges of the past to the large multiversity with its complex administration is first of all the history of the presidency. The third views the twentieth-century period of organizational expansion and consolidation. A concluding section identifies very briefly the evidences of dysfunction that have emerged in recent years.

CORPORATE ORIGINS By the twelfth century in Europe the church not only reigned supreme as a ruler of man's conscience but also exercised great temporal power over his mundane affairs. Rare were the individuals who would, when threatened with excommunication, choose to face an uncertain future in the hereafter. As the arbitrator of an ultimate destiny which included the possibility so vividly described in Dante's *Inferno* and as the only effective organization for all Europe, the church entered into the total life of the culture. But early in the thirteenth century, the more astute popes began to feel the rumblings of a shift of temporal power to political states and kings. The remote threat of hell began to give way to the more tangible thrust of the sword. As a result, the church hierarchy moved to bring its scattered organizations—religious orders, cathedral chapters, and universities—under more effective papal control. To this end, canon lawyers looked back to Roman law and its concept of corporations as fictitious legal entities. Their learned investigations led to a number of papal statements in the first decades of the thirteenth century and in 1243 to the famous bull or

proclamation of Pope Innocent IV. The central idea in the Innocen-
tean doctrine was that each cathedral chapter, collegiate church,
religious fraternity, and university constituted a *Universitas,* i.e.,
a free corporation. Its corporate personality, however, was not
something natural in the sense of a social reality but rather "an
artificial notion invented by the sovereign for convenience of legal
reasoning," existent only in the contemplation of law. This was
a theoretical conception but nonetheless a very real one, since the
corporation thereby derived its right to exist from an external
authority and not from the intrinsic fact of its being (Brody, 1935,
pp. 3–4).

The efforts of the papacy, the need of universities for protection
against the immediate threats to their freedom from local bishops
and townspeople, and the fact that the kings also intruded on their
sovereignty—all these supported the corporate idea. The theory
of corporate existence meant ultimately the end of the guild system
and, for universities, of the idea of an independent association of
scholars. The history of this development is complex and detailed,
certainly beyond the scope of this particular analysis. It is sufficient
to note that Emperor Frederick II rivaled Pope Gregory IX during
the later years of the thirteenth century in the issuance of grants of
authorization to universities, which in turn did not hesitate to
strengthen their own hand by playing off pope against king (Rashdall, 1936, vol. 1, pp. 8–9). As national states gained dominance,
however, universities ultimately had to look solely to kings for their
charters, and what the king gave the king could take away.

The concept of corporations which served as precedent for the
early colleges in this country matured in England during the fifteenth and sixteenth centuries. It provided an effective legal means
by which the king and later parliament could delegate in an orderly
way authority for designated activities, not only to universities but
to municipalities, trading companies, charitable establishments,
and various other institutions. Charters provided for perpetual
succession and the freedom for corporate bodies to set up and maintain the rules and regulations which in effect constituted internal
or private governments. They also carried the right of supervision
and visitation by representatives of the state. They established, in
addition, legal protections associated with the rights of individuals
in the sense that the corporation existed as an artificial or juristic
individual. This conception of governmental grant of authority
served also as the basis for the charters and statutes of the colleges

of the English universities, which in general included provisions for external visitors or overseers, a head elected by the teaching staff or fellows, and a formal body constituted of these fellows which "exercised the legislative powers" (Davis, 1961, pp. 303–305).

The influence of this English college model was evident in the founding of the first two colonial colleges, Harvard (1636) and William and Mary (1693). For example, the language of the 1650 charter for Harvard is very similar to that of the royal charters for the colleges of Oxford and Cambridge (Morison, 1935, p. 10). Both these institutions were formed with governing councils composed of internal members (the presidents and teaching fellows) in tandem with external supervising boards that held final approval powers and the right of visitation.[1]

Another medieval precedent, however, came to the colonies with the early settlers and caused a significant modification of the English practice. In place of immediate control of the colleges by the teachers or professors, the practice evolved of granting complete corporate power to governing boards composed of external members. The origins of the use of external control lie in the medieval universities of northern Italy. Initially guilds of students who hired their professors, universities proved good for local business. The Italian towns competed for their presence in part by subsidizing salaries of outstanding teachers. The inexorable result was a blunting of student economic power and the establishment of municipal committees, in effect the first lay governing boards, to guard their financial interests (Rashdall, 1936, vol. 2, p. 59). Again, the detailing of the history of this tradition goes beyond the scope of this chapter. The lay board of control proved an appropriate mechanism for the direction of advanced education under the Calvinists at Geneva in the early sixteenth century, at the

---

[1] These arrangements for the College of William and Mary were stated in a manner that led to conflicts between the two boards during its early years, although essentially they remained in effect until it became a state institution shortly after 1900. At Harvard, however, practice nullified the apparent intent of the 1650 charter, so that by the eighteenth century the immediate governing council (the Corporation) had passed into the hands of external members. The practice was disputed from time to time by tutors until an 1825 vote of the Overseers finally and formally stated that "the resident instructors of Harvard University" did not have any exclusive right to be chosen members of the Corporation (Quincy, 1860, vol. 2, p. 324).

Dutch University of Leyden a few years later, at the Scottish universities of that same era, and finally at the Protestant Trinity College in Dublin. It was in part from these Dutch, Scottish, and Irish sources that the concept of lay boards came to the colonies (Cowley, 1964; 1971).

The English pattern of internal control by academics which was followed by Harvard and William and Mary did not set the precedent for university government in this country. That distinction fell to Yale College, established in 1701. Whether because of direct influences from the European Calvinistic practices noted above or simply because of parallel sectarian desires to maintain religious orthodoxy, the founders of Yale petitioned for a single nonacademic board of control. As a consequence, the colonial legislature of Connecticut granted authority to a board of "Trustees, Partners, or Undertakers" to "erect a collegiate school." Renamed in the revised 1745 charters as the "President and Fellows of Yale College," it continued as an external board with the right of self-perpetuation and with final control of the affairs of the institution (*The Yale Corporation,* 1952; see also Brody, 1935, Ch. 1).

Meanwhile, yet another deviation from English precedents also had begun to emerge. The right of the king and parliament to grant a charter carried with it an equal right to withdraw this charter. In fact, during the times of religious conflict in England this did occur, as first a Protestant and then a Catholic sovereign reconstituted the organization of the English universities in terms of religious biases. In the eighteenth century a new philosophy, that formalized by John Locke, gained acceptance, especially in the American colonies so strongly committed to a separation of church and state. This view stressed the nature of government as a compact among individuals, with sovereignty held by the people. In these terms of reference, having legal status as a person in law, although a fictitious or juridical person, corporations gained protection from legislative intrusions associated with the rights of individuals. Early in the nineteenth century court decisions began to interpret charters as contracts equally as binding upon the state as upon their recipients. The first intimation of this position regarding corporate autonomy appeared in the 1763 statement of President Clap of Yale to the colonial legislature. He was protesting a threatened legislative visitation of the college on the grounds that such action would be contrary to the nature of the charter and the private legal nature of the institution.[2] Clap's position was novel in his day, but after the turn of the eighteenth century support of a judicial theory which interpreted charters to private corporations as contracts or compacts between the state and the founders began to appear. This point of view received its legal, judicial confirmation in the famous Dartmouth College case decision of the Supreme Court under Chief Justice Marshall. In that decision, the Court viewed the college as a private institution and interpreted its charter as a contract binding upon the state of New Hampshire as well as the trustees, "a contract, the obligation of which cannot be impaired without violating the constitution of the United States" (Wright, 1938, p. 45).

The Dartmouth College decision led to a reexamination of the state-college relationship. Faced with a loss of control, legislators understandably questioned the award of public funds to private corporations. As a result there emerged in subsequent decades a number of public or state colleges, but not as agencies of state government under ministers of education in the continental tradition. Rather, the early public colleges took the form of public corporations parallel in their general organization to the private colleges. In the nineteenth century, it became common practice for legislatures to delegate governing power over state institutions to boards of control established as public corporations.[3] These boards received authority to control property, contracts, finances, forms of internal governance, and relationships with internal personnel — students, faculty members, and administrative employees (Brody, 1935, Ch. 6).[4]

---

[2] Yale historians apparently have tended to credit Clap with a successful defense. Recent investigation of this incident by Professor W. H. Cowley, however, discloses that a visitation was made the following year, about which one of the visitors later observed that "we touch'd them so gently, that till after ye Assembly, they never saw they were taken in, that we had made ourselves Visitors, & subjected them to an Annual Visitation" (a point made in correspondence with this author).

[3] This precedent has undergone modification in more recent decades as state budget bureaus, civil service commissions, and coordinating boards have intruded directly into the internal affairs of public institutions.

[4] Exceptions to these rights do exist, particularly in connection with the control of property and the borrowing of monies. Frequently special corporations are set up within the control of state universities to handle private funds. Actual practice varies among the states, some of which limited the powers of boards in the founding legislation.

MODIFICATION
OF BOARD
CONTROL:
FACULTY AND
ALUMNI PAR-
TICIPATION

Whatever the legal authority inherent in lay governing boards, continuing modification of their actual power is documented by a history of university organization. Early in the nineteenth century, accounts of the administration of Jeremiah Day at Yale College attest to the influence of faculty members with whom Day conferred regularly on policy decisions. Students, while rarely a direct component of government until recent years, have traditionally participated as alumni.

Earlier precedents than Yale exist. Professor W. H. Cowley (1964, Ch. 7) has uncovered a number of such instances. Overall, it is clear from his analysis and from histories of the leading universities that faculties greatly expanded their influence over academic affairs during the nineteenth century. The period from 1869 to 1900 illustrates the gradual but decisive involvement of professors in academic policies (Morison, 1930, p. xxxiv). The trustees at Cornell in 1889, for example, established a University Senate of the president and full professors (Kingsbury, 1962, pp. 263–264). Similar arrangements existed at Michigan, Illinois, Wisconsin, and other Midwestern institutions. At Johns Hopkins and Chicago, professors were accepted as the guiding force for all matters concerned with education and research. Faculty influence reached the point that, by the 1890s, President Jacob G. Schurman of Cornell saw his influence in educational affairs limited to final approval of appointments and his role as "the only man in the University who is a member of all boards, councils and organizations" (Kingsbury, 1962, p. 323).

By the turn of the century the trend to faculty participation was definite in the larger universities and major colleges. The decades that followed have chronicled the extension of faculty control over academic affairs, a development influenced by the policies and pressures of the American Association of University Professors subsequent to its founding in 1915.[5]

During the nineteenth century, alumni also entered actively into the government of colleges and universities. In doing this, they had well-established precedents in both England and Scotland,

---

[5] In recent decades the growth in academic status and influence of the disciplines and professional departments and schools has further strengthened faculty power within institutions. The status associated with productive scholarship and research has given faculty members a greatly improved position vis-à-vis administration in internal affairs, a condition documented by Theodore Caplow and Reece J. McGee in their classic study, *The Academic Marketplace*, 1958.

though little evidence exists to support a causal relationship. It is probably more accurate to explain alumni participation as the result of a unique commitment epitomized by the spirit of alma mater and reinforced by recollections of campus camaraderie. The college class has constituted a primary social as well as academic unit which, early in the history of the colleges, led to campus reunions and thus served regularly to reinforce the loyalty of graduates. In turn, it was natural for the members of governing boards and leaders of state governments to look to graduates of colleges for service on these boards when openings occurred. "From the very beginnings," Professor Cowley (1964, Ch. 10, p. 10) has written, "alumni have contributed to the support of private colleges and universities; and as legislators, lobbyists, and moulders of public opinion they have strategically influenced the subsidizing of civil institutions." Formal representation by means of elected members to governing boards first appeared at Harvard in 1865, a pattern that was followed by many other institutions in the subsequent decades.[6]

In summary, university government had coalesced into the pattern we know today by shortly after the turn of the century. It reflected a continuation of medieval and English precedents whereby institutional autonomy received a high degree of protection, modified perhaps in American higher education by a more overt sense of commitment to societal needs. Private colleges and universities had the protection afforded them by their status as corporations under law.[7] In practice, public institutions obtained much of this same autonomy through their status as public corporations under the control of boards established by state constitution or

[6] Amherst in 1874, Dartmouth in 1875, Rutgers in 1881, Princeton in 1900, Columbia in 1908, Brown in 1914. (In the 1865 modification of its charter, Harvard adopted a plan whereby alumni gained the right to elect all new members to the Board of Overseers, the body with ultimate responsibility for that institution.)

[7] Little attention is given, unfortunately, to the uniquely significant role of the governing board in this country as the agency that both has protected internal autonomy and intellectual freedom and has served as a force to keep institutions relevant to the general society. This history badly needs doing. Despite occasional intrusions into internal affairs and matters related to academic freedom, the governing board has served as a point of balance for that essential dualism between institutional and academic autonomy and public accountability which has characterized American higher education. Current forces pressing for greater internal participation on the one hand and increased public control on the other need tempering by the experience of the past in this connection.

legislative law. But even before the end of the nineteenth century, evidences of growing restrictions upon the actual power of governing boards had begun to emerge. Over and above any incipient faculty militance, the practical result of growing size and complexity necessitated the delegation of some policy-making and managerial responsibilities to presidents and faculties.

Finally, the unique role and influence of presidents during this era require recognition. In contrast to earlier periods when presidents served more as principals responsible for campus conduct and morality—of professor and student alike—and trustees sat importantly at commencements to examine graduating seniors, by 1900 presidents had become a positive force. Every university to rise to major status did so under the almost dominating influence of such presidential leaders as Charles W. Eliot at Harvard, Andrew D. White at Cornell, Daniel Coit Gilman at Johns Hopkins, Charles R. Van Hise at Wisconsin, William Rainey Harper at Chicago, David S. Jordan at Stanford, and Benjamin Ide Wheeler at California. The office of president emerged as the central force that has given United States higher education a distinctive character among systems of higher education in the world. Whether one viewed the president as the alter ego of boards or as a discrete unit in institutional government had little bearing on practice. Whatever faculty voices may have been raised to the contrary, university government by the twentieth century centered upon the office of the president.

ADMINIS-TRATIVE STRUCTURE In his history of Williams College, *Mark Hopkins and the Log* (1956), Frederick Rudolph vividly portrays a typical college from 1836 to 1872. President Hopkins presides as the paternal head of a small and personal college family, responsible for the character of its children, the students. The curriculum was fixed and limited. In any event, what the students studied was secondary to the quality of personal moral life. In contrast, the "new education" of the last half of the nineteenth century reflected the new morality of the times, a turning away from Christian theology as the basis for life's judgments and toward values oriented far more to the marketplace and material success. In the words of Veysey (1965, Ch. 2), "discipline and piety" gave way to "utility" as the hallmark of a college education. Specialized knowledge replaced the "disciplining of the mind and character" as the raison d'être for higher education. Adherents of reform rallied to elective ideas which supported, to a degree at least, the rights of students to choose their subjects and thus to open the universities to the new studies of science and technology and of specialization in the humanities, all of which stressed the advancement of knowledge and a utilitarian commitment. By 1900 graduate studies, professional schools, and professors whose careers rested upon their published research rather than upon their role as teachers were moving to positions of the highest status in the academic hierarchy. Harvard University offered good evidence of the impact of this influence upon the curriculum. The 1850 catalog described the entire four years of undergraduate study on four pages; in 1920, 30 times that number of pages were required to list the courses offered at the university.

Two shifts in organizational structure inevitably followed. On the one hand, by the turn of the century departments and professional schools had become the basic units for academic affairs. The academic structure of the university coincided with the structure of knowledge. On the other hand, the impact of this "new education" fitted the times. In contrast to the declining enrollment of the 1840s and 1850s, the latter half of the nineteenth century marked the beginning of what has become a constantly increasing rate of college attendance. More students meant more professors, more buildings, more facilities and equipment, and, above all, more money from private and public sources. As chief executive, the president inherited the responsibility both for securing this support and for coordinating and managing the inevitable internal complexities that resulted. Initially, a vice-president and a few professors who served as part-time registrars, bursars, and librarians assisted him. By 1900, however, such staffs proved insufficient; the managerial burden of the president had begun to necessitate what has become a burgeoning administrative bureaucracy.

Academic Organization Some intimations of the specialized departments and professional schools which have become the basic organizational units of universities do appear in the early colleges. The University of Virginia, for example, opened in 1825 with eight schools, each headed by a professor and each offering a program of studies. In that same year, the statutes reorganizing Harvard College established nine "departments" for instruction, each of which (in the pattern already set for medicine, law, and divinity) would be "governed by a board of its full professors" (Cowley, 1964, Ch. 7, p. 4). The use of departments appeared also in 1826 at the University of Vermont, a decade later at Wisconsin, and at Michigan in 1841. But these departments served only as progenitors of the disciplinary and professional units that fashioned the academic organization of universities later in the century.

The appearance of departments as organizational entities accompanied the expansion of knowledge—particularly scientific and technological—and the elective system, by means of which the adherents of specialized study forced their point of view into institutions with traditions of a fixed, classical curriculum. But the reason for the association of departments of scholars in this country (in contrast to the chair held by one professor in foreign universities) has not been documented historically. That they had become the established structural units by 1900 is evident nonetheless in the histories of all major universities.[8]

A similar development occurred in the various professional studies, which appeared with few exceptions first as departments and later as schools, which in turn procreated their own departments. Certainly by 1900 professional specializations in more than a dozen areas were well established, ranging from the traditional trinity of medicine, law, and theology to such new areas as business administration, veterinary medicine, journalism, librarianship, and architecture.

The departmental structure that followed in the wake of specialized knowledge was accompanied by other evidence of disciplinary and professional segmentation, such as journals and national societies. Professors, as the authorities for their respective specializations, assumed more and more control over academic affairs. This revolutionary change from the earlier colleges had evolved by 1910 to the extent that a study of physics departments complains about their having "too much autonomy." The report describes the department as "usually practically self-governing" in control of its own affairs—that is, its students, staff, and curriculum (Cooke, 1910).

[8] For example, Harvard established 12 divisions, each including one or more departments, in 1891; Chicago had 26 departments in three faculties in 1893; Cornell, Yale, Princeton, Johns Hopkins, and Syracuse, among others, all reveal the trend toward departmentalization during the decade of the 1890s (Forsberg & Pearce, 1966).

Responding to the pressures of office work, travel, supervising new construction, employing new faculty, and initiating educational programs, in 1878 President Andrew Dickson White of the new Cornell University appointed a professor of modern languages and history, William C. Russel, as vice-president. Russel functioned as a kind of executive associate—hiring and dismissing junior faculty members, answering correspondence, and carrying out routine responsibilities as well as acting as institutional head in White's absence. The same year, a presidential colleague at Harvard, Charles W. Eliot, appointed Professor Ephriam W. Gurney as dean of the college faculty. In contrast to Russel's initial tasks, Dean Gurney's primary responsibility was to relieve the president of the burden of contacts with students.

These appointments at two major universities signaled the beginning of a trend. For the college growing into a large and complex university, the office of the president quickly ceased to be a one-man job. Those part-time assistants, usually professors, who served as librarian, bursar, or registrar had by 1900 turned into full-time administrative officers, and by the 1930s they were supervising large staffs. A 1936 study by Earl J. McGrath documents the trend. The author charts the growth from a median of three or four administrative officers in the 1880s to a median of nearly sixty for the larger universities by 1930. As noted previously in this chapter, the decades from 1890 to 1910 proved to be the turning point. The lines on McGrath's chart after 1890 turn upward abruptly, showing a doubling of these officers from an average of about 12 in that year to 30 in 1910.

What brought about this transformation of American universities into complex administrative systems, especially in contrast to the much simpler organization of European universities? Many determinants exerted influence, of course. In large part, administrative expansion responded to the need to coordinate and, to a degree, control the expansion of the academic structure. In part, it grew out of a relationship with the general society, unique to this country, which imposed on the university the task of securing financial support from both public and private sources and concurrently of attending to public relations. In part, the enlarged administration implemented an intricate credit system for student admissions and educational accounting.

Fundamentally, however, the administrative organization of

universities resulted from the managerial role of the American college president, the coincidental result of the fact that early founders looked to the colleges of the English universities for their patterns. In doing this they carried over the concept of a permanent headship, designated in the English colleges as *warden, master, provost, president,* or *rector* (Cowley, 1971, Ch. 11, p. 10; Davis, 1961, p. 304).[9] In contrast to the English custom of election by the fellows of the college, the presidents in this country from the very beginning have been appointed by governing boards. Thus, the presidents of the early colleges had responsibilities as executives for boards. For the first two centuries this constituted a relatively simple and personal, almost paternal, relationship with student and teachers. When, after the Civil War, colleges ceased to be small and universities appeared with expanded enrollments, academic fragmentation, and diversified relationships with the external society, presidents found their responsibility elaborated and their need for staff assistance imperative.

By 1900 it could be said that the general administration had developed something like its full measure of force in American higher education. In 1902, President Nicholas Murray Butler assumed the presidency of Columbia complete with clerical staff, abetted by well-established offices for the registrar and bursar (Veysey, 1965, p. 307). Probably typical of its times, the University of North Carolina administration included a registrar, bursar, librarian, and part-time secretary for the university. The office of alumni secretary was not unknown by 1900 (McGrath, 1936). Although largely a product of this century, business officers commonly served as bursars or collectors of fees. By the turn of the century, librarians had established themselves on a full-time basis and had begun to employ assistants—in contrast with the rudimentary condition of these services 40 years previously. The first press bureau appeared at the University of Wisconsin in 1904 (Seller, 1963, p. 3). The office of registrar was nearly universal. The office of vice-president, usually assigned to handle specific functions such as university relations, academic affairs, medical affairs, or similar constellations of administrative services, had appeared in some numbers by the First World War.

[9] Actually, the first head of Harvard had the title of *master* and that of Yale, *rector.* The Harvard custom lasted two years, that at Yale about forty. Both colleges shifted to the title of *president.*

Concurrently, presidents turned to the title of *dean* to further delegate their academic responsibilities. By 1900 this title was used for the heads of professional schools, especially medicine and law, and of schools or divisions of arts and sciences. The office of dean served in smaller colleges to designate the "second in command." In an 1896 reorganization at Cornell, for example, President Schurman appointed deans of academic affairs and of graduate studies. All the universities and two-thirds of the colleges included in the McGrath study had academic deans by 1900. The designation of the title of *dean* for student affairs also has precedent in the late nineteenth century. At Harvard, Eliot's appointment of Dean Gurney, as noted above, was a response to the pressures of his responsibilities for students. Similar appointments were made at Swarthmore, Oberlin, and Chicago in the 1890s. The same forces that had fragmented the unitary curriculum of the early colleges in support of specialized knowledge made the orientation of faculty members more intellectual and pushed into secondary or tertiary importance their concern with students. Into this void came the forerunners of contemporary student personnel services. Deans of women began to meet annually in 1903; directors of student unions appeared in 1914; the National Association of Deans of Men was organized in 1917.

In summary, then, the organizational structure of American universities was etched clearly enough by the first decade of this century. Its two mainstreams flowed to and from the offices of presidents: one an academic route to deans and thence to departmental chairmen; the other a managerial hierarchy. Whatever the organizational charts designated, as early as 1910 it had become apparent that initiative on the academic side had begun to rest heavily at the departmental level.

TWENTIETH-CENTURY EXPANSION If the late nineteenth century constitutes the formative years of American higher education, the present century has been an era of growth and consolidation. During the decades following the Civil War, colleges began their search for a personality appropriate to the times and to their position in society. As the years of maturity approached, each found its particular role in what has become a spectrum from small, unitary schools to large, complex universities which set the pace and pattern for the whole system. Diversity became the pervasive quality of the new era—diversity among institutions and within the major universities.

Expansion in this century has led to colleges and universities that number faculty members in the hundreds and thousands and students in the thousands and tens of thousands. Society's commitment to send youth to college as a major preparation for adult roles is evident in the steady increase from 52,000 students in 1869 to 2,650,000 in 1949 to more than double this by the 1970s. The less than 2 percent of the age group who attended college at the close of the Civil War has grown to more than 40 percent and approaches 50 percent. This expansion in numbers has carried with it a similar expansion in functions. By the early 1960s Clark Kerr, then president of the University of California, could comment that his university employed more people "than IBM . . . in over a hundred locations, counting campuses, experiment stations, agricultural and urban extension centers, and projects abroad involving more than fifty countries." He pointed to "nearly 10,000 courses in its catalogues; some form of contact with nearly every industry, nearly every level of government, nearly every person in its region" (Kerr, 1966, pp. 7–8). The "multiversity" has proved to be the ultimate outcome for the "new university" of 70 years ago.

Since 1900 no radical departures have altered the form of university organization or changed in any substantial way its function. In the retrospect of the last 60 years, the major thrusts that have characterized this era are the following: first, the expansion in numbers of both personnel and of units of the administrative structure, both academic and managerial; second, the consolidation of departmental control over academic matters; and, third, the diffusion of participation in government with a concurrent lessening of the influence of boards and presidents.

Administrative Expansion

Aside from the study by McGrath (1936) and a recent article by David R. Witmer (1966), little documentation exists to delineate the specifics of administrative expansion in this century. But the outward manifestations are obvious. What university of any size today lacks that imposing administration building located near the center of the campus? Within its walls dozens and even hundreds of clerks, typists, secretaries, bookkeepers, accountants, staff assistants, and a variety of administrative officers labor diligently over correspondence and reports, accounts and records, and a variety of managerial services—frequently in a high degree of efficient isolation from the classroom, laboratory, and library across the campus. In addition, one finds a plethora of service positions ranging from dietitians and delivery men to personnel for institutional research.

Paralleling the managerial services, the academic organization has had its own expansion of new functions and offices appended to departments and professional schools. It takes only a quick glance at the telephone directory of a major university to spot such activities as the animal facilities, athletic publicity and promotion, black studies program, carbon research, program in comparative literature, council for international studies, continuing education division, cooperative urban extension center, and creative craft center at the top of the alphabet through to technical research services, theater program, upward bound project, urology studies, and urban studies council at the bottom. Each of these activities has its director or head who reports to a chairman, a dean, or a vice-president. Each has a professional staff of one to a dozen individuals aided by secretaries and research assistants. The totality presents a bewildering complex of functions requiring administrative coordination and control.

As one looks over charts for the period, what stands out clearly is the steady, inexorable increase in administrative personnel and services paralleling the increase in numbers of students and faculty members.

Departmental Influence Specialization of knowledge has its counterpart in specialization of departments. But more than this it has led to what amounts to a monopoly of the expert. This specialization has left the university-wide administrators, and at times deans as well, unable to do more than respond to initiative on matters of personnel, facilities, teaching, curriculum, and research. Authors Paul L. Dressel and Donald J. Reichard (1970, p. 387)[10] observed in their historical overview that the department "has become a potent force, both in determining the stature of the university and in hampering the attempts of the university to improve its effectiveness and adapt to changing social and economic requirements." As early as 1929 a study of departments in small colleges demonstrated that they exercised a major influence in matters related to teaching, curriculum, schedule, and promotion (Reeves & Russell, 1929). More recent studies confirm the trend toward departmental autonomy and control over

[10] This report anticipated a more complete study by Dressel, Marcus, and Johnson entitled *The Confidence Crisis,* Jossey-Bass, Inc., San Francisco, 1970.

its own affairs (Caplow & McGee, 1958), evidenced by what David Riesman (1958) has called an academic procession in which the less prestigious institutions have followed the leadership of the major, prestigious universities.

This departmental autonomy has come as a logical outgrowth of size and specialization and of the pressing necessity to delegate and decentralize if major administrators were not to find themselves overwhelmed. A new kind of professor, the specialist and expert and man of consequence in society, has replaced the teacher and has augmented his (the specialist's) influence with a national system of professional and disciplinary societies. Together they have set the standards and the values, both oriented to productive scholarship, that dominate the universities.

Diffusion of Government

Following hard on the downward shift of academic power, governing boards have withdrawn extensively from active involvement in university affairs. This condition was incipient in 1905, as noted by James B. Munroe, industrialist and trustee at Massachusetts Institute of Technology. The trustees, he observed then, "find less and less opportunity for usefullness in a machine so elaborate that any incursion into it by those unfamiliar may do infinite harm" (Munroe, 1913). Fifty years later, in the same vein, the 1957 report on *The Role of Trustees of Columbia University,* (Columbia University, 1957) stated flatly that, while governing boards may hold final legal authority, their actual role in government leaves them removed from the ongoing affairs of their institutions. And as Trustee Ora L. Wildermuth, secretary of the Association of Governing Boards of State Universities, commented in 1949: "If a governing board contents itself with the selection of the best president available and with him develops and determines the broad general principles . . . and then leaves the administration and academic processes to the administrative officers and the Faculty, it will have done its work well." It serves best to select a president, hold title to property, and act as a court of last appeal, he summarized (Wildermuth, 1949, p. 238).

Pressing up from a departmental base, faculty members have moved into governmental affairs via the formalization of a structure of senates, councils, and associated committees. Evidence supports the contention that by 1910 professors were not hesitant to refer to their "rightfully sovereign power" (Veysey, 1965, p. 392). President Harper of Chicago formally stated in his decennial report that it was a "firmly established policy of the Trustees that the responsibility for the settlement of educational questions rests with the Faculties" (Bogert, 1945, p. 81). During the first half of this century the precedent of the major universities slowly carried over to other institutions. In 1941 a survey of 228 colleges and universities by the AAUP (American Association of University Professors) Committee T on College and University Government led to the comment that "in the typical institution the board of trustees appointed the president, the president appointed deans, and the deans in turn designated executives. . . . Consultation concerning personnel and budget . . . took place between administrative and teacher personnel through departmental executives" ("The Role of Faculties . . . ," 1948). A decade later, however, the same committee reported an increase in faculty communication with trustees, participation in personnel decisions, influence on personnel policies, consultation about budgetary matters, and control of academic programs ("The Place and Function . . . ," 1953). By the late 1960s the basic position of the AAUP had the strength of general tradition; in the eyes of a new breed of faculty radicals it had become a conservative force. In essence, the AAUP's position was based upon five principles: (1) that faculties have primary responsibility over educational policies; (2) that they concur through established committees and procedures in academic personnel matters; (3) that they participate actively in the selection of presidents, deans, and chairmen; (4) that they are consulted on budgetary decisions; and (5) that appropriate agencies for this participation have official standing.

Precedents for student involvement in university and college government (distinct from extracurricular campus activities) have gained a new force, although their roots lie deep in the history of higher education. Professor Cowley (1964, Ch. 11, p. 16) has described the abortive two-year "House of Students" at Amherst in 1828 as a legislative body concerned with security on campus, study hours, and similar matters. In this century, something of the same spirit has appeared sporadically. At Barnard during the academic year 1921–22, students carried out a sophisticated analysis of the curriculum. At Dartmouth in 1924, a committee of 12 seniors submitted a critical review of the education program. At Harvard in 1946, following the publication of the faculty report *General Education in a Free Society* (Harvard Committee, 1946), students published an equally formidable document. Overall, as

Cowley (1964, Ch. 11, p. 47) observes, "American students have continuously and sometimes potently affected the thinking and actions of professors, presidents, and trustees." Historically their influence has been an informal one. Their drive for direct participation on the governing councils and boards of colleges and universities generated real potency only during the late 1960s.[11] Its effectiveness remains conjectural, although the evidence suggests that the student drive for participation will tend to dissipate further the influence of boards and presidents.

Alumni have maintained their traditional voice in government, although one can perceive an undermining of the spirit of alma mater and the significance of financial contributions so long associated with their institutional commitments. This participation was substantiated by a 1966 survey of 82 public and private universities and colleges which reported that 31 of the institutions have elected alumni trustees and an additional 24 have trustees nominated by alumni. Nearly all had alumni on their boards, however.[12] Cornell University's situation is typical of private institutions. In a 1966 letter the president of the Alumni Association noted that "a trustee is not required to be an alumnus of the University unless he is elected by the alumni. At present, however, of the 40 members, 35 are alumni."

In retrospect, then, higher education is moving into the final decades of the twentieth century with a pattern of organization similar in its major dimensions to that with which it entered the century. The question readily comes to mind whether this form will continue to prove effective.

CONCLUSION That the American university, the hallmark of the American system of higher education, has flourished as an institution uniquely fitted to its times stands without question. Its commitment to the

---

[11] In his 1970 book, *Should Students Share the Power?* Earl J. McGrath reports a survey of existing practice, noting that more than 80 percent of 875 institutions admit some students to membership in at least one policy-making body. In the same year the University of Tennessee admitted students to its trustee committees. A House bill submitted in 1969 in the Massachusetts legislature proposed an elected student member of each of the governing boards of public universities.

[12] Conducted by Howard University with the sponsorship of the American Alumni Council. The questionnaire was mailed to 112 institutions, from which 82 usable responses were received.

expansion of knowledge and its application are emulated throughout the world. Similarly, its organizational arrangements have
grown out of and suited well its particular kind of educational
enterprise. Inevitably governing boards and presidents had to
delegate as institutions expanded. That they did so in a manner
that enhanced the effectiveness of the academic endeavor has
proved to be no minor achievement. Departments, in turn, have
served well by translating the essence of specialized knowledge
into workable organizational forms. Student personnel administrators, in their turn, have filled that void between individual and
organization left by the impersonalism inherent in a faculty pre-
eminently concerned with the extension of knowledge. A faculty
governing structure has given an organizational channel to the
exercise of professorial influence, in turn an academically essential
counterbalance to the authority of governing boards and external
constituencies. In sum, universities have proved an effective organizational means by which scholarship and learning could flourish
within the confines of large, complex organizations.

Yet, as the decade of the 1970s unfolds, a sense of uncertainty
about just how well universities do perform has begun to settle
over the campuses of the nation. Students in large universities,
and even to a degree in smaller institutions, find themselves caught
in a complex of increasingly impersonal relationships and an
educational endeavor which enhances advanced study and research
more than student learning. Both influences tend to dull any sense
of intellectual awakening or of personal meaning for life on the
part of students. Most faculty cling hard to the traditional fields
of knowledge and to specialization despite a societal need for
synthesis and application of what is known. As, historically, cultures and nations in their greatest flowering have begun to show
their inherent weaknesses, so the university in the last few decades
has provided evidence of its limitations. The changing nature of the
social order, as it too reaches a pinnacle of scientific-technological
achievement, amplifies these weaknesses.

A historical survey such as this would be inadequate indeed if
it did not at least suggest some clues to the future. In conclusion,
therefore, we note three pervasive organizational inadequacies.
One can be attributed to size and complexity, a second to specialization and departmentalization, and the third to the shifting
pattern of institutional government. All were incipient but gen-

erally underway as higher education emerged from the First World War.

The size and complexity of United States universities seem to dictate that they have become large bureaucracies. Actually, however, one finds two bureaucracies. On the one hand, over the past 50 years faculties have created a hierarchy of departments, schools, and senates or executive councils well larded with a variety of permanent and temporary committees. This bureaucracy claims rights of control over the totality of the academic function. On the other hand, administrators have formed a separate hierarchy to grapple with the immense tasks of management of essential yet supportive services which maintain the university, not the least of which are budget and finance. The lines of relationship between the two bureaucracies have become tenuous. The different attitudes and values associated with each have driven a psychological wedge between faculty members and administrators. Faculty remain committed to a traditional ideal of the university as an integrated community, at the same time giving constant evidence that they fail to grasp its real operational nature and managerial complications. Administrators find their managerial tasks so consuming that they become forgetful of the nature of the academic enterprise.

The second evidence of dysfunction stems from the nature of the department as the organizational unit for disciplinary and professional specialization. The commitment to specialization energizes centrifugal forces that tend to push faculty loyalties out from the universities. Thus the university is often merely a base, temporary or permanent, from which the scholar pursues his primary concern with research activities. Specialization has produced a similar tendency toward fragmentation of the academic organization. While exercising a dominant influence on instruction, curriculum, research, and other academic matters, schools and departments show a low regard for university values and a high concern for disciplinary and professional values. Despite many evidences to the contrary during the student disruptions of the last few years, this condition is reinforced by academic condescension toward administrators, who are viewed as servants rather than leaders of the professoriate. It reflects what one might call a faculty schizophrenia which categorizes administrators as minions while condemning them for failure to stand firmly as defenders of the academic faith in times of crisis.

At times this divergency threatens an atrophy in leadership for large universities in an era when leadership is of utmost importance. The remedy, however, inevitably must lie beyond the bounds of organizational factors. Forms of government serve only as well as they are supported in the general values and commitments of those affected by them. Any rectification of this condition, therefore, must stem from deep within the higher education enterprise. In particular, there must be some resolution of the conflict between the clear and direct rewards that accompany achievement in scholarship and research and the nominal recognition, despite societal expectation, accorded to the education of students. From this base line one moves into explorations of reward systems that conform to stated purposes. One also has to reflect upon organizational systems that prove responsive to changing conditions as against those that support existing arrangements.

The third problem—the shifting power in institutional government—was anticipated in 1903 by President Schurman of Cornell when he characterized his role as that of a mediator. Sixty years later Clark Kerr made the same observation with greater force. Presidential deference to faculty expertise in academic affairs is only one facet of the situation, however. The history of university organization in the twentieth century has been an account of the disintegration of the traditional form of government conceived in terms of formal authority granted to governing boards, which have exercised it through the president as executive officer.

The diffusion of government by means of dissipation of boards and presidential influence and dispersion of operating control to departments, administrative offices, and faculty governing bodies has been accompanied by the intrusion of external forces. Professional and disciplinary associations, accrediting agencies, agencies of the federal government for all institutions and state executive offices for public ones—all have tended to bypass presidents and boards. It appears that higher education has experienced one of those historic circles. Governing boards today serve much the way the original visitors or overseers did. What is lacking is a new corporation in the sense of a controlling or managerial council to fill the vacuum. As one English observer phrased it, organizationally American universities have tended to become "confederations of largely autonomous departments." It adds up to what he has characterized as "the hole in the centre" (Shils, 1970).

As universities enter the decade of the 1970s, the pressures on the established organization are evidenced in student dissent and the public reaction to it. The movement toward decentralization of control over educational and administrative functions has begun to come up against external demands for more forceful central authority to the end not only of "law and order" but of a "more efficient use of resources." Mass higher education and the possibility of almost universal higher education exacerbate the problems. More fundamentally, one finds growing evidences of academic inadequacies in the face of the need for new kinds of education and scholarship. These must relate to the role of the university in a society pressed by ecological and social dislocation stemming from scientific and technological achievement. One readily suspects that the organizational forms effective in 1900 may serve but poorly for the year 2000.

3. Similarities and Differences among Universities of the United States

by John D. Millett

In the literature of recent years about higher education in the United States, one theme has been constant: that of diversity. There is little evidence of a common pattern in the mission, in the structure, or in the operation of the more than 2,500 institutions of higher education in this country.

Private associations of concerned citizens, various religious groups, the 50 state governments, and certain local government units have all played some part in establishing colleges and universities to provide higher education throughout the nation. The federal government has restricted its role to the creation of military academies, including a merchant marine academy, and the sponsorship of some institutions of higher education within the District of Columbia.

The complications in endeavoring to classify more than 2,500 institutions of higher education clearly indicate diversity and variety. (Throughout this chapter the subject of attention is institutions of higher education and not the subcategory of universities as a separate type.) The most important first distinction to make among institutions of higher education in the United States is that between public and private sponsorship. In turn, these two broad categories are often subdivided as follows: in the public category into federal government sponsorship, state government sponsorship, and local government sponsorship; and in the private category into nonsectarian sponsorship, Protestant sponsorship, Roman Catholic sponsorship, and other sponsorship. The second major distinction to be made among institutions of higher education is by the type of student body served: coeducational, men only, women only, and predominantly black students. The third major distinction is by the type of instructional program offered by an institution of higher education: two-year programs, general baccalaureate programs, professional baccalaureate programs, master's degree programs, graduate professional programs (such as law and medicine), and doctor's degree programs.

Commentators have suggested other distinctions from time to time. One such distinction is that of qualitative standards of instruction maintained by institutions of higher education. Another is that of expenditures, as indicated by average compensation paid to faculty members or average expenditure on instruction per full-time student. Indeed, there is in the United States a general assumption—for which there is little if any empirical validation—that the greater the expenditure per student, the higher the quality of instruction. Geographic location is a further distinction. There are colleges and universities that are predominantly residential in character; others serve a predominantly commuting student body drawn from the urban area where the institution is located. Institutions may be defined by function: some are predominantly involved in instructional activity; others are heavily engaged in research and in the performance of various kinds of public service, from care of patients to public broadcasting, from continuing education to operation of museums and art galleries.

In recent years still another distinctive feature has appeared on the American higher educational landscape: the multicampus institution. This phenomenon is more prevalent among public universities than among private colleges and universities. Today a considerable number of public institutions identify themselves as a single institution, such as the University of California with nine campuses, the University of Texas with nine campuses, and the University of Missouri with four campuses.[1] On occasion private colleges have opened branch campuses or have sponsored satellite colleges.

The U.S. Office of Education classifies institutions of higher education in the United States according to three basic characteristics: control (public versus private, the level of government in public sponsorship, church-relatedness in private sponsorship); program offering (less than four-year, four-year, first professional degree, master's degree and beyond, doctoral degree); and type of student body (coeducational, men and women).[2]

The Carnegie Commission on Higher Education has developed a

---

[1] Cf. Lee & Bowen, 1971.

[2] Cf. National Center for Educational Statistics, 1971.

classification structure with 17 primary categories ranging from leading research universities to other specialized professional institutions. It is noteworthy that the Carnegie Commission classification introduces a qualitative differentiation among universities and liberal arts colleges, that its primary emphasis is upon program offerings of various institutions, and that it ignores any differentiation between public and private sponsorship of institutions.

In his study of the financial condition of 41 colleges and universities, Professor Earl F. Cheit utilized a six-category classification for comparative purposes: national research universities, regional research universities, state and comprehensive colleges, liberal arts colleges, primarily black colleges, and two-year colleges. This is a convenient grouping, but it ignores the considerable number of separate United States professional colleges. Further, it omits any reference to sponsorship as an important characteristic of an institution of higher education.[3]

There is no classification scheme yet devised that can bring order and simplicity out of the many diversities that inhere in the structure of higher education in the United States. Each classification is at best a partial ordering of institutional characteristics — a considerable simplification of reality.

QUANTITATIVE DATA   As of 1970–71, the Office of Education listed 2,573 institutions of higher education in the United States. This number includes the separate locations of various state universities having multiple campuses. In terms of control, there were 1,101 institutions under public control (enrolling 5.5 million students) and 1,472 under private sponsorship (enrolling 2.1 million students).

The following table summarizes the data about the number of higher education institutions enumerated by the Office of Education. This table combines data on control, level of program offerings, and type of student body.

Several conclusions are immediately evident from these data. Public institutions of higher education are preponderantly state sponsored; the role of local government has been primarily that of establishing two-year colleges and technical institutes. Of the 1,472 privately sponsored institutions of higher education, more than half are church related in some degree. Private higher educa-

[3] Cf. Cheit, 1971, p. 26.

	Total	Less than four years	Four-year	First prof. degree	Master's and beyond	Doctoral degree
Public						
Federal	8		6			2
State	618	205	77	6	196	134
Local	344	327	4		6	7
State and local	131	127	2			2
Private						
Nonsectarian	655	117	266	36	147	89
Protestant	485	75	264	21	95	30
Catholic	300	44	149	8	74	25
Other	32	2	5	6	10	9
Student body						
Coeducational	2,226	828	605	60	453	280
Men only	197	15	60	17	47	15
Women only	210	54	108		28	3

SOURCE: National Center for Educational Statistics, 1971, tables 1 and 2.

tion is predominantly education in a four-year college or in a college offering the master's degree. Numerically, the smallest segment of higher education is the school offering a first professional degree, followed by universities or specialized institutions offering a doctor's degree. Most United States institutions of higher education provide coeducational instruction. As of 1970, of a total higher education enrollment of 7.6 million students, 4.5 million students were male, 3.1 million were female.

Institutions of higher education are widely distributed throughout the 50 states, the District of Columbia, Puerto Rico, and three territories. The number of public institutions ranges from 113 in California to 1 each in Alaska and Hawaii. Only 13 states have fewer than 10 public institutions of higher education. The number of privately sponsored institutions ranges from 145 in New York; 111 in Pennsylvania; 90 in Massachusetts; and 88 in Illinois to 4 each in Arizona, Delaware, Idaho, and Utah; 3 each in New Mexico and North Dakota; 2 in Alaska; and 1 in Nevada.

About 1.5 million students were enrolled in two-year colleges, with all but 100,000 of these students attending public two-year colleges. Nearly 900,000 students were enrolled at the graduate level. These data mean that 5 million students were enrolled in baccalaureate programs in the arts and sciences, in business and teacher education, and in various professional fields of study.[4]

The essential issue is the extent to which differences in type result in differences in operation. Our attention will concentrate upon four major elements of operation: (1) mission or program, (2) financing, (3) governance, and (4) consensus or sense of community.

MISSION The major objectives of an individual institution of higher education are ordinarily stated in terms of five categories: instruction, research, public service, auxiliary service (from residence halls to intercollegiate athletics), and student assistance. Actually, this classification is a listing of activities rather than of purposes. As a statement of mission, each institution needs to set forth with some precision the actual objectives it seeks to achieve in terms of student instruction, research projects, public service endeavors, auxiliary services, and financial assistance to students. United States institutions of higher education are seldom precise about their actual purposes or about the quality of student achievement expected in each field of study.

In terms of mission, the most important distinction to be made among institutions of higher education in the United States is that of degree programs offered to students. Although a precise categorization of programs does not exist (the Office of Education classification is misleading in its statistical treatment of professional degrees awarded), essentially, United States institutions of higher education offer five kinds of instructional programs which correspond roughly to the types of institutions that offer them: (1) the two-year programs in general studies and in technical education (given in two-year colleges); (2) the baccalaureate programs in arts and sciences and in business management and teacher education (given in baccalaureate colleges); (3) the specialized baccalaureate programs in professional studies (agriculture, architecture, art, engineering, dramatic arts, forestry, journalism, music, nursing, pharmacy, social work); (4) the specialized graduate professional programs in such fields as medicine, dentistry, law, optometry, theology, and veterinary medicine (given in graduate professional schools); and (5) the graduate programs at

---

[4] Data from American Council on Education, 1971, pp. 71.8, 71.16, 71.17, and 71.34.

both the master's degree level and the doctor's degree level in th
arts and sciences and in professional fields where there is also
baccalaureate program (as in architecture, engineering, journa
ism).

There is no area of conflict within United States institutions c
higher education more virulent or more persistent than that betwee
academic and career objectives in instructional programs. Thi
conflict has been present in American higher education since th
years of Jacksonian democracy. The conflict is still with us an
its ramifications are many.

The academic perspective of higher education encompasses tw
interrelated concepts or ethical commitments: "knowledge for it
own sake" and development of the "renaissance man" cultivate
in the genteel tradition.[5] This perspective about the mission c
American higher education was inherited from the seventeentl
and eighteenth-century university education in the United Kingdo
with which the American colonists and early citizens were familia
The perspective is still preserved by thousands of American pr
fessors who are probably unaware of its historical origin and of it
class-interest context related to an elite social and political stru
ture. The persistence of the perspective may well be traced t
faculty reaction to the recurrent manifestations of anti-intelle
tualism in American history.

The career perspective of higher education is concerned wit
knowledge as a social utility, as a practical means to social progre
in meeting problems in such areas as health, agricultural produ
tion, economic growth, technological improvement, managemei
proficiency, national security, and, more recently, environment:
protection. The career perspective of higher education has helpe
to develop the professions of American society (law, medicin
dentistry, architecture, engineering, agricultural and forest scienc
management, accountancy, social work, teaching, the biologic
and physical sciences, and higher education), which have done :
much to advance social welfare through knowledge, skill, ar
ethical obligation. Higher education today is turning its attentic
to furthering new paraprofessional competencies in various tec
nologies (health, engineering, business, public service).[6]

[5] See the very perceptive discussion of educational norms, educational ethi
and social interest in Lowi, 1971, Ch. 6.

[6] For a survey of current faculty attitudes about the conflict between academ
and career purpose in higher education, see Heiss, 1970, Ch. 3.

The conflict between academic and career emphasis is reflected in the structure of United States higher education. For example, the land-grant colleges developed with the assistance provided by the federal government's Morrill Act of 1862 were supposed to emphasize career objectives, especially in agriculture and the mechanical arts. With few exceptions, most of these land-grant colleges sooner or later became state universities where the academic point of view won dominance.

Statistics of the Office of Education show that approximately 700 to 800 institutions of higher education in the United States can be identified as private liberal arts colleges. The Carnegie Commission suggests that these colleges should be divided into two types: "highly selective" and "other." Probably as many as 200 of these colleges would fall into the first type. The instructional program of "highly selective" colleges emphasizes academic values in higher education, and the college selects a student body of academic talents clearly consistent with its particular mission. It is usually overlooked that these colleges seldom provide the breadth of educational instruction they profess to honor, but do, in fact, provide an academic specialization appropriate to career preparation at the graduate or graduate professional level of education for certain professions (law and medicine) and for the academic profession itself. The "other" liberal arts colleges cannot so readily assume that their graduates will enjoy the luxury of graduate preparation for careers and so must introduce a career emphasis or orientation at the undergraduate level.

The research interests of particular universities likewise tend to reflect an academic as opposed to a career orientation. According to the enumeration of the Office of Education, about 300 universities in 1970–71 were offering the Ph.D. or a similar doctoral degree. Of these universities, 145 were publicly sponsored and 155 were privately sponsored. From time to time the National Science Foundation has identified the 100 universities receiving the largest amount of federal government support for research. For the fiscal year 1969, the amount of federal government research funding for the 100th university came to $3,739,000 (National Science Foundation, 1970, table 22). This was the line of demarcation between research-oriented universities and other universities offering the doctoral degree. Research interest tends to be associated with the university having a strong academic interest. Other doctoral-granting universities must be satisfied with a career orientation, and the hope that they might sometime advance into the magic circle of a research university and its concomitant academic commitment.

The question of qualitative evaluation of universities tends to be related also to their research and academic orientation. For example, studies made of the quality of doctoral degree programs have been confined to the academic disciplines and have not included evaluation of doctoral programs in such career fields of study as the agricultural sciences, engineering, teacher education, management, and medicine (Cartter, 1966; Roose & Anderson, 1970). It may well be that universities achieving a "high" rating in the academic disciplines will also enjoy a similar assessment in the more definitely career-oriented fields of study. Yet the implication is strong in the judgment of many faculty members that only achievement in an academic discipline is an indication of high quality at the doctoral program level.

The academic versus career conflict in higher education institutions has further evidenced itself within the two-year college. Some states have developed technical institutes in preference to the community college because technical education specialists have feared that their career interest would be neglected or submerged by the academically minded in a community college. This fear can scarcely be ignored or belittled; there are too many instances within community colleges where virtual battles have appeared between those interested in the so-called college transfer program and those interested in the career-oriented technical education program.

The program diversity of higher education is evidenced in more than the matter of degrees offered. This diversity is to be found in judgments of quality and in the academic as opposed to the career orientation of various institutions. Apart from research funds provided in the professional field of medicine, federal research support to universities has tended in general to flow toward those institutions with a strong academic tradition and faculty members of recognized academic achievement. Colleges have been rated according to the number of their graduates entering graduate programs in the academic disciplines. Universities, colleges, and two-year institutions with a strong career orientation are often dismissed as contributing little to the reputation or even the accomplishment of American higher education. Needless to say, the separate professional school avowedly dedicated to the exclusive mission of professional education (whether this mission be technical, engineering, law, art, music, optometry, theology, or medicine) is generally considered to suffer from a lack of association with the academically qualified faculty of a more comprehensive institution.

There are other objectives of institutions of higher education in the United States besides instruction and its corollary activity of research. We have already mentioned public service, auxiliary service, and student aid. Public institutions of higher education tend to undertake a greater array of public service endeavors than private institutions, if for no other reason than the importance of these activities to public financial support. A residential institution undertakes a more extensive volume of auxiliary services than an institution with a commuting student body. The scope of student aid activities within any given institution depends upon several factors: the concern of the institution to encourage students of special talents to enroll in that institution; the extent of institutional commitment to seek out and assist students of some higher educational promise to overcome economic barriers impeding their access to such education; and the magnitude of the resources available to the institution for student aid.

All in all, considerable program diversity is to be found among United States institutions of higher education.

FINANCING There is substantial diversity in the financial support available for the instructional, research, public service, auxiliary service, and student aid activity of institutions of higher education. This diversity results from varied circumstances. In turn, this diversity affects the relative financial "affluence" or "depression" of these institutions.

Insofar as the instructional activities of higher education are concerned, the essential distinction is between those institutions having public sponsorship and those that are privately sponsored. In general, as of 1970–71 public colleges and universities derived from 60 to 80 percent of their instructional income from state government tax support. The remaining 40 to 20 percent of instructional income was obtained from charges to students and from miscellaneous sources. On the other hand, private colleges and universities in general obtained from 70 to 90 percent of their instructional income from charges to students. The remaining 30 to 10 percent of available instructional income came from philanthropy (endowment and current giving) and miscellaneous sources.

This difference in the source of instructional income was reflected in the considerable variation in charges to students between public and private institutions. As of 1970–71 it was quite common for the instructional charges of public institutions to amount to around $300 to $450 for an academic year of two semesters or three quarters. At private colleges and universities the charges to students tended to range between $1,500 and $2,500 for one academic year. This substantial differential has been criticized as a positive economic incentive to encourage enrollment expansion at public institutions in preference to enrollment at private institutions.

It must not be supposed that public institutions as a group enjoy a common financial well-being. And the variation in the financial condition of private colleges and universities is quite considerable. The 50 state governments vary a great deal in their per capita and their per-student appropriations for public institutions of higher education. In 1971 a report of the Education Commission of the States (1971, vol. 2, pp. 68–71) showed the magnitude of these variations.

Appropriations for the current operations of public higher education from state tax funds in 1970 varied from a high of $81 per capita in Alaska to a low of $18 per capita in Pennsylvania; the average for 50 states came to $36 per capita. Measured in per-student terms, appropriations ranged from nearly $6,000 per student in Alaska to $1,000 per student in California; the average was close to $1,600 per student. These data must be subjected to careful interpretation; for example, the magnitude of the state subsidy to junior colleges affects the outcome, as in California. But there is considerable variation in the amounts of funds provided as well as in programs undertaken among the higher education activities of the 50 state governments.

The research activities of United States institutions of higher education are largely financed by grants and contracts administered through several agencies of the federal government, agencies which essentially make no distinction between public and private universities. The distinction rather is supposed to reflect the qualitative standing of an institution, and, more particularly, the research capability of its faculty. Of the top 10 universities in magnitude of federal research support in fiscal year 1969, 4 were privately sponsored and 6 were publicly supported. Of the next 35 universities, 15 were privately sponsored and 20 were publicly sponsored. These qualitative judgments about research quality did tend to be correlated with the relative standing of the public universities in terms of state government support and of the private universities in terms of philanthropic support.

Although federal government research support was supposed to defray the direct and indirect expense of particular research projects, there is ample evidence that in fact this support did assist in the financing of instruction at the Ph.D. level. Graduate students were often employed in these research projects. Research grants helped also in the purchase and operation of equipment essential to the research component of Ph.D. education. In some instances, research grants supported in whole or in part the salaries of scholars who carried on the research instruction of doctoral students. As the federal government curtailed the support of research projects, the leading doctoral-granting institutions, which were for the most part also the leading research universities in terms of dollar value of federal research grants, experienced severe financial difficulties. Similar difficulties were not experienced by universities with little involvement in extensive federally supported research.

Public service activities have involved primarily continuing education. As mentioned above, public universities have tended to undertake more extensive continuing education activities than have private colleges and universities. The land-grant tradition after 1862, along with federal government funds starting in 1914, encouraged the development of an agricultural extension service attached to Morrill Act colleges and universities. Later, continuing education became a concern of most professional colleges of public universities. Educational broadcasting via radio and television has been another form of continuing education. Teaching hospitals provide public service through patient care. Experiment stations have helped to translate research findings into practical application to agricultural and other problems. To some extent, charges to the beneficiaries of public service, supplemented by state and federal subsidies, have helped to defray the costs of these activities.

Within public universities, state higher education policy has dictated that residence and dining hall facilities should be self-supporting from room rents and board charges. The capital costs of the facilities have usually come from bond issues repaid from these same rents and charges. Private colleges and universities have obtained the necessary operating income for residence halls from charges to students but have often utilized gift funds to assist in the capital expense of the facilities. Student health services are usually maintained from a compulsory health insurance charge to students. Bookstores and similar services are also supported by charges to users. The financing of intercollegiate athletics is looming as a major financial problem in two kinds of circumstances: (1) where gate receipts from athletic events are insufficient to meet the costs of an extensive array of intercollegiate sports participation and (2) where the costs of intercollegiate athletics have been supported in part by a compulsory charge upon all students.

Student aid financing has represented a complication for institutions of higher education under two conditions: (1) where the institution has desired to use financial inducements (scholarship and fellowship awards) to persuade particular students of high ability (academic, athletic, or artistic) to enroll and (2) where an institution has made a commitment to enroll an increasing number of students from poverty and minority groups. Both the federal and state governments are now providing extensive funding of this second objective, although these efforts may still be inadequate to the numbers needing financial assistance. Federal government student aid programs generally make no distinction between private and public institutions. The student aid programs of state governments tend to recognize the instructional charge differential between public and private institutions and so provide a larger amount for the student enrolled in a private college or university.

One further financing complication deserves mention here. Within public universities and state governmental systems of higher education, fairly systematic and sophisticated attempts are being made to develop cost data for various instructional programs. It is apparent that private colleges and universities have been under less pressure to undertake this kind of analysis or have been less aware of the utility of such data. State government budgeting for higher education has clearly revealed that there are substantial differences in the cost factors for various instructional programs as between levels of instruction (associate, baccalaureate, master's, and doctoral) and as between fields of instruction (general studies, technical, arts and sciences, teacher education, law, dentistry, medicine, etc.). These findings are bringing to the fore some pressures for differential pricing to students enrolled in different instructional programs. It seems likely that differential pricing will become an important issue in higher education financing during the

1970s, if not at the private universities then surely at the public universities.

There is diversity within United States higher education in terms of the income resources available to various institutions, in terms of the scope of the instructional and other activities which they finance, and in terms of the corresponding expenditure commitments of these institutions. There is little indication that this diversity has become less pronounced in recent years. It seems likely to continue in the years ahead.

GOVERNANCE Institutions of higher education in the United States also vary one from another in their structures of governance.[7] It may seem to some that these differences are slight and almost meaningless in practice, but they do exist and must be recognized.

The most important difference in governing structure is in the selection of members of boards of trustees for public as distinct from private institutions. To be sure, both kinds of institutions have their respective boards in whom the legal authority of government is vested. Yet the size and the method of selection tend to be quite different between the two types of institutions. The board of trustees of a public institution is frequently composed of 9 persons, although in some instances it may be larger (one consisted of 100 persons). The board of trustees of a private college or university frequently numbers from 25 to 50 members. The board of trustees of a public college or university is usually appointed by the governor, subject to senate approval, and each member serves for a staggered term of years (often 7 to 15). The board of trustees of a private college or university is self-perpetuating (members elect their own successors). Board members often serve for life or until a fixed retirement age. In a church-related college or university, all or part of the board may be selected by a church body. A minority of board members in a private institution may be elected to a term by the alumni of the institution.

Although the authority of boards of trustees tends to be the same for both public and private institutions of higher education—both kinds of boards are usually vested with the authority of government—the role of each kind of board is essentially different. The

---

[7] The reader is referred to Part 3 of this volume, Corporate Authority: Trustees and Regents.

difference arises from the inherent nature of an enterprise under public sponsorship contrasted with an enterprise under private sponsorship. The public board serves as a substitute for the executive and legislative power of state government. The board of trustees enacts rules and ordinances governing the operation of the public institution which otherwise might be the subject of executive direction or legislative enactment. The public board of trustees is an instrument of political insulation, a device one step removed from the political process of public election. It represents the public interest in a political sense, but it bespeaks this interest as a board not subject to direct electoral accountability.

On the other hand, the board of trustees of a private institution of higher education exercises its collective judgment in a social rather than a political setting, concerned with the public interest as guided by the principle of trusteeship. In making its decisions, the board of trustees of a private institution bespeaks a collective social conscience, enlightened by personal experience and an individual code of ethics. The private trustee represents all society and not just the political process of a pluralistic society.

Unfortunately, the nature and the role of trusteeship in both the public and the private institution of higher education have not been analyzed and articulated in the only context of importance to each: the context of the trustee role in the political process on the one hand, and in the context of the social or nonpolitical process on the other. The absence of a well-defined doctrine of trusteeship is all the more critical today because of the demands made by students and by faculty members for membership on boards of trustees. These demands are made in the name of participatory democracy. Superficially, their claims appear reasonable.

In public institutions of higher education, however, the crucial issue is that of the relationship of the board of trustees to the political process. Students and faculty members are participants in this political process, and the elected representatives of the people have a voice in the selection of trustees for public institutions of higher education as well as a voice in the determination of the scope of authority to be exercised by these boards. If all or some of the board members were not selected through this general political process but through a more particularized political process, what would be the consequences in terms of the willingness of state executives and legislatures to refrain from extensive external control over board behavior?

In the instance of the private institution of higher education, the crucial issue is the relationship of the board of trustees to an external social process. Without doubt, many trustees of private institutions are selected as such in the expectation that they can and will be instrumental in assisting to obtain the philanthropic support upon which the institution depends. If all or some board members are elected by students and faculty of an institution, what would be the consequences in terms of the willingness of friends and alumni to contribute voluntarily to the support of the enterprise?

It must be noted that private institutions of higher education have a greater freedom to make changes in the size and selection of board members than do public institutions. If a private college or university has been chartered as a nonprofit educational corporation under general state law, it is usually a relatively simple process to change the charter or bylaws of the corporation. In this way the private institution may decide to enlarge its board membership, to lengthen or reduce the term of service, and to provide for various classes of membership, including student and faculty election. There is thus a potential for experimentation in governance within the private institution of higher education.

This same potential for experimentation does not exist within the public institution. For the public college and university, the size, term of office, and method of selecting members of the board of trustees are determined by law or even, in some instances, by constitutional prescription. Changes can be made only through the legislative process or through the procedure of constitutional amendment or revision.

The entire subject of governance for both public and private institutions of higher education deserves much more extensive discussion than can be undertaken here. It is sufficient for our present purpose simply to point out the important differences in governance between public and private institutions of higher education.

COMMUNICA- TION AND CONSENSUS The academic community that constitutes any particular college or university consists of various primary groups: administration (board of trustees and administrative staff), faculty, students, and nonacademic staff. In addition, the interest of alumni in the institution of which they are graduates, although the exact nature of this interest has seldom been clearly defined, is a concern that requires some accommodation. This academic community is a unique enterprise or unit of social organization. Its objective is to provide an environment of learning, a setting in which the scholar communicates his knowledge to students, pursues the advancement of his own knowledge, and interacts with colleagues and students in advancing the cognitive capacities of each participant. The goal of the student is to become a graduate who individually demonstrates for his own satisfaction and for the benefit of others his mastery of knowledge, his skill in the utilization or advancement of knowledge, and his commitment to the values of learning and service.

Our question here is how these various individual academic communities differ one from another in the communication and consensus essential to achieve that degree of cohesion necessary for an effective environment of learning. In the past 10 years public attention has been directed to the evidence of conflict among administration, faculty, students, nonacademic staff, and alumni that has disrupted the academic community. Is such disruption more likely to arise within one kind of academic community than in another?

One factor that has been identified in the effort to answer this question is size. It appears that communication, an indispensable procedure in achieving shared understanding of a shared purpose, is more difficult to accomplish in a large institution of higher education than in a smaller one. This is undoubtedly one reason for suggesting an upper limit in enrollment size for any one institution.

Another factor is quality. It appears that faculty members in particular tend to derive much personal satisfaction from association with an academic community having a reputation for intellectual quality. As we have noted earlier, quality is at best an elusive element in an institution of higher education, but it tends to be associated with a selective university having extensive research and doctoral degree programs in academic disciplines and medicine; it also tends to be associated with a selective liberal arts college having a high cost of instruction and a low student-faculty ratio. In any event, faculty satisfaction seems to be an important factor in helping to achieve communication and consensus within an academic community, and academic quality appears to be related to certain institutions of higher education and not to others.

Interestingly enough, it also appears that a highly selected student body of superior academic promise is more likely to be disruptive than supportive of consensus within an academic community. This circumstance seems to result from a variety of conditioning influences. Students from more affluent families with high socioeconomic status and a family tradition of higher education tend to be more critical of the learning process and the learning environment of the academic community than students from less affluent families with a lower socioeconomic status and no family tradition of higher education. The second kind of student is particularly concerned with higher education as a means to upward social mobility and remunerative professional employment in society. The first kind of student is more concerned with knowledge as power to achieve change in society.[8]

It has also been suggested that students with a specific career objective in their higher education tend to be more concerned with preserving consensus within an academic community than students whose career goals are less certain. It appears that a tendency toward disruption is more evident among students in the humanities and the social sciences than among students in the biological sciences, physical sciences, and mathematics.

There is also some evidence to suggest that institutions of higher education that are church related, and especially those related to a church with a considerable tradition of authority, are more likely to achieve consensus among administration, faculty, students, nonacademic staff, and alumni. In colleges and universities related to churches with a recent tradition of a liberating theology, a sense of academic community based upon a common strong religious faith is somewhat less likely to be evident.

Here again there is an immense range of circumstances and conditions relating to communication and consensus within an academic community that call for extensive research and consideration. We can do no more here than to suggest that differences in the cohesion of particular individual colleges and universities need to be correlated with differences in objectives, programs, size, quality, affluence, and sponsorship.

CONCLUSION   Society in the United States has developed a considerable array of varied kinds and types of individual institutions of higher education in order to meet the needs of that society for higher learning.

---

[8] On class definitions and distinctions in American society, see especially Banfield, 1970, Ch. 3.

The determination of those needs throughout American history ha been undertaken in a manner consistent with the pluralism an individualism of American society. Voluntary groups and churc groups have sponsored various kinds of institutions in variou parts of the nation. State governments have from time to tim usually by law, expressed the prevailing political sentiment of th state about higher education needs. Local governments have spoi sored some institutions of higher education, primarily at the tw year level. The federal government has tended to support th diversity rather than to direct or to supervise it.

Particularly in recent years, state governments have begun t seek means for a more "rational" planning of higher educatio objectives, programs, location, and support. This planning nece sarily has had to cope with the historical background, group loya ties, and other circumstances enforcing political constraints upo such planning.

At the beginning of the 1970s, diversity was still a major cha acteristic of American higher education: diversity in programs, i financing, in governance, and in communication and consensu Moreover, there remained a strong belief among those concerne with higher education in a political, administrative, or instructiona role that this diversity had intrinsic value and should be preserve Time and change would have to decide whether or not this beli could and would survive.

4. The University as a Community

by Irwin T. Sanders

The traditional view of the academic community provides only a partial understanding of the organization of the modern university. Such a view stresses "the community of scholars," the dominance of the faculty, the separation of academia from worldly affairs, and a sense of a common heritage. It also involves the idea of a *functional community,* a concept that emphasizes not merely what everybody has in common but also a recognized division of labor and mutual interdependence which takes differences into account. Even a very homogeneous community is based on some division of labor and interdependence, and even an extreme type of functional community—such as one's home town—can operate only because people share a common value system and use the same facilities and services, subscribe to the demands that the local government makes upon its citizens, and bind themselves together in an intricate cross-cutting network of organizations, associations, and informal structures.[1]

Three characteristics of a sense of community deserve special attention. They are shared sentiments and values; reciprocal roles, including a recognized division of labor; and acceptance of a system of authority.

SHARED SENTIMENTS AND VALUES Every institutional complex is tied to the overall society of which it is a part. It reflects and at times modifies the major values recognized within that society. Usually, a university, a business corporation, or a government bureau, in keeping with its avowed purpose,

---

[1] For variations in the definition of community, see Hillery, 1955, pp. 111–123. Other references include Minar & Greer, 1969; Arensberg & Kimball, 1965; Sanders, 1966; and Warren, 1963. Also see Nisbet, *Community and Power* (formerly *The Quest for Community*), 1962, p. 77.

may emphasize some values more than others, but those working within that institution supposedly share such common values. One way to test the existence of a sense of community on any given campus is to find out the degree of acceptance of shared sentiments and cherished values, some of which might be beliefs about the purpose and goals of higher education, the importance of freedom of scholarly inquiry, loyalty to the institution or collectivity, and agreement about certain day-to-day emphases operating within the university itself.

Purposes and Goals of Higher Education

Members of an organization have no sense of community if they do not agree in general on the purpose of that organization. In its early days, the university had a central purpose: that of providing a rationale for medieval society. It marshaled evidence to support leading church dogmas and to construct theologically oriented views of man and the world. It trained young men in these skills. Later, with the shift from acceptance of truths as handed down by the church to the stress on the scientific method as the basis for discovery and accumulation of new knowledge, it had to redefine its purposes to become more in accord with a society moving toward industrialization. In *The University in Transition,* James A. Perkins (1966, pp. 9–10) described the threefold mission of the university as the acquisition of knowledge in the mission of research, the transmission of knowledge in the mission of teaching, and the application of knowledge in the mission of public service.

But general agreement about goals does not presuppose accord on other matters. In the Middle Ages as well as in the Enlightenment, universities were the sites of bitter debates, but these were not usually about goals of the institution. Rather, they often dealt with such fine points and shades of difference that those outside the university had difficulty in following what the argument was all about. But even when debates centered upon some highly controversial topic, they did not divide the community of scholars over the issue of their central purpose as scholars.

More recently, the purpose of the university has become blurred and the "community of scholars" is at times a figure of speech rather than a reality. Structurally, the increase in size and the heavy financial burdens of a modern university have greatly expanded the administrative apparatus. On many campuses there now is a clear-cut dichotomy of interests between the administration and the faculty which plays havoc with the cozy ideal of shared sentiments and common values. A further breakdown in the traditional sense of community is found in the differences between younger and older faculty members; between those who do not have tenure and those who do; and between a minority who feel that the university ought to be involved in social action, in giving direction to our society, and the majority who prefer to play the more conventional professorial role. Also, with the shift from the view of the student as an embryonic scholar and an apprentice to the concept that he should be processed through an academic maze of courses and credit hours, the identity of interests between faculty members and most students declined. This discrepancy between faculty and students increases as our society more and more views the chief role of the university as a certification mechanism for a highly professionalized society. In such a case, the student is not as interested in knowledge for its own sake as he is in getting the diploma which is a prerequisite to the accomplishment of a professional goal.

This utilitarian emphasis is a great departure from what Talcott Parsons calls the "cognitive orientation," or the cultural matrix out of which the present university has derived. The university's stock-in-trade has been knowledge: the students come to the college or university to gain it, the administrators help the faculty finance research to further it. Many consider the professor's major concern to be with the student's mind and, according to Edward Shils (1969, pp. 47–48), he should teach the best knowledge that has been attained by mankind on what are thought to be the most important subjects. Others, like Martin Meyerson, argue that intellectual life includes an affective character as well as a cognitive character—a student's emotions are important too (Meyerson, 1969, p. 52). How a student *feels* toward his society and toward the main issues involving mankind is highly significant, along with what he *knows* about them. Most professors have been trained to deal only with the cognitive aspect and to play down emotional overtones. Therefore, to the extent that they are asked to express in their teaching a commitment to some pressing social issue, they become confused about the nature of the university and their own role in it. If the cognitive purpose is denigrated, they begin to lose their sense of community.

Differences in the values of faculty and students are noted by William Letwin, a British professor, who prefers to think of the university as a family run by its mature members rather than a community, which he sees in terms of identity of interests. He com ments:

> The demand for democratic universities is absurd also because it assume that a university is a single community in the sense that its members shar a common principal goal. In fact, they obviously do not. The goal of mos teachers is to work in the university the rest of their lives; the goal of mos students is to get out as soon as possible. . . . A university in England to day is not a community; it is rather an institution where two communitie meet. . . . (Letwin, 1968, p. 148).

To summarize, although the general public still tends to view the university in fairly traditional terms — as a community of scholars — those who face campus problems daily and intimately are impresse by erosion of the sense of community, especially with respect to the general goals of higher education, the purposes of any given in stitution, and the parts different members of the university com munity should play in carrying out these purposes.

Freedom of Inquiry   A sentiment shared at the most prestigious universities has bee that the scholar has the right to inquire freely into topics of interes to him and to come out with conclusions which run counter to popu lar opinion or even to what many would consider the public interest Today, a professor who seeks to explain racial or sex difference in intelligence largely on the basis of genetics does so on th presumption that he is entitled to freedom of inquiry and, as a scholar, is obligated to publish his findings. But when one does so as recent events centering around Richard J. Herrnstein at Harvar University have shown, students and others protest because of th social implications of these findings for programs designed to eliminate inequality in a society ("Harvard Professors . . . ," 1971 p. 12). According to the accepted academic mores, those who dis agree with a position advanced as scientific truth are supposed to challenge such a position with convincing evidence to the con trary. But when nonrational, highly political factors enter into th debate, as they did in the case of evolution half a century ago, the the concept of freedom of inquiry as a value is called into question On such matters in the past the academic community tended to b united; today, with the acceptance of social commitment as an over riding value by some members of the university community, the righ of free inquiry into controversial and unpopular questions may ex perience serious erosion, thereby reducing one value around which a sense of community developed in the past. New values may take its place, but not without serious strain within the academic community.

The right of the professor to expound unpopular doctrines in his classroom is periodically challenged as a parent learns of the exposure of his child to a point of view different from that of the parent; when a student finds his intellectual complacency disturbed; when a member of the board of trustees becomes upset by the views of a political scientist advocating drastic change; or when a university administrator fears that highly publicized, unpopular ideas presented in the classroom will cut down alumni and foundation giving. Thus far, the faculty ranks have remained firm in resisting encroachment on the professor's right to teach what he thinks appropriate to his course and subject matter.

But a new trend is under way which may lead to some weakening of the concept that the professor is master of his classroom. As a result of student protest against poor teaching, which is all too prevalent, teaching ability is taken more seriously in the overall evaluation of an individual professor for promotion or tenure. Many attempts to carry out such evaluations have relied primarily upon student opinion, without the traditional visits to the classroom by administrators, department chairmen, or senior colleagues. Such visits to the classes of the younger professor whose promotion is at stake could inhibit not only how he teaches but what he teaches, since outside visitors for a single session may judge statements out of the context of the course as a whole. The measure of his performance would then move away from student progress to how his colleagues assess his teaching ability. Yet the opening of a class to qualified visitors is a small surrender of professorial sovereignty if it actually results, as it inevitably will, in greater attention to good teaching.

Loyalty to the Institution or Collectivity The academic ideal as grounded in the public mind is that a professor settles down on a congenial campus and devotes the rest of his life to participating with fellow scholars in teaching, research, and occasional forays into public service. His main focus, according to this ideal, is unselfish contribution of time and abilities to the institution, though he may not be paid very well. In fact, his badge of prestige and penury may be patched elbows on a favorite sports jacket.

The majority of professors no longer share, and maybe they never did, this sense of permanence, this colleagueship through time. Academics are now decidedly peripatetic. Like the diplomat or the corporation executive, they do not let their roots grow too deeply wherever they happen to be. In our highly specialized society, a professional's career is tied in with the favorable judgment of his colleagues as well as with the approval of the administration of the university where he is currently teaching. But the faculty are not the only ones who are mobile. In fact, the top administration may actually move more than the professors, often lasting no longer than a single college generation. Nevertheless, many professors do have a long record of service to a particular institution, not necessarily because they expected their career to develop this way or because loyalty to the institution was the chief factor preventing a move.

For a few highly publicized professors, the university provides a forum from which to deal with (in some cases to pontificate about) the larger social issues of the day. They move in and out of government and the larger foundations, and they serve on major commissions. They also advise business and foreign governments and promote one good cause after another. Their loyalty is to the broader national need, although they would argue that their activities also bring luster to, and thereby serve, the institution that affords them a base.

Loyalty has another twist that can affect the sense of community. Sometimes the loyalty is primarily to a unit of the university rather than to the institution as a whole. Departmental loyalty reflects the professor's disciplinary emphasis; loyalty to a professional school indicates that this is where a professor considers his future to be. The department or professional school may thus become a subcommunity in which people try to recapture or recreate the sense of community that they find lacking in the institution as a whole. When professors no longer share a common humanistic tradition, the division into competing loyalties is not unexpected. But it does indicate that the specialization of the larger society reaches into the university and runs counter to the earlier academic ideal which had its beginning in the liberal arts colleges three or four generations ago.

Any sense of community built primarily on institutional loyalty is apparently in for rough going. Harold L. Hodgkinson (1971) predicts that there will be little or no institutional trust in the next decade of higher education and that appealing to the loyalty of either faculty or students will not be a good administrative strategy.

Agreement about the Character of the Institution

The existence of a shared value system or its lack shows up in agreement or disagreement within the university community about some matters that set the tone of the institution.

One of these is the balance struck between curricular and extra-curricular activities. How does the student, for instance, perceive his role? Is it primarily in terms of course work, or is it related even more to a wide range of extracurricular activities? In those liberal arts colleges noted as much for their production of "gentlemen" and "ladies" as of scholars, a rich social life has loomed as important as the life of the mind, and campus organizations provided a fertile field to develop those leadership qualities necessary for success in business, the professions, or government. In this connection, athletics often assume much importance, with the result that a basketball or football coach may be given a silver-plated Cadillac by his fond admirers while the most eminent professors find it difficult to finance a modest research project. When everyone in the institution agrees on the value of a winning football team, then the arrangements made to tutor athletes, whose practice schedule allows little time for laboratories or study, are readily accepted by the instructors concerned. But when many professors resist efforts to favor the athletes, sharp value differentiations become apparent and the sense of community is weakened.

Admissions policies also set the tone of an institution, especially as they stress either elitism or universal access. Should only the brightest, most capable, most privileged be admitted, or should the student body comprise a cross section of students more nearly representative of the larger society? Open admissions procedures, which have been forced upon reluctant faculties by the political realities facing some public institutions, can and should erode the idea of a "community of scholars" to the extent that this idea is based on elitism and exclusion of students from the "community."

Another split in common values is represented in the debate over the relative importance of teaching and research. In the past, the professors with much weight have been those who could get research contracts which helped build up not only their own reputations but also the department or center with which they were connected. The university administration enthusiastically laid claim to its share for overhead, though arguing that even the amount gained was not full compensation for indirect expenses incurred. Some of the well-known professors whose offerings had attracted students to the university were, to the disappointment of the students, periodically absent from the campus on research leaves, thereby causing some students, faculty, and administrators to question the balance between teaching and research. At times, a false dichotomy was raised, as though the choice were between one or the other when, in reality, it was a question of which emphasis the institution as a whole should take. Certainly there is little sense of community between the research entrepreneur who works with four or five graduate students a year and the professor who instructs large sections of undergraduates in the rudiments of a discipline. They are all housed on the same campus, but they reflect in their work, willingly or unwillingly, different sets of values. Fortunately, many faculty members are able to combine advanced research with undergraduate teaching.

The few selected examples cited above indicate that on many campuses there does not exist common agreement about the goals and purposes of the institution nor about the emphases in its daily operation. Universities and even colleges have grown so complex in their response to demands being made upon them that the values at the center of "the community of scholars" are no longer at the heart of many major decisions made in behalf of the institution. The traditional sense of community popularly thought to characterize a campus is thus weakened. This state of affairs can be even more clearly illustrated as we move from a discussion of values to a description of the reciprocal roles that members of the university community are expected to play with each other.

RECIPROCAL ROLES   In addition to common values, the heritage of any community also includes a set of statuses, or positions, and prescriptions as to how people occupying these statuses should behave toward each other. Norms or rules governing this behavior are also a part of this heritage. The sense of community is affirmed when there is agreement on these rules; it is shaken when people do not share the same expectations as to how others should respond or do not agree on the norms that apply to that behavior. We can, therefore, look at the university community in terms of its basic social relationships: those among faculty members, those between students and faculty, those between faculty and administration, and those between students and the administration.

Relationships among the Faculty

The idea of a community of scholars carries with it the notion of collegiality, marked by a sense of mutual respect for the opinions of others, by agreement about the canons of good scholarship, and by a willingness to be judged by one's peers. The ranking of faculty into full professors, associate and assistant professors, and instructors affects collegiality to the extent that those in lower or junior ranks supposedly defer to those above them, or those in higher ranks condescend when dealing with those more junior. Such differences need not mean any loss of community feeling as long as the younger members aspire to senior status and are willing to use the accepted means for climbing the academic ladder. Today, however, the whole process of ranking and the basis for moving from one rung to another are being debated, and no agreement has yet been reached.

More divisive than the issues of seniority, rank, and age is the high degree of specialization represented on the university faculty. The humanist, the social scientist, and the physical scientist lack a common medium of discourse as far as their professional fields are concerned. They are in no position to evaluate the performance of colleagues outside their own domain. They may even deplore the expenditures granted another field seemingly at the expense of their own: new and bigger laboratories for the scientists at the expense of library acquisitions for the humanists, or increased computer facilities for some of the social scientists at the expense of support for research based on nonquantitative methods. Representatives of the different disciplines also vary in their emphasis upon research as opposed to teaching and upon graduate as opposed to undergraduate education. In some disciplines, such as chemistry, outside professional organizations prescribe what must be taught if the degree awarded is to have national recognition; other disciplines would resent such interference and attempted standardization. A further strain is that between an emphasis upon liberal arts content and vocational or preprofessional content.

The result of such difference is that in official sessions, such as committees or faculty meetings, individual faculty members often play the role of disciplinary representatives rather than that of colleagues in a common educational enterprise. Though this may not be new in higher education, it can be disruptive of the community.

In the traditional setting, the faculty member sought to reproduce his own kind, particularly at the graduate level. A professor sought to move even undergraduates as far as possible toward an appreciation of the values and the facts that he held most dear or considered most important. The student sought to discover what the professor expected him to learn or do and then sought to carry out the expected task.

Today, many students are developing their own expectations of what the college experience should provide, which may differ from those of their supervising professors. Supposedly a dialogue ensues for which both parties are the richer in the end. Cases are even more numerous in which the professor will not abandon the traditional role (lecturing, setting the demands) when some students want a much more flexible participative student role. Even more confusing and detrimental to a sense of community is the case of the professor who has moved into a nontraditional role in his efforts to activate students who themselves cling to the traditional, submissive student role.

Adding to the confusion on contemporary campuses is the fact that the student body now includes substantial numbers of students from segments of our society that are gaining college education for the first time. Their home life and other contacts have not prepared them for the comfortable, traditional college experience associated with the well-to-do "educated class" of two or three generations ago and with roles that faculty members accepted as part of their training in the past. Such students, unwilling to accept or untrained for traditional student roles, are demanding that higher education be changed to meet their needs at the level of their preparation and to give them the credentials that will move them into better jobs than they could have aspired to without the college degree. Many faculty members are understandably resistant to what they interpret as a "watering down" of the educational program, but they find it hard to make such a case with students who lack an appreciation of the nature of scholarship or of the historical role played by the university in the past.

The emphasis on student evaluation of a professor's performance does much to challenge the superordinate position he once enjoyed. More and more he finds himself asking the students what they would like to do in the course; what books they find interesting and helpful; and whether or not they want to grade each other, receive only a pass or fail grade, or be graded by the instructor.[2] At its best, this new emphasis enables the student to make a creative contribution to his education; at its worst, it reduces traditional standards of scholarship to the level of the worst-prepared and most poorly motivated students. In any event, it breaks down the earlier idea of a college community in which the students were the pliable partners in a one-sided relationship with the faculty, were molded intellectually by the classroom experience, and were "prepared for life" by having shared in the wisdom of those who had studied in detail some aspect of "the world" into which they were to proceed upon graduation.

Faculty-Administrative Relationships Many faculty members feel genuine ambivalence toward administrators. The faculty member may view administrators as people who exist to help him carry out his professorial role more effectively. At the same time, the faculty member increasingly recognizes the existing power structure of the university and the ability and power of the central administration to affect his future. Consequently, faculty feel they must treat not just deans but vice-presidents and the president with a certain degree of circumspection, if not cordiality.

John R. Seeley (1967, p. 34) has characterized administrators, including boards of trustees, in caustic fashion and in keeping with the views held by many faculty members:

The "administrators," depending on their relations to their boards of trustees, are generally rulers or procurators, set over against their "underlying populations," holding their powers and offices in plenary independence of those populations, receiving them at alien hands, answerable (if at all) to alien bodies, and limited only (like any other illegitimate ruler) by the propensity of the population to rebel if pressed too far—which in any university that I know is quite a ways.

In close conspiracy (in most places) and unholy alliance with these successors to the sultanship, we find another body of men calling themselves "trustees." These, too, do not derive their powers (or alleged rights)

---

[2] These changes in faculty-student relationships are more prevalent in some disciplines than in others. In some colleges and in some departments instruction is carried on much as it was in the past.

from the underlying population, or, indeed, from any academic population. . . . To these there is commonly no access by the governed, and from their decisions, no appeal. Commonly, they determine their own succession. And, usually, they do not publish (or publish properly) their own proceedings, so that the light of day cannot, in principle, light up their goings-on. . . . In most cases, they derive their power legally and actually either from the fount of unregenerate power, the state, or from mere money—or access to—and a claim to represent the men of might or money.

With increasing layers of administration, necessitated by the complexity of higher education, a separation of interests has developed between administrators and faculty. The division of labor each represents is based upon different functions, different methods of accountability, different preparation and recruitment, and a somewhat different reward system. Thus, the conventional "community of scholars" has expanded to the point at which it can no longer accommodate those with administrative responsibilities; a fission has occurred.

When the administrators are ex-professors or even attempt to teach a course or two, they find this demarcation most unwelcome. The character of the central administration is strongly colored by the hard-nosed accountant types who have never thought of themselves as academics but who have to make the professors (and the units they represent) toe the line financially if the institution is to maintain fiscal integrity. The professors' view of the "administration," though based largely on experience with deans and vice-presidents, is also influenced by contacts with or perceptions of bookstore managers—who may seem cooperative or uncooperative—purchasing agents, the security force, the deans of men and women, the alumni secretary, and the public relations office.

In effect, then, the university community consists of three networks: faculty, administrative, and student. Role changes occur within each of them, with the administrative being reorganized more frequently and with new statuses being added as needed.[3] The interaction between the faculty and administrative networks varies with the president, who may choose to work through established channels, such as the university senate or similar forums,

---

[3] François Bourricaud (1969, p. 5) has noted that "in the French university the various strata are being more and more separated; they each have their own views, their own goals, their own values. . . ." See also Bourricaud (1971).

or may act on his own initially and then use the faculty-administrative groups as communicating links for messages that come from the top down. Such behavior further confirms the distrust faculty members have for the administration, particularly if those faculty still cling to the belief that they themselves should be running the institution or that they *are* the institution.

Unless major segments of the academic community feel that they are part of the decision-making process, they do not gain a real sense of community. For certain kinds of decisions, one network may have major responsibility—for example, faculty may have primary jurisdiction over academic questions. But there needs to be some understanding about just what the responsibilities are and how problems relating equally to both networks—faculty and administrative—are to be handled. As the pendulum swings between autocratic and democratic decision making, so the sense of participation and affiliation of those affected goes down or up. Lost in the shuffle, all too often, are those unpublicized individuals known as the staff—the secretaries, clerks, custodians, and others needed to keep the institution in operation. That they are a part of the community is not always recognized, a fact that underlies efforts at staff unionization on many campuses. Indeed, one indication of the breakdown of the traditional community but the broadening of the functional community is the effort by a group of employees to seek a new identity and an increased voice in university affairs.

Administrative-Student Relationships There are, of course, numerous and crucial points of contact between the student network and the administrative network. As the college or university acted in the nineteenth and twentieth centuries *in loco parentis,* it had to provide not only for course instruction but for the total living environment of the young people entrusted to its care. S. M. Lipset (1968, p. 44) points out:

. . . the increasing amount of time required for educational development inherently means the prolongation of adolescence. Although physiologically mature, and often above the age legally defined as adult, students are expected to refrain from full involvement in the adult world. Dependency is, of course, built into the very essence of the university system . . . . Hence, the student who leaves home to attend the university finds that he remains in a highly controlled situation, even while society is urging him to become independent.

Dormitories, health and counseling services, chaplains, and recreational outlets are but a few of the services universities have provided for the dependent student. And in all of these, student at one time or another could find some cause for complaint. They have had to conform to rules that they did not make or did not like, accept services below those they thought they were entitled to, and pay charges which they could not understand. With the affluence of the 1960s and early 1970s, students indicated their dissatisfaction by moving in large numbers to off-campus facilities so that universities whose enrollments have grown tremendously in the past few years nevertheless have empty dormitory rooms.

The concerns of the students—expanding in the case of many to political and social issues of the day—now transcend the parochial concerns of a given campus. Sometimes radical students are credited with politicizing the university, but they claim instead that the university had already become politicized through administrative arrangements with off-campus agencies. Nobody, they argue, recognized this until the students called it to public attention. Repercussions can follow whether the university does or does not assist job recruiters from the Department of Defense or prominent United States corporations, whether or not black students have their own center where they can withdraw from the white-dominated environment, and whether or not students have a voice in the selection of a dean or a president. Even though the majority of students may not feel involved or even want to be bothered by some of these concerns, their elected or even self appointed student leaders know how to manipulate or work within the student network to influence or checkmate the administrative network. This is done at times by making the students feel that their interests are antagonistic to those of the central administration or even the faculty. Student leaders may play down the sense of community of the institution as a whole in order to create a sense of community among the students alone, which can be marshaled in behalf of some immediate student goal.

AN ACCEPTED SYSTEM OF AUTHORITY

A sense of community is possible only where there is an accepted system of authority along with the previously mentioned shared sentiments and values and agreement as to roles. Inherent in reciprocal social relationships is a recognition that, in a given social situation, some are more competent and others less competent some are leaders and others followers.

The Nature of Authority

Robert A. Nisbet (1962, p. xii) mentions social function and social authority as the two supports upon which community, in any reasonably precise sense, can alone exist and influence its members. He explains the meaning of authority as follows:

> By authority, I do not mean power. Power, I conceive as something external and based upon force. Authority, on the other hand, is rooted in the statuses, functions, and allegiances which are the components of any association. Authority is indeed indistinguishable from organization, and a sense of organization becomes a part of the human personality. Authority, like power, is a form of constraint, but, unlike power, it is based ultimately upon the consent of those under it; that is, it is conditional. Power arises only when authority breaks down.

This passage explains why university officials, as well as faculty members, seem impotent at times to cope with campus violence. They rely on members of the academic community to accept the system of authority, and their response is in terms of their position in that system of authority. The calling in of police is a recognition that external power, rather than authority, is needed, but this very act is a public announcement that the university is no longer a community —at least during that time.

Authority, however, needs legitimacy if it is to have ready acceptance within the community. Daniel Bell has pointed out that the older authority of the university was the traditional authority, whose role was "that of expressing the central value system of a society, which was not the ideology of any particular social body, but the maintenance of the tradition of free inquiry and the idea of civility." He notes, however, a recent move by the university toward a rational-legal authority, "namely the assertion of a particular expertise (as the source of rational authority) and the self-conscious service to the society in pursuit of socially defined goals (the basis of its claim to legal support)" (Bell, n.d.).

Related to such a transition in the social definitions of university authority is the growing amorphousness of the United States university itself (Bell, n.d.). While the legitimacy of traditional authority figures is being questioned in society at large, we find people in the academic community—as was mentioned earlier—uncertain as to what component of the university they owe any loyalty. Is a faculty member's primary loyalty to his students, as the doctor's is to his patients? Or is the faculty member's loyalty chiefly to his

disciplinary colleagues or to the central administration? The answ
to such a question is of vital significance when legitimacy is qu
tioned, when the traditional authority system is undergoing chan
For example, under what circumstances does the chairman of 1
board of trustees speak *for* the university and when does this l
come the right and duty of the president? Under what circu
stances, if any, should the faculty member who is president of 1
university senate speak in the name of the university? As indica1
earlier, increasing faculty professionalization has tended to curb 1
authority of governing boards and administrative officers (N
Connell, 1969). At the same time, the authority of the teacher l
been lessened by the increasing maturity, real or superficial, of 1
student and by the obsolescence of much of the training that ol
professors received prior to World War II (Corson, 1970). Ev
within the student network, the traditional role of once-power
student governments has been weakened by the refusal of radi
student groups to accept their legitimacy.

Reshaping the Authority System
To try to regain a sense of community, persons from all segmen
of the university are busily engaged in setting up new social mec
anisms to replace the old. In a few cases, this has been done
simply adding students or faculty to existing committees or age
cies; often, the effort has been made to give a new legitimacy
changing the nature of representation. Edward Shils (1969, p.
maintains that the basic need is not greater participation but rath
a clarification of the responsibilities of the different levels of t
university. He argues, therefore, for a rewriting of the constitutio
of American universities.

Harold Hodgkinson sees much of the remedy in "selective c
centralization," or a principle in terms of which decisions affecti
individuals' lives and commitments would be made in the smalle
possible units, while matters of logistics and support servic
would be made in the largest context available. Such a princip
also recognizes that no single hierarchical structure can solve a
problems confronting a university, but that the university con
munity will have to rely on more ad hoc decision making by rapid
shifting groups. He writes:

This program of selective decentralization will clearly result in more sh
ing membership in decision-making groups and fewer committees that v
endure forever, creating enough work to justify their existence. [T

modification of our governance systems] could increase the dimension of trust and loyalty, not to the huge super organization of the total university, but to the meaningful subunit in which the individual participates (1971, pp. 150–151).

Such observations lead directly into the question of decision making within a university community.

Decision-making Models

In the traditional view, the university as a community relies basically on a consensus model of governance. One assumes a sense of community based on the elements that have been described. A few deviant faculty characters are either tolerated or dealt with when reappointment times comes around; students who do not wish to abide by the rules are reminded of their freedom to go elsewhere and may even be excluded from the community. To achieve consensus, much time is spent in discussing all the fine points of every issue, which, in itself, makes a faculty meeting unlike that of any other deliberative body, since this kind of elaborate discussion is what the Ph.D. finds most congenial to his training and temperament. To foreclose an issue before all facets have been explored is not only bad governing policy but it is aesthetically and intellectually unacceptable to the academic mind.

To get consensus, therefore, within a given college or professional school faculty is difficult enough; to arrive at such a consensus when faculties from several schools are involved, chiefly in a representative body such as a university senate, calls for necessary accommodation of diverse views. The situation becomes much more complicated when faculty and students or faculty and administration seek to reach a consensus, particularly if they labor under the assumption that they have a common goal, a common set of interests.

With the emergence of "student power," allied with the demands of junior faculty, the traditional consensus model has proved inadequate to meet all situations. For some problems a *conflict* model of decision making is needed. This starts with the assumption that there may be antagonistic interests, not just common interests, that must develop some modus vivendi if the community—viewed in terms of function rather than communality—is to operate in a manner satisfying to its members. A conflict model has built into it a set of procedures to be invoked if agreement cannot be reached; it calls for collective bargaining, not necessarily in the trade-union sense of drawing up a final legal contract but in the sense of accommodation and compromise to the point that each party feels that it has done the best it can under the circumstances. A conflict model may be basically juridical in that it provides a means for appeal to successively higher organs within the community for a ruling. Or, it may be localized or specialized to the extent that one competent body alone is expected to come up with a resolution to a particular issue, no matter how long it takes. There may be various kinds of bodies for different kinds of issues, but each body is expected to exercise its competence.

Of course, no decision-making model works unless the parties to the issue communicate with each other in an effort to end an impasse. Should communication break down and one party withdraw then the rules of the game become changed and the community has to take other action in the interest of continuity and safeguarding the interests of others who may not be involved in the dispute. With the predicted tendency for staff, teaching assistants, and junior faculty to turn increasingly to formal unions as a means of accomplishing their demands, the university community will find the conflict model more and more called into play.

Just as no community is ever in a state of full harmony, so it is never in a state of total conflict. Many decisions can be made from day to day with the use of the consensus model; others may periodically require a conflict model. The modern university administration and leaders of the faculty and student networks, if they are to prove effective in discharging their responsibilities, will have to be familiar with both kinds of models. In particular, they will have to exercise judgment in deciding when one model rather than the other is appropriate. One can even predict a seeming paradox to the extent that the conflict model proves workable, members of the community may develop a greater sense of community based on functional interdependence rather than merely on communality.

CONCLUSION   The discussion of the sense of community on university campuses today has forced consideration of a wide range of topics related to the university as an organization. Two additional topics deserve brief treatment in conclusion: one is the utility of viewing the university as a local community and the other is the connection between the academic community and the other communities with which it is linked.

The University as a Local Community

An appropriate organizational model for the university might well be the local community.

First, the campus is a physical fact, just as the boundaries of any community are a fact, often determining by their shape and physical features what is possible and not possible in the way of community life. Campuses that are fragmented or very large must provide transportation systems. The physical plant and its operation involve the same problems encountered in the management of the public buildings of a small city; the use of space to best advantage and even the acquisition of additional space require planning skills of the quality and magnitude required for most towns.

Second, the university community, like the local community, has tended to become a *total* community in the sense that the inhabitants can satisfy most of their basic needs within the community. Food and shelter, supplementary employment, health care, religious activities, family counseling, communication through newspapers and radio, police protection, and a wide range of recreational outlets are under the general supervision of the administrators of any large university. This combination of services, along with the staff to provide them, moves the university a long way from being merely a community of scholars and confronts it organizationally with concerns similar to those found in local communities of comparable population size.

Third, procedures for allocation of resources within a town or city may provide useful models for the university. Some of these resources flow through local government, others through quasi-governmental bodies, and still others through private or nongovernmental channels. In what circumstances does decentralized decision making work best? The great number of studies done by sociologists and political scientists on community power structure have much to say to university administrators on the problems of wrestling with the influence of various leaders and the means by which a complex collective arrives at decisions on controversial issues, such as fluoridation of water supplies or a bond issue for a new elementary school.

Fourth, the allocation of resources calls for the exercise of political leadership. In fact, Daniel Bell (n.d.) argues that the university must become, more formally, a political community in which the making of policy decisions is open and subject to debate and to some form of confirmation by the relevant constituencies in the university. He cites three major areas that require exploration:

1 The structure of representation. This will vary from school to schoc

2 The relevant constituencies. Who is to have a voice and of what kind i
university deliberations?

3 The division of powers. What decisions, if any, are reserved for the trustee
who are often the legal custodians of the corporation?

In moving toward the recognition of the political factor, the un
versity community is becoming more like the local communities tha
surround it. Drawbacks to the analogy between a university and
local community lie in the fact that the university is specialized i
its societal purposes and caters primarily to a particular age se:
ment of the population; nevertheless, the analogy could be carrie
to considerable length. For example, in each community form
associations play a role in creating public opinion, in carrying ou
certain needed functions, in giving members a sense of belongir
and therefore greater satisfaction within the community, in dealir
with problems before they become large enough to affect sever.
segments of the community. Another example is the manner i
which new arrivals to a community are "socialized" into the pa
ticular folkways and expectations of that community. A final e
ample is the manner in which social change is initiated and tl
community is kept responsive to new needs and receptive to expe
mentation with new procedures for serving the members of the cor
munity. Far too often university administrators and faculty mer
bers who play an active part in off-campus community life do n
apply to their university responsibilities either the models or i:
sights they use in trying to make their home town a better place
which to live.

**Relationship
between the
University and
Other Com-
munities**

A key feature of the academic community in the past has been th
of autonomy. The university administration was responsible f
what occurred within the campus confines; outside police did n
enter without prior approval. The larger society, through legisl
tion or special charter, granted it a tax-exempt status so that it cou
conduct its facilities for students with minimum external inte
ference and could even handle its business properties with co
siderable freedom. Thus, fiscal autonomy in the use of its own r
sources came to be accepted. In the intellectual enterprise, of whi
it tends to have the monopoly at the higher levels, it brooked litt
interference. In its dealings with the young people sent to it f

"preparation for life," it also wanted much freedom, even to the point of suggesting that pranks of college students be viewed in a different light from similar deeds of noncollege young people.

But the student disorders of the 1960s, along with other factors such as shrinking urban tax bases, changed this relationship to the rest of the community. The taking over of university buildings by student groups was no longer viewed as a prank but as a political act; the calling in of the police—often with serious misunderstanding between the university and local authorities as to what police behavior would be—broke down the pretense that the university could handle its own affairs. The additional pressure that the university provide gymnasium and other facilities to those, often disadvantaged, groups living in proximity to it made university administrators keenly sensitive to off-campus relationships.

What is needed, of course, is a redefinition of what university autonomy really means. It does not mean a lack of involvement with its immediate economic and political environment, since it cannot escape facing local issues. It has become too big a power on the local scene. Its ties to the surrounding community are even more pronounced as students register to vote in the same place they attend college. Moreover, the university is an important provider of jobs to local people, a purchaser of supplies, a sponsor of athletic and other entertainments, a payer or nonpayer of taxes on income-producing property.

Each university, then, must increasingly adjust to the local conditions it faces. This is happening at the same time that universities as social institutions are confronting problems of funding from national sources—governmental agencies and private foundations. Such funding is based on some rationale of social purpose and it becomes translated into the terms of specific program, terms which often depart from what the university community two or three generations ago would have considered appropriate.

A redefinition of roles such as those mentioned above is reflected in modifications in university organization. A sense of community based on an awareness of a common heritage, a shared purpose, an acceptance of the canons of good scholarship, and the need for rigorous testing of new ideas advanced will vary in intensity from institution to institution and within points in time. It may even transcend a given campus and describe bonds among intellectuals in diverse fields. But the emphasis upon communality is no longer sufficient as the organizing principle. To this must be added the view of the functional community, which depends, internally, upon division of labor, interdependence, and conflict-resolving mechanisms. Externally—in society at large—the university also has a functional interdependence with large institutional complexes. Though its own organization may remain unique, the university will nevertheless have to interact with other large-scale organizations— corporations, private foundations, and government bureaus—upon which it is dependent for the discharge of its major responsibilities. In doing so, however, the basic nature of the university must not be lost. Martin Meyerson (1970) puts this into focus:

The college and university best serve the city and best serve civilization as the intellectual base for action, rather than as the arena of action. Some are tempted, in moral causes, to make the college a piece of contested turf or turn the campus into warring terrain. Colleges and universities, however, do not serve best as battlefields but as places for dreams and plans to begin, that new responsibilities and responsiveness may ensue from them.

5. Comparisons of Four Foreign Universities

by Barbara B. Burn

This chapter compares governance at the universities of Freiburg, Paris, Toronto, and Cambridge and the place of these universities in their respective systems of higher education. These universities were selected primarily because, excluding the Soviet Union and Eastern Europe, they represent models of major university systems found outside the United States. Paris exemplifies the Napoleonic university which was grafted onto the medieval guild of masters; Freiburg, the research-dominated university dating from the founding of the University of Berlin by Wilhelm von Humboldt in 1809; and Cambridge, the collegial model developed at Oxbridge. Toronto illustrates a more recent amalgam of influences from the church-related college, Oxbridge, Redbrick, the federated University of London, and perhaps even the contemporary American multiversity. Almost all universities share in some measure the features of these four institutions.

The four representative universities are also comparable in certain specific respects. Freiburg and Paris have until recently had little autonomy in fiscal affairs and are now acquiring more. Toronto and Cambridge until recently enjoyed substantial fiscal autonomy and are now having to relinquish some of it. In Germany and Canada, both federal states, higher education falls primarily under the jurisdiction of the state governments, whereas in France and Britain the national governments have jurisdiction. Cambridge has a collegial structure, Toronto a mix of college and faculty organization. Freiburg and Paris are theoretically organized on the basis of units that combine allied disciplines.

All four universities have traditionally accorded considerable priority to research and little to continuing education. All four are now large institutions: Enrollments vary from about 10,000 at

Cambridge to more than 27,000 at Paris VI.[1] The following section sketches in the background of each of the universities to provide a perspective for subsequent comparisons.

**BACKGROUND
OF THE
UNIVERSITIES**

The University of Cambridge

After Paris, Cambridge is the oldest of the four universities, and it cherishes its antiquity. The college system dates from 1284; the university from 1318. Originally, the colleges merely provided housing for scholars coming to sit at the feet of the masters. Not until the Tudor period, when all students were required to be members of a college, did the colleges take their present form. They evolved into self-governing and largely self-contained societies. Headed by a master and comprising fellows and scholars, each college provided most of the teaching for its small band of undergraduates.

Before the 1850s the heads of houses or colleges virtually ruled the university and selected the vice-chancellor from among themselves. In effect, the colleges were the university, and the central administration had few functions. Although there have been major changes since then, the vice-chancellor still has no office in "Old Schools," the central administration building, but performs his duties as vice-chancellor in his college, where he continues to serve as master. The collegial model, a major factor in the university system today, is only now being seriously questioned. Critics note the weakness of the central administration, the alleged elitism and relatively high costs of the colleges, their outdated ritualism, and the possible incompatibility between the traditional self-sufficiency of the colleges and the urgent need to coordinate total resources in a period of steeply rising costs.

A second major factor in the university's present organization is its origin as a guild, a society of masters and scholars. Other English universities (except Oxford) were typically established at the initiative of local and regional interests, government and lay. Their chief governing bodies reflect this origin by including representatives of local government, community interests, professional bodies, and other similar groups. Cambridge is founded on the con

---

[1] In 1970 the University of Paris was divided into 13 separate universities comprising the old University of Paris plus other newer institutions. The term *University of Paris* as used in this chapter refers collectively to the 13 new universities.

cept of a self-governing society of scholars. Some are graduates— the senate; some are senior members—the dons; and some are junior members—the students.

Among British higher education institutions Cambridge (along with Oxford) is commonly acknowledged as leading the academic procession. This eminence is variously attributed to the quality of its teaching staff, the caliber of its students, its major research role, the tutorial teaching system enshrined in the colleges, its allegedly superior faculty-student ratio, its architectural splendor, and its renowned if somewhat antiutilitarian tradition of intellectualism.

The proportion of all British university students enrolled at Cambridge has declined from about 10 percent before World War II to less than 5 percent today. Although university enrollments will probably double nationally during the 1970s, Cambridge does not expect to increase its enrollment by more than 2,000–3,000 students. In fact, yet another difference between Cambridge (and Oxford) and other British universities, perhaps the most significant, is that Cambridge assumes that it can still largely control its own destiny despite the urgencies of rising enrollment demand and costs, the need to coordinate resources, and the mounting pressures on all higher education institutions for stricter public accountability.

The University of Toronto

Like Cambridge, Toronto has residential teaching colleges, an international reputation for excellence, and, among Canadian universities, relative antiquity. It too emphasizes research. Beyond these general characteristics the similarities are slight, the differences profound. Toronto's internal governance and its relations with external government are the product of a very different history and different social forces.

Toronto was born out of religious dissent. It was launched by the Anglican Church in 1827 as King's College. In order to draw it and other denominational colleges into a single provincial and nondenominational system, King's College was secularized in 1849 and its name changed to the University of Toronto. In 1853, when University College was established as Toronto's teaching arm, the university itself adopted the University of London's external degree-granting pattern. The theory was that, as a nonsectarian and purely degree-granting institution, Toronto would encourage the denominational institutions to affiliate with it by conferring its degrees on their students, thus reversing the trend toward proliferation of denominational institutions.

The need to reconcile the divergent interests of the denominational institutions with the concept of a single secular institution explains the University of Toronto's complex pattern of federated universities and colleges. Various denominational institutions gave up their degree-granting powers in most fields but through federation kept their separate identities as legally independent institutions.

Apart from religion, ethics, and related subjects in which the federated universities offer their own degrees, their undergraduate programs (and those of University College) can include courses only in the so-called college subjects enumerated in the University of Toronto Act. These include English, ancient history, classical and Oriental languages, French, and German, and hence tend to reflect more the rhetoric of the senior common room of 60 years ago than current needs. The university Faculty of Arts and Science, whose course offerings are not similarly restricted, now teaches about 80 percent of the students in arts and science. The colleges of the federated universities figure little in the power structure of the university because their staffs teach in relatively few fields and constitute a minority of the Faculty of Arts and Science of the university. The colleges are important chiefly as communities offering some diversity within the university. Toronto's federated and constituent colleges also have little influence on universitywide decision making.

Since the 1906 University of Toronto Act, the university has had a two-tier system of governance comprising a lay Board of Governors appointed by Ontario's lieutenant-governor and a Senate composed largely of academics, with the president serving as the pivotal link between them. In 1971 this two-tier system was replaced by a single governing body.

As the largest university in Ontario—a leading province in higher education development in Canada—and as a university heavily oriented toward graduate training and research, Toronto has traditionally been viewed mainly as a national rather than provincial university. In the last decade, however, Toronto has become more provincially oriented. Rising enrollments and costs of university education have been accompanied by a vastly increased public concern and financial investment on the part of the provincial government. Since the Federal-Provincial Fiscal Arrangements Act of 1967, the federal government, which all along has lacked constitutional jurisdiction in education, has mostly withdrawn from the higher education scene. Direct subsidies to universities on a formula basis have been replaced by the transfer of federal fiscal resources to the provincial governments. Now, except for research, the universities deal almost entirely with the provincial governments for financial support.

Toronto's position within Ontario has also changed. One of only five universities before World War II, it is now one of sixteen. Whereas 92 percent of all students in postsecondary education in Ontario were at universities in 1951–52, close to half are now in other institutions. Toronto currently enrolls about 26,000 full-time students; its enrollments, however, have increased proportionately less than those of other universities in the province, and its share of graduate enrollments in Ontario dropped from about one-half to only one-fourth during the 1960s. Although these quantitative changes may testify to Toronto's sustained quality in the face of pressures to dilute resources, they also suggest Toronto's reduced leverage within the higher education system of the province.

The rapid growth of university institutions in Ontario in the 1960s made necessary the establishment of more elaborate government machinery to advise on and fund this expansion and prompted the universities to set up their own arrangements for interuniversity coordination. It is ironic that Toronto, which played a major part in pressing for both of these developments, now confronts a situation in which, both within the voluntary coordinating scheme and vis-à-vis the provincial government, it is an equal among equals and no more equal than the other universities. Like Cambridge, Toronto is less able to control its destiny than it was in the past.

The University of Paris

The University of Paris, which in 1970 enrolled 180,000 of the nation's 647,000 university students, has undergone profound transformation—and in fact no longer exists as a single university. In accordance with the 1968 *Loi d'Orientation de l'Enseignement Supérieur* (Orientation of Higher Education Act), the university was dismantled and restructured into a series of new universities. The five faculties constituting the former central university in Paris were broken down into about two hundred *Unités d'Enseignement*

et Recherche (UERs)—units roughly comparable to departments
in United States universities—and regrouped among the new
universities known as Paris I through VII. University centers that
emerged during the 1960s on the outskirts of Paris now comprise
the new universities of Paris VIII–XI. Two more new universities
mostly in the planning stage as of 1971, are Paris XII and XIII
Although Paris no longer exists as a single university, a common
framework governs Paris I–XIII (and all the new French univer
sities). Paris III, IV, and VII are the chief successors to the Sor
bonne.

Before the 1968 reforms, French higher education was based on
centuries-old traditions. Like Cambridge, the Sorbonne—the most
widely known faculty in the old University of Paris—had its roots
in the Middle Ages. Its origin as a university of privileged masters
led to traditions of professorial power that survived the university's
subjection to the Crown in the fifteenth century, its virtual elimina
tion by Napoleon, and even the 1968 reform law. France's pre-1968
university system dates mainly from the 1808 decree that set up the
Napoleonic Imperial University and made faculties, not universities
the central unit in the higher education system. Only in 1896 were
the faculties regrouped into universities, and even then the faculty
remained the dominant unit. The present system assumes that sep
arate disciplines share common interests and can work out com
mon solutions. In 1972 this assumption was still in doubt.

Another ancient tradition—that universities prepare an elite for
society—is no longer in force. And the underlying assumption that
a central authority could know and should determine the nation's
needs for university-trained people has been largely discredited
Such a large proportion of young people now go on to the university
that society cannot guarantee them the jobs they train for, much
less elite positions.

Enrollments in France rose from about 135,000 in 1950 to
647,000 in 1970; continued rising enrollments are plaguing efforts
to reform the university system. All young persons who success
fully graduate from the university stream in secondary school and
obtain the baccalaureate are entitled by right to enroll in a univer
sity—a practice that makes it impossible for universities to stem
the tide of increasing numbers of students.[2]

[2] A step toward selective university admissions was taken with the passage on
June 21, 1971, of a law amending the 1968 *Loi d'Orientation* to provide selection in admission to UERs in medicine.

Before the 1968 reform law, the French university system was highly centralized. The Ministry of National Education determined curriculum and degrees and had the final authority for faculty appointments as well as finances.

The 1968 reforms were designed to give universities flexibility in determining course offerings and, through decentralization, autonomy in order to make them more responsible to local and regional needs. But university autonomy does not appear overnight. Lacking the people, processes, and traditions needed for the effective exercise of autonomy, the new universities still look to the Ministry of National Education for guidance.

Finally, it should be noted, the 1968 reforms did not include the Grandes Écoles, the elite of all higher education institutions in France. Autonomy, participation, and political and organizational freedom, the main themes of the new reforms, were apparently not judged appropriate for this most selective sector of higher education in France. Even here, however, some change is now brewing.

The University of Freiburg

Albert-Ludwigs Universität in Freiburg, founded in 1457, is one of Germany's oldest and most distinguished universities. It does not, however, have a place among German universities comparable to that of Cambridge, Paris, or Toronto within their respective university systems because Germany traditionally has had a number of universities sharing equal repute.

The von Humboldt University continues to be a nostalgic ideal for Freiburg as for all German universities. It was research-oriented, proclaimed the freedom of both teacher and student to pursue science and learning as ends in themselves, and saw as its essential task the training of scholars regardless of the immediate needs of the state. This background explains the dichotomy between universities and other postsecondary education institutions in Germany and the ambivalence of the universities today as they confront rising pressures to be more "socially useful."

Traditions of university governance in Germany also derive from von Humboldt. Full professors, known as *Ordinarien,* enjoyed enormous power within the universities and prestige in the wider society. Within certain limits they directed their individual institutes as they wished. The central administration had little power in academic affairs. Junior teaching staff depended on the personal backing of their professor patrons for advancement, and opportunities were limited because "chairholders" were appointed for life and new chairs rarely created.

This system began to erode in the late 1950s. The doubling of university enrollments between 1955 and 1965 in the absence of a commensurate increase in permanent teaching staff brought a sharp increase at the assistant rank. Assistants now handle the bulk of teaching and, not surprisingly, demand much more say in decision making. The universities launched in the 1960s are establishing new patterns in structure and governance, and student protest, headed by radical student leader Rudi Dutschke in the late 1960s, catalyzed the recent nationwide reforms giving students a part in university governance.

Freiburg University is changing more slowly than many other German universities. Located in Baden-Württemberg, a relatively conservative state, the institution reflects political forces within the *Land* (state). But it too is bowing to national and local pressures for reform.

In 1970–71 Freiburg enrolled about 11,500 students. One of 39 universities in the Federal Republic (including West Berlin), it is financed mainly by the *Land* government. Under Germany's federal system, the *Land* government has had primary jurisdiction over university affairs. With the recent amendment of the national constitution, however, the federal government can now set guidelines for university development. The Commission for Educational Planning *(Bund-Länder Kommission für Bildungsplanung)*, established in 1970, can recommend on the future of all education in Germany, including higher education. Although the commission is only an advisory body, its recommendations are not lightly ignored because its membership includes equal numbers of federal and *Länder* government representatives.

The national government has been the initiator of reform in Germany. The *Wissenschaftsrat* (Science Council), an advisory council of representatives of federal and *Länder* governments and research and lay interests, lacked the necessary power to effect change. The Conference of University Rectors and the Conference of *Länder* Ministries of Education have been more conservative than reformist. But as a result of the increasing federal involvement in the last decade, a national system of higher education is at last beginning to emerge. Traditions of professorial power, faculty autonomy, and *Land* government dominance are giving way to the power of the students and assistants, to societal demands and needs, and to federal government pressure.

RELATIONS TO EXTERNAL GOVERNMENT
Relations between these four universities and their governments have been determined little by the structure of government. Cambridge and Paris are in countries with a unitary system of government, yet there are few similarities in their relations with their governments. Freiburg and Toronto are in federally organized countries, but again there is surprisingly little commonality in their relations to governmental authorities. On the other hand, there are significant similarities between Paris and Freiburg, because their governments have traditionally influenced university affairs, and between Cambridge and Toronto, which have had great autonomy.

Freiburg and Paris

Before the recent reforms in France and Germany, the French Ministry of National Education and Ministry of Education *(Kultusministerium)* in Baden-Württemberg made the final decisions on faculty appointments, the selection of senior administrators, and how funds were spent. Degrees and major examinations were also governmentally determined. In France the national government even decided on the courses to be taught. The rector of the *académie* of. Paris[3] and the *Kanzler,* an administrative official in the rector's office at Freiburg, represented their governments to the universities. In both countries permanent teaching staff had and still have civil servant status.

Freiburg had a greater illusion of autonomy because German professors, unlike the French, could determine what they taught and not merely how they taught it. At both Freiburg and Paris the sense of autonomy was reenforced by the practice of government authorities to accept the universities' recommendations on most matters even though government had the last word.

The main change in Freiburg's relations with the ministry is not so much that the latter has relinquished authority but that reforms under the 1969 Baden-Württemberg *Grundordnung* (constitution) aim at strengthening the central administration of Freiburg University (and other universities in the *Land*) and achieving more unity in what was a highly decentralized system. The rector's term of office has been increased from one year to four, and there are now four prorectors instead of one. The faculties are expected to reach

---

[3] The *académie* of Paris was one of the 23 educational districts into which France was divided before the 1968 reforms. The rector, appointed by the Ministry of National Education, was the chief administrative official at the University of Paris and supervised all education in his *académie.*

agreement on universitywide interests; their recommendations are then pressed on an institutional basis with the ministry rather than directly by individual faculties. (Faculties are not, however, quickly abandoning their habit of dealing directly with the ministry.)

In France the 1968 *Loi d'Orientation* in principle encourages more institutional autonomy within the universities and allows lay and regional interests to have a role in institutional governance. The rector (now called chancellor) of Paris is no longer head of the University Council,[4] the top governing body of the University of Paris, but coordinator of all the universities in his *académie*. The universities now report their expenditures after the fact instead of being told by the government how they may allocate funds. And they may set up new courses and degrees rather than fit all their curricula to national degrees.

No longer is the Ministry of National Education virtually the only body influencing the universities in France. A new National Council for Higher Education and Research, composed of university representatives and others and chaired by the Minister, assists and advises the Ministry of National Education at the national level. Once established, parallel regional bodies will have a similar mandate at the regional level.

With only 54 university representatives among its total of 90 members, the new National Council cannot give equal representation to all 67 universities. The presidents of the universities consequently have pressed for official recognition of the Conference of Presidents as a second organ to represent the universities nationally. This new permanent conference was established by ministry decree in January 1971 and, together with the National Council, constitutes a bicameral system for coordinating university affairs in which, however, the National Council is preeminent. Neither body has more than advisory power.

Cambridge and Toronto

Both Cambridge and Toronto are in principle autonomous. However, as in France and Germany, government concern with university affairs has expanded in Britain and Canada, especially in the 1960s, because of the dramatic increase in the need for public funding. In Britain the University Grants Committee (UGC), which

---

[4] Before the 1968 reforms the council was made up of deans and professors elected by the faculties plus outside members chosen by the University Council.

reviews the universities' financial needs, makes periodic recommendations to the government on its support to the universities. No longer do UGC recommendations receive the relatively unquestioning acceptance typical of past decades. In negotiating with the Department of Education and Science, the UGC must be able to justify its recommendations in detail. In turn the UGC demands more detailed justification from the universities for their expenditures.

Cambridge is less susceptible to government pressure than the other British universities (except Oxford) because only the university, and not the colleges, receives Treasury funding via the UGC. In principle, therefore, the colleges have no public accountability. In fact they are supported in part by the university because most of their regular teaching staff have faculty appointments and hence receive the bulk of their salaries from the university.

Since 1964 Ontario has had its version of a UGC, the Committee on University Affairs (CUA). It includes academics and lay representatives and advises and recommends to the provincial government on the development, operation, expansion, and financing of the universities. Also in 1964 Ontario established a Department of University Affairs, changed in 1971 to the Department of Colleges and Universities (it is now responsible for the 20 colleges of applied arts and technology as well as the universities), which serves as secretariat to CUA and staffs the Ministry for University Affairs. This dual function of the department distinguishes it sharply from the UGC in Britain, which has a permanent staff separate from the Department of Education and Science and which does much of its work through subcommittees composed mostly of academics. The CUA, however, maintains close working relations with Ontario's universities and, in fact, carries out much of its work through joint committees with the Council of Ontario Universities, the coordinating body of the universities. The recommendations of these joint committees are regarded by both the government and the universities as binding.

The CUA differs from UGC in respect to its role as well. Whereas the UGC bases its recommendations for funding the British universities on details of programming, staffing, enrollments, and other needs, the Ontario government provides funds to the 16 provincial universities on the basis of formulas devised by CUA that allot certain amounts per number of students enrolled in different kinds of programs and at different levels. The CUA therefore is oriented toward the universities as a system. One can conjecture that formula financing and CUA's role produce more coordination among Ontario's universities than occurs in the British system.

Known as "collective autonomy," this coordination in Ontario was formalized in 1962 with the establishment of the Committee of Presidents of Universities of Ontario. Since then the committee has developed remarkable vigor. In 1971 the committee changed its name to the Council of Ontario Universities, reflecting the fact that participation has for some time extended well beyond the presidents of the 16 institutions.

INTERNAL STRUCTURES

This section first compares the relative authority of Freiburg, Paris, Cambridge, and Toronto with respect to funding, academic appointments, curriculum and admissions, the selection and role of heads of institutions, and the handling of financial affairs. It then reviews the overall structure and dynamics of each of the universities.

Functional Authority

Funding

All four universities are overwhelmingly dependent on public funds for their support. Cambridge and Paris are in theory free to allocate funds as they wish, but hanging over them is the prospect of justifying future needs. Toronto's income is tied to enrollments but it can decide how to allocate funds. Freiburg is the least autonomous in financial affairs. An annual line-item budget, authorized and audited by the *Land* government, leaves it little flexibility. Individuals and units, however, are still relatively free to seek outside funding. They also have some leeway within their individual budgets to transfer funds from one account to another.

Appointments

In the selection and promotion of teaching staff, Cambridge is limited only by UGC-determined ratios and salary ranges for staff at different levels. Toronto also has considerable autonomy in this area. Although the Governing Council (formerly Board of Governors) formally appoints teaching staff, it rarely overrides faculty recommendations. At Freiburg faculty also recommend on personnel matters. However, the Ministry of Education in Baden-Württemberg has considerable leeway in the extent to which it follows faculty recommendations. For example, rather than merely rubber-stamping the faculty's first choice, it may choose to appoint the second or third person suggested. The universities at Paris are limited in nominating candidates for permanent teaching positions by the requirements that a national committee approve their qualifications and that the ministry make the appointments.

Admissions and curriculum

In student admissions and curriculum, Toronto and Cambridge determine their own policies. In fact, at Cambridge each college determines admissions autonomously. Paris and Freiburg must implement the national policy that guarantees university admission to all who are successful in academically oriented secondary schooling. However, Freiburg can set quotas in overcrowded fields. The system of state examinations set by bodies outside the university limits Freiburg's freedom of teaching. At Paris, since 1968, universities are free to innovate in curriculum and establish their own university degrees. However, students mostly want nationally recognized degrees for which the ministry approves curriculum.

Institutional heads

The four universities differ significantly in the term of office, powers, and influence of their chief executive officers, particularly at Cambridge, Freiburg, and Paris on the one hand and Toronto on the other. The vice-chancellor at Cambridge has a two-year term, the rector at Freiburg a four-year term, the presidents at the Paris universities five-year terms, and the president at Toronto no fixed term. At Cambridge, Freiburg, and Paris the university heads tend to be *primus inter pares,* and much of their influence comes from chairing major bodies rather than from the special powers of the office. In each case, they are elected by the institution's chief legislative unit. The vice-chancellor at Cambridge by tradition is the head of a college, the Freiburg rector must be a full professor, and the new presidents at Paris must be full professors and members of their university councils unless the ministry approves an exception.

At Toronto the president is appointed by the Governing Council and there are no formal restrictions on who may be considered. Until 1971, when a single governing body replaced the separate Board of Governors and Senate at Toronto, the president had almost impossible responsibilities, far more onerous than those of his counterparts at Freiburg, Paris, and Cambridge, where the university head was and still is more an administrator than initiator, mediator, or executor. He had to bridge the separation of powers between the

board and the Senate, a separation similar to and much sharpe
than that in universities in the United States. Under the new sys
tem the president still has more authority than his counterparts a
Paris, Freiburg, and Cambridge and may well have even mor
onerous responsibilities and more influence than was true unde
the previous bicameral system.

Financial authority

Responsibility for financial affairs follows no common pattern in
the four universities. Day-to-day supervision of financial affairs fall
under the *Kanzler* at Freiburg, the secretaries general at the uni
versities of Paris, the treasurer at Cambridge, and a comparabl
senior administrator at Toronto. Except at Paris, major polic
recommendations on finance are made by a body with limited mem
bership, mainly senior administrators and academics, which pur
ports to represent the universities' overall interests. At Freibur;
it is the *Verwaltungsrat,* the administrative council on which th
Kanzler serves ex officio and which includes as nonvoting member
one representative each of the assistants, students, and non
academic staff.

A comparable body at Cambridge, but without student members
is the General Board of the Faculties together with its Needs Com
mittee. Charged with advising the university on educational polic
and chaired by the vice-chancellor, the General Board recommend
how total resources should be allocated. The Needs Committee,
subcommittee of the General Board, is expected to make many c
the hard financial decisions. In theory the General Board and Need
Committee represent the university as a whole. However, becaus
they do not represent all faculties at any one time, they are reluctan
to reject proposals from the faculties.

At Toronto, until 1971 the Board of Governors in principle de
termined financial policy. Budgetary recommendations put forwar
to it were prepared and approved by the President's Council and b
the Presidential Committee on Budget. Under the new governanc
system, the president's role in recommending on the financial need
of the university to the board may be modified to adapt to the uni
cameral system.

The alleged new autonomy and participation of the French uni
versities in financial affairs is less than complete. The authorit
of the University Councils to determine the distribution of resource
within the universities excludes the funding of research. Furthe

more, if the chancellor of the *académie* determines that a university budget fails to conform to ministry guidelines, he can require the University Council to reconsider it, and in extreme circumstances can himself take over the financial powers of the University Council.

Structure and Dynamics of Institutional Decision Making

Just as all four universities have undergone changes in their relations to external authorities, so too have they each experienced change in internal structure and especially in the decision-making process. The broadened participation of students is only one of the universities' many internal transformations.

Paris

In 1971 the new Universities of Paris were still sorting themselves out after a traumatic transitional period. Faculties in many cases split into *Unités d'Enseignement et Recherche* (UERs), and the UERs then clustered to form new universities (often on the basis of the ideological concepts of the university held by key professors). In drafting the new university statutes, some constitutive assemblies, racked by tension and mistrust, aimed at limiting as much as possible the University Council's jurisdiction. The Ministry had to be vigilant in refusing proposed statutes that, under the guise of decentralization, would eviscerate the University Councils and perpetuate the old faculty system.

At the new Paris universities the UERs have a quadripartite council consisting of permanent teaching staff and researchers, non-tenured staff, students, and representatives from outside the university. There may be as many as 40 members. Sixty percent of the professors must normally be from the upper ranks. The number of students may equal but not exceed the number of professors.

The councils also include administrative personnel. Electoral colleges for each group elect their respective representatives except that the council chooses the outside members. The UER councils elect the University Council, also quadripartite in structure and including up to 80 members.

Student power is now official but restricted. Students vote in only one UER, and if less than 60 percent vote, student places are reduced.[5] Students are excluded from personnel decisions, but since

---

[5] The 1971 amending act attempted to reduce the required vote to 50 percent, but without success.

these are made on the principle of judgment by peers, for the first time assistants—on up—can participate when an assistant position is being filled.

The new structures do not yet function as intended by the 1968 law. Student parity with the professoriate exists almost nowhere. Whereas some 52 percent of students voted in the 1969 elections for the constitutive assemblies, student participation in the UER council elections in 1970 was only 32 percent nationally, 25 percent in Paris. Student apathy and a sense that the new structures fail to live up to promises of student parity were among the factors for declining participation.

Some professors, reformist well before the events of 1968, also became disenchanted by new restrictions set by the ministry that appeared to circumscribe the autonomy of the UERs in curriculum and governance, by the indifference of most students, by the obstructionism of the *Gauchiste* (radical) minority, and by the ministry's failure to provide the resources needed to remedy some of the more glaring deficiencies in the university functioning.

Nevertheless the changes accomplished are remarkable. The "Parisian monster" is no more. Professorial power is having to come to terms with student power, and, even more important, with the power of the assistants who now have an important influence on the deliberations and decisions of the UER and University Councils. A new breed of university head has taken over the internal administration of the universities, professors in different disciplines must now talk to each other and reach consensus on new areas of common concern, and the broader society can at last have a direct input into decision making through the external representatives in the UER Councils, the University Councils, and the National Council. If the situation in 1971 left much unresolved, it was a dramatic change from the situation in 1968.

Freiburg

Recent changes at Freiburg resemble those at Paris in several respects. The 1969 *Grundordnung,* as already mentioned, strengthened the central administration. It diminished the scope of individual faculties by increasing them from 5 to 15, set up a new universitywide representative body, reduced the power of the professors within the faculties, gave entry into decision making at all levels to the junior faculty, students, and nonacademic staff and, in principle at least, lessened the domination of professors over assistants by attaching the assistants to departments rather than to individual professors.

Whereas before the recent reforms faculty councils were made up mostly of full professors, they now comprise four full professors; two middle-level professors *(Dozenten)*; two junior faculty *(Mittelbau)*; and two students, in each case elected by their peers; plus the dean, who is a tenured professor elected annually. The council determines course offerings, the awarding of degrees, and budget requirements, and it generally handles faculty administration. Although outnumbered in faculty councils, professors still dominate in recommending new appointments.

Before the new *Grundordnung,* deans and *Ordinarien* dominated the senate, which handled few universitywide questions, since the faculties decided most issues. Even though senior administrators and full professors are a majority of the new senate, it now includes three representatives each from the middle-level teaching staff, students, and nonacademic staff. Its jurisdiction encompasses all university affairs not explicitly delegated to other organs, and it elects certain key officials including the senate representatives on the *Verwaltungsrat.*

The *Grosser Senate* (large senate) has final authority on major issues: for example, constitutional amendments. It elects the rector and deputy rector and reviews the annual statement of accounts. However, with close to 100 members, including 10 *Mittelbau,* 30 students, and 6 nonacademic representatives, the *Grosser Senate* is too unwieldy to be active in ongoing decision making.

The power structure at Freiburg has changed less than at many other German universities, but it has changed significantly. Students, assistants, and *Dozenten* have on occasion joined forces in faculty councils and the Senate to carry the vote. The policy monopoly of the full professors has weakened and some professors even vote with the students for fear of opposing them in public. Full professors have lost much of their individual power in matters relating to curriculum and budget resources and in their relationship to assistants.

Where the center of decision-making power at Freiburg lies is unclear. The rectorate has more authority than formerly but the weight of tradition combined with meager staffing inhibit its leadership. This is intensified by the division of authority within the rectorate between the rector and *Kanzler.* Nor is it clear how conflicts between the Senate and *Verwaltungsrat* are resolved. As at

Toronto until 1971, this system, which separates responsibilit
for finance and academic matters, has anachronisms.

Toronto

At the University of Toronto the communication gap resulting fror
the former two-tier system of governance was aptly described b
former president Claude Bissell as "double innocence": innocenc
of the Board of Governors of academic problems and of the Senat
of financial affairs. The University of Toronto Act of 1971 has mad
the new Governing Council supreme, empowering it to "do all suc
acts and things as are necessary or expedient for the conduct of it
affairs and the affairs of the University and University College
The council has 50 members, all Canadian citizens: the chancellc
and the president; 16 members appointed by the government;
appointed by the president; and, by election of their constituer
bodies, 12 faculty members, 8 students, 8 alumni members, and
administrative staff. Initial reaction to the new system was tha
faculty had lost much power while students may have gained son
and the provincial government has gained much.

Governance at the faculty and department levels at Toronto
readily intelligible to the American observer because it shares mar
of the patterns of schools, faculties, and colleges, and within the
departments and institutes that typify many United States ui
versities.[6] In the last few years senior teaching staff have dominate
less than formerly, and student participation at all levels has su
stantially increased.

Governance at Toronto is plagued by problems of size. As facul
councils usually include all teaching staff, they tend to be unwielc
(e.g., the Faculty of Arts and Science has about 1,125 members
Consequently they meet infrequently, delegating much of the
work to deans and committees. Size also impeded the functioning
the now defunct Senate, formerly the supreme academic bod
With a membership of about 190 persons, it became too large ar
heterogeneous to function effectively.

Even before the Duff-Berdahl report of 1966 (Duff & Berdal
1966) called for reforms in university structures, Toronto wa
changing. Protracted negotiations finally led to the establishment
1968 of the Commission on the Government of the University
Toronto, a body chiefly representing faculty and students plus tl

---

[6] Toronto comprises 10 faculties, 8 schools, and a college of education.

president. Its 1969 report, *Toward Community in University Government* (Commission on Government . . . , 1970), recommended staff-student parity at all levels of governance, student participation in faculty personnel decisions and research policy, enforceable rules on faculty consulting, and a single governing body with equal numbers of lay, academic, and student representatives. The report provoked widespread internal criticism. Energetic efforts to work out an institutional consensus on its major recommendations were only partly successful. This absence of consensus, particularly on staff-student parity, was interpreted by the provincial government as giving it considerable latitude in deciding on the composition of the Governing Council which, as indicated, now has a 3 to 2 ratio of faculty to students.

Cambridge

As at Freiburg, though for different reasons, governance at Cambridge presents no neat pyramidal pattern. It presents a bewildering array of different organs whose mutual relationships are largely defined by custom and whose members and functions often overlap. In fact, the Cambridge Student Union, in pushing for student representation, has difficulty determining who makes the major decisions.

The Senate has basic legislative authority and includes as members all registered holders of the university's Master of Arts or higher degree. It elects the chancellor, confers degrees, and votes on appeals from Regent House decisions. But as the chancellorship is mostly ceremonial, the conferring of degrees largely automatic, and the right of appeal never exercised, the Senate's role is limited.

Regent House includes the 2,000 university administrative and teaching staff who belong to the Senate. It elects the vice-chancellor, enacts university statutes and ordinances, and is the final arbiter in university affairs. Regent House cannot initiate but can only act on "graces" (rules and motions concerning the conduct of university affairs and falling under the general authority of the university as set forth in its statutes) submitted to it by the Council of Senate. That more than 99 percent of graces are automatically approved suggests that the tough decisions are made elsewhere.

The Council of Senate, Financial Board, and the General Board of the Faculties are the central policy-making and executive bodies of the university. The council acts as spokesman for the university, is the contact point with Regent House, and is concerned with long-range development. The General Board is responsible for academic policy, the Financial Board for the administration of financial affairs. Although the lack of a sharp definition of the relationships among these bodies and some overlapping of their activities does not make for administrative tidiness, the system works. Each body is small and is chaired by the vice-chancellor or his deputy. The requirement that at least three members of the Financial Board and General Board be on the Council of Senate promotes communication.

Faculty governance is well summarized by the verse (Brook 1965, p. 185):

Along these lines, from toe to crown,
Ideas flow up and vetoes down.

In both the colleges and faculties democracy prevails—for the dons. Unlike Freiburg and Paris, the full professors have not dominated. At the colleges, heads and fellows constitute the governing body and elect a council to direct affairs. Few college councils include students, on the theory—not wholly endorsed by students—that the close relations between fellows and students make this superfluous. Instead the colleges have joint faculty-student consultative committees through which students articulate their views.

The colleges know no higher authority, neither the central administration nor the faculties, and above all not the Colleges Committee in which the Masters convene periodically to discuss common interests. But coordination is congenital at Cambridge. Nearly all dons wear at least two hats, as they belong to a faculty and a college. The problem is to know which hat a don is wearing.

The Faculty Boards, not the faculties as a whole, elect representatives to the General Board. All members of the twenty-odd faculties elect Faculty Boards without consideration to rank. At the next level democracy is indirect. As only eight faculty members represent the Faculty Boards on the General Board at any one time (two each from the four groupings of the faculties), members on the General Board are loathe to reject their absent colleagues requests. The General Board tends to endorse recommendations of the Faculty Boards on the principle of mutual back-scratching.

As with the colleges, students are represented on few Faculty Boards but participate in faculty-student consultative committees

There are no student representatives on the three central bodies. Nevertheless, Cambridge offers to students as well as dons a variety of contact with decision making. Despite or perhaps because of the complexity of governance at Cambridge, there is an astonishing degree of communication, which may well be its major strength.

Direction of Recent Change

Among the four universities reviewed, Paris has changed the most and Cambridge the least in the last decade, but all have changed. Similar pressures have produced more similarity in their internal governance and their place in their respective higher education systems. Internally and externally the bodies participating in the decision making are now more diverse and numerous. They also agree less than formerly on the nature and role of the university.

A major change internally is that students are now everywhere included, although to varying degrees. Traditional elitist notions of the university are crumbling in the face of new demands and expectations of the university as well as the sheer weight of vastly increased numbers. The emphasis is shifting to preparing students for a variety of jobs in society.

The large increase in junior-level teaching staff and their expanded participation in governance, especially at Paris and Freiburg, are also changing the concept and role of the university. The old system of mutually isolated faculties and institutes dominated by the professors is being replaced by a system based on community, the drawing together of separate units, and the participation in decision making by all members. Toronto, too, is moving in this direction. Cambridge, heretofore the most democratic of the four institutions in its governance, may end up being the least so because it does not include students in most of its chief organs.

Accompanying these changes in internal decision making has been an expansion in the external forces affecting university affairs—again less so at Cambridge. Pressure from the public to admit increasing numbers of students, especially at Freiburg and Paris, which are less able to limit enrollments than Toronto and Cambridge, may require more emphasis on teaching at the expense of research. This pressure may drive some research out of the universities into government and other research institutes.

The biggest change in external forces affecting the universities is the increased concern and influence of government. The exception is Paris, where the new autonomy of the universities has altered but not appreciably diminished the role of the Ministr; It is ironic that a second external force beginning to emerge ma be the university system itself. The arrangements set up by tl universities to coordinate their interests in their relations wit government, in order to ward off government interference, lesse the freedom of action of the individual institutions.

CONCLUSIONS Each of the four universities surveyed in this chapter has unde gone significant change in recent years, resulting from both intern; pressures toward reform and external pressures from the larg(society—particularly the state or central governments. As in tl United States, rising enrollments and costs, coupled with tl inadequacy of traditional structures and methods, have create widened concern for the reshaping of higher education. Althoug there are important variations among the four universities exan ined, there are also parallels in their changing organizationt patterns, which in many cases resemble changes in United State universities. The principal changes of the last decade are outline below.

Strengthening of Central Administrations The central administration of the universities has been strengtl ened, especially at Freiburg and Paris, where it was weakest, an even at Cambridge, although it still maintains the independenc of the colleges and a brief term of office for the vice-chancellor.

The growth in enrollments and costs and in the complexity of th university's functions has required more people and more profe; sionalism at the center. Of greater significance, the central admir istration has acquired more executive authority as a result of th increased pressures—and scrutiny—from outside the universit and the need for the university to speak with one voice to its cor stituents within and without. Even though the central administr; tion in the European universities (but not at Toronto) remain woefully understaffed by United States standards, its executiv authority is much greater than in the early postwar period and wi doubtless continue to grow.

Declining Professorial Power Senior teaching staff have lost power, and except at Cambridg(middle- and junior-level staff have gained. At Freiburg and Pari the oligarchy of professors is on the way out, for professors n longer have a monopoly in the determination of curriculum, in th selection of representatives to various university bodies, or in the appointment of new teaching staff. These powers are now shared with junior staff and to some extent with nonacademic personnel and students. As the central administration has gained authority at the expense of deans and faculties, the professoriate has lost.

The professor is losing ground even with respect to his most cherished tasks, the personal supervision of advanced students and the pursuance of research. The sheer weight of student numbers and of proliferating committee and administrative work necessitates mass teaching and leaves scant time for research.

In the United States university, one also finds a diminution of the power of senior professors and more democracy in decision making. Most recently there are parallel trends in the United States and abroad toward modifying the status of academics: in continental Europe through the recruitment of staff whose functions are permanently restricted to teaching and exclude research; and in the United States by the growing support for limiting or even abolishing the systems of faculty tenure. In the United States and abroad these tendencies are exacerbated by measures taken or contemplated to increase the teaching load of academic staff.

Growing Student Influence The provision for student participation in university governance has everywhere received the most publicity among recent university reforms, but its practical impact has not lived up to its publicity. These reforms have enlarged the students' opportunity to influence but not to determine university affairs. Their influence depends upon their willingness to devote themselves to often time-consuming and tedious committee work and, as a minimum, to vote in elections of various university bodies.

The student generation of the early 1970s did not pick up the banner of the student activists of the 1960s. In 1970 and 1971 students were more docile or even apathetic, and presumably were devoting themselves to their studies rather than to the demands of university governance. The decline in job opportunities for university graduates was an important factor, less so in Germany than elsewhere.

Nevertheless student participation has brought change, especially when the students have joined forces on issues with junior teaching staff, as at Paris and Freiburg. Furthermore, the mere presence of student representatives in various organs of governance

has affected decision making, as some professors have been relu
tant (or even afraid) to take positions publicly that are unpopula
with the students.

Emerging Systems of Higher Education

Internal pressures to widen decision making may in the long ru
prove far less consequential to university organization than th
external pressures imposed by the emergence of national or stat
systems of higher education. Rising costs and enrollments ar
compelling individual universities in a given country to justif
their expenditures, growth, and functions in terms of their co
tribution as part of a higher education system. To compete fc
resources, the individual institution may increasingly have to coo
dinate with others in the system, for it is through the system that
may be able to apply the most leverage.

Although much coordination has already evolved, especially i
Ontario, it will be some time before any of the four universitie
surveyed in this chapter presses its needs more as part of a wide
higher education system than as an individual institution competin
with others in the system. But the imperatives of coordination wi
in time take priority over the competing ambitions of individua
institutions, and these in turn will have to achieve more intern
centralization and self-discipline in order to make coordinatio
work.

Broadening of Higher Education

Hanging over individual universities in Europe and North Americ
is the growing threat that conventional higher education institution
may lose their relative monopoly over training the highly qualifie
manpower needed by society and providing certification for thi
training. Already the developed countries are groping toward ne
approaches to advanced education that may bypass or at leas
compete with contemporary academic institutions. Not only ar
the conventional institutions increasingly costly but also the
may not be doing the job.

On the one hand universities and colleges are failing to kee
pace with the rapidly changing needs for trained people. On th
other hand few countries can afford the luxury of enrolling i
conventional higher education an increasing proportion of youn
people who lack defined professional goals but wish to postpon
their entry into adult society or at least to obtain the socia
approval that university degrees offer. Current concern in th
United States with making higher education more job-related b

extending the apparatus of academic certification to practical experience and the mounting interest in Europe in alternatives to higher education testify to the need for change.

If academic higher education is to satisfy the growing demands made upon it, it must achieve much more coherence in its functions, imagination in its methods, and rationalization in its use of resources. In mapping the future of higher education, priority must therefore be accorded to developing higher education as a system capable of responsiveness and self-discipline, as much at the system level as in the individual institutions within the system. In the 1960s significant first steps were taken in this direction in Europe and North America.

Part Two
Variations on a Theme

6. A Comparison of the University with the Corporation

by Ralph M. Besse

The increasing financial troubles of institutions of higher learning have prompted many people to suggest that universities would all be better off if they were managed as businesses are. Inherent in the suggestion is the assumption that universities can be managed as business corporations. This assumption, in turn, implies that a strong parallel exists between the factors that control or significantly affect the management of the two types of institutions. Since the financial needs of our colleges are so great, the transferability of validated business practices should be examined.

Actually there is no simple way to compare the organization and operation of institutions of higher learning with business enterprises. There is too much variety within each category. Businesses are both large and small, simple and complex, concentrated and dispersed, closely held and widely owned, specialized and complexly integrated, and, last but far from least, successful and unsuccessful. Institutions of higher learning have an equal range of variants. They are large and small, specialized and comprehensive, publicly and privately supported, limited or unlimited in the level of education offered and subject matter covered, adequately and inadequately endowed, generously and stingily supported, and variously integrated by race, sex, religion, and talent. Any general comparison of the two classes of institutions is subject to these variants as well as to the specific differences discussed below.

SOURCE AND STRUCTURE OF AUTHORITY Perhaps the most important area of comparison is the structuring of the authority to manage the two types of institutions and the accountability for the use of such authority.

In the structuring of authority, the business corporation has a clear advantage over the university. It has a clearly defined common interest group with ultimate power over the enterprise: the shareowners. By standardized procedures they select a board of direc tors charged with achieving the corporate mission through th employment of full-time managers.

The corporate process results in well-defined sources an channels of authority and is buttressed both by the fact of being single source and by the universally agreed-upon underlying mis sion of making money. Unity is the normal order of affairs.

Where there is dissent in the granting of corporate authority ther are two methods of solution. One is the simple device of majorit voting control; the other is economic escape through a sale of th dissenting shareowner's interest.

The result is that a corporation for profit is always an author tarian organization. It is structured to achieve its dominant purpos the making of profits. Unity of mission requires unity of actior Unity of action requires a well-defined process of authoritative de cision making built around a hierarchy that is well known to a members of the organization and reasonably well accepted. En ployees expect to have bosses in a business corporation; they expe to be bound by higher authority. Like football players, they knov that signals can't be called by the whole team when the entire tea is needed for every play. Because organizations are subject t human weaknesses, the result is far from perfect, but the potenti for a high correlation between responsibility and achievement always present and is normally achieved in well-managed con panies.

In comparing the authority structure of business corporation with that of the university, we may first compare the basic cor stituency. What group in the university corresponds to the shar owners, that ultimate source of all corporate control and prim beneficiary of its success? The alumni? The students? The facult and administration? The public? The sponsoring church? The les islature that allots funds? The governor who appoints trustee: Some combination of these? Or, in some cases, no one?

It seems obvious that there is no authority-granting group for th university that is quite parallel to shareowners. There are, howeve authority-granting sources. Except for a few cases in which truste are self-perpetuating, they must be appointed by someone in a cor stituency of sorts. Thus, like the corporation, the appointmer source can in the long run exercise control over malfunctionir trustees. It does so, however, with several handicaps not common shareowners' control over corporate directors.

Authority for the management of a university is often fragmented. Consequently a variety of objectives have an impact on the selection of trustees: governors who appoint trustees often have political purposes in mind; churches often select trustees as a reward for religious activity rather than educational competence; alumni selections are keyed to various types of popularity; and the trustees selected by the board itself quite often have a dominant financial orientation. When students and faculty are common appointment sources, activism is probably a key to student selection and self-interest to faculty selection. In any event, many trustees of universities are selected for reasons foreign to any demonstrated ability to contribute to the management of an academic institution. The directors of a business corporation, on the other hand, are normally selected because of an ownership of the corporation, management responsibilities in it, or some career-demonstrated capacity to help it. This gives a strength of purpose to their action that is hard to match in universities.

Thus, the possibility of strong, unified, experienced trustee direction in a university is handicapped by the very nature of the appointments. When a board so structured attempts to endow a president with the managerial responsibilities and authority to operate a university, additional hurdles to the strong exercise of authority are encountered.

The first hurdle is the basic dichotomy of an academic structure and an administrative structure. Actually the board of trustees does not possess complete authority over the academic structure and cannot, therefore, delegate the exercise of complete authority to the university president. The faculty in the sanctuary of academic freedom and tenure tend to think of themselves as being the university. This leaves the board of trustees with little authority over the prime function of a university, instruction.

Not only is there a lack of authority to guide and control many facets of academic activity, there is also a lack of unity in academic activity itself. The academic endeavor of a university is divided into students and faculty, and the faculty is divided among schools which in turn have both undergraduate and graduate levels. The graduate level, especially in science, has the dual mission of teaching and research.

No two of these fragmented segments have missions entirely in common. This is compounded by the fact that a faculty member's career depends as much on his reputation among peers in his discipline as it does on the ratings of his superiors (or his students). He serves many masters: students, peers, supervisors, and often those who buy manuscripts, fund research, hire consultants, or book lecturers.

Virtually all the diffusion of authority and mission within a university is essential to the accomplishment of its objectives. No conceivable model of academic authoritarianism is consistent with the freedom required to enable a university to serve a democracy. A mere statement of the situation suggests that the authoritarian posture of the business corporation does not fit.

TECHNIQUES FOR ACCOUNT-ABILITY The ambiguous authority structure in a university suggests the closely related difficulty of holding the faculty and administration accountable for the exercise of the authority granted to them.

In a business corporation there is always one quantifiable measure of performance, variously stated as the rate of earnings on the capital invested, the percentage of profit per dollar of sales, or the earnings per share of stock outstanding. Because dollar profits are both the objective of the activity and the measure of performance, the operation of a company is keyed to accountability for the profit achieved. This leads to the clear identification of areas of responsibility; to a responsibility accounting system; to cost accounting and cost control; to periodic reporting, analysis, and review of everything that affects profit results; and to an understanding and acceptance by employees of the importance of all these measures.

A university has no such characteristics. Its mission is often blurred and, even where clearly stated, it varies for different people. Students themselves come to college for purposes that vary not only among students but among generations of students. Society at large cannot state specifically what it wants universities to do. What degrees of emphasis, for example, should be accorded the three phases of knowledge—discovery, preservation, and transmission? For whom is the university maintained: The dull as well as the bright? The indifferent as well as the motivated? The unqualified as well as the qualified? The poor as well as the rich? The students only or society at large? What should the university teach after it decides whom to admit: General knowledge or specialized knowledge? Philosophy or skill? Problem solving or organized information? How should resources be divided among teaching, scholarship, and research? If the questions were answerable, should the answer apply equally to all universities? What is the proper allocation of the faculty member's resources and energy among such varying tasks as scholarly preparation for classwork, actual class-work, student counseling, research, publication, extracurricular campus activity, and community activity?

Universities simply have nothing comparable to the mission-defining force of profits. Harvard's obligation to staff the brain trust of the federal government is quite different from that of her West Coast sister, Stanford. The influence of the church at church-founded Notre Dame is quite different from that at church-founded Southern Methodist.

Even if all the varied and conflicting missions could be clearly defined, the measurement of performance would be very difficult. The quality of a teacher's performance can be judged but it cannot be quantified except as the number of hours spent in a classroom. The number of hours spent outside the classroom in order to qualify for good performance within the classroom depends on a great variety of things that cannot be meaningfully quantified: the new-ness of the course, the rapidity of change in the field, the range of talent and previous academic preparation among the students, the size of the class, the difficulty of the subject matter, the amount of paperwork needed, the student counseling involved, etc. In addition, a university teacher has many other campus-related responsibilities —few if any of which are subject to mathematical measurement even in terms of time. Thus, no system of accounting is available on which to base corporation-type accountability techniques. The diversity inherent in the activities just described is one of the great strengths of higher education both in its underwriting of free thought and in its contribution to social needs. These are objectives of a higher rank than optimum efficiency.

The results of research, however, can be measured. But the weak-ness of the measure is that university research is oriented toward results rather than cost. It is certainly not profit oriented, although much research ultimately results in substantial profit to someone other than the researcher or his university. Thus the accountability impact of cost and profit are not available as tools of management in the academic efforts of the university, even in research.

Good cost accounting is perhaps the most transferable element of the corporate model. Many university research projects have been funded with no real knowledge of the overhead costs imposed on the institution both during and after the project. Corporate cost-accounting procedures would give university administrators the information needed to apply better control to such project research costs.

In the area of business administration there is much more opportunity for the application of corporate accountability techniques. Most principles of organization structuring are applicable and many work functions are as measurable as they are in industry. Both historical and engineered standards of performance can be developed, and market standards of performance should be much more readily available in the university than they are in competitive industry.

Thus we conclude that in administrative matters there is a solid case for application of business methods. In the construction and operation of buildings; purchasing of supplies; control of costs; selection, retention, training, and promotion of employees; investment of funds; the designation of control centers; use of cost accounting; and many other operations; the basic rules of business management should apply. Many universities do not apply business methods with anything like the care that attends a good business-for-profit application. It is often only some financial stringency that results in better management practices.

Actually the failure of universities to benefit from the efficiency model of industry is easier to explain than to justify. Some of the explanations are these:

First, the necessarily loose control of academic affairs tends to influence the style of business administration.

Second, the continuing prod that comes from a need to show a dollar profit is missing. Increasingly, however, this prod is being supplied by the necessity to eliminate deficits.

Third, the university rarely has enough money to compete for the best business administration talent, and virtually no type of incentive compensation is available.

Fourth, the expenditure of capital funds in universities is based on considerations that are utterly different from those in business.

PERSONNEL The impacts of authoritarianism, accountability, and profit motivation are probably the most fundamental characteristics that distinguish the business operation from the academic operation. There are nevertheless a number of other activities, functions, and characteristics that justify further comparison.

One of these is the method of selecting, developing, and motivating personnel. The single activity of greatest importance within this category is the selection of a president.

Business corporations do not use a single standard method to develop and choose chief executives. The most common method for major corporations is the progression of professionally trained people through the ranks over a relatively long-term career. This gives the corporation the opportunity to implant a thorough knowledge of the business in the individuals competing for top jobs, to test them at increasing levels of responsibility, to give them specific training to overcome weaknesses, and to judge their abilities in competition with their peers.

Even this seemingly foolproof approach often fails, and the corporation must go into the market and buy executive talent. The talent it buys, however, has almost invariably been developed by the process that failed within the company purchasing the talent. In a few major corporations and in many small corporations the chief executives are selected because of substantial family ownership in the company. In more than a few cases the chief executive's job is filled as a result of merger and affiliation deals. Nevertheless the standard process remains a progression through the ranks.

A college president is almost never selected this way. He normally starts his career as a teacher with high academic training in his specialty and proceeds through the ranks of teaching to a full professorship and often to a deanship. At this point he receives his first administrative experience, although it is often somewhat restricted compared with the wide range of administrative duties of a university president. Obviously the original objectives in this type of career are teaching, scholarship, and perhaps research rather than administration. Presumably the individuals who ultimately become presidents trained for the objectives of their early career because they thought that this was where their aptitudes lay. In any event the career-ladder process is quite different from the corporation process.

Since a university president has responsibility for both the academic and business administration activities of a university, there is much to be said for the type of experience indicated in the selection process. It is, however, unreasonable to expect that presidents with an academic career would be as well trained in the arts of business administration as the presidents of business corporations are. There are basic differences in the skills and aptitudes required for good teaching on the one hand and good administration on the other. The good teacher is open-minded and willing to explore all sides of all issues. The good administrator must be decisive and single-purposed. The college president must harmonize these somewhat inconsistent requirements and apply one of them to the academic side of his responsibilities and the other to the business side.

There is another difference in the selection of executive personnel. The corporation president has normally come up through the corporation of which he becomes chief executive, although he may have changed employers when younger. The university president is normally sought from the entire field of higher education. Acceptable candidates are sometimes found within the institution seeking a president, but this happens in a minority of cases. Thus the motivation of the career within a single institution, if not missing, is much weaker than in the business corporation, where promotion from within is universally considered a vital prod to ambition and performance.

Administrative deans follow a course comparable to presidents. They are almost always selected because of academic training, aptitude, and performance. They seldom wanted to be administrators: they wanted to teach and study, possibly to write and lecture. Disciplined for these arts, they discover the high status of deanship and change course. As deans, they are expected to devise the skills and tools of administration and apply them to an "employee" group that is quite unwilling to be regimented.

In the selection, development, motivation, and control of other personnel there are other great differences between the university and the business corporation. On the academic side perhaps the most distinguishing feature is tenure. Tenure imposes on university management a control, motivation, and selection limitation unknown to businessmen in their management of supervisory and professional people. In some respects, it is comparable to the seniority provisions of business-labor contracts and is about as difficult to alter.

Universities have another and favorable force at work in motivating their faculties. This is the achievement of status among peer groups in other institutions, a powerful influence almost unknown in industry. It is complemented by the fact that universities have a kind of first draft choice among the talented super-IQ group who attain Ph.D. degrees. Great universities probably have a higher average level of intellectual talent among their professors than great corporations have among their executives.

Thus tenure limits control, but the freedom guaranteed by tenure attracts talent. Talent and freedom are more important in the achievement of academic objectives than accountability for use of time. The offsetting values between greater freedom and talent on the campus and greater control and motivation more closely keyed to performance in the corporation are difficult to determine. The common charge that all men in academia lead sweatless lives and all men in business develop ulcer cultures from overwork is clearly not true. It is far more probable that charted curves of effort for both groups would produce normal bell curves almost indistinguishable from each other. In any event there are common forces at work in both types of institutions. An individual's pride in achievement, commitment to his job, ambition, and God-given metabolism are not primarily dependent on the type of institution he serves.

One other variant deserves comment. The scholarship and research functions of faculty members call for major activity outside the classroom. While this benefits the classroom, much of it has prime objectives which are in no way related to the classroom; some of it is entirely nonparietal. Alleged abuse of the freedom to pursue such activities is a subject of much current controversy, but no sophisticated person advocates its elimination. No adequate method of control has been devised that is consistent with the ideals of academic freedom and the university mission to develop knowledge. Even if perfect control mechanisms were available, the mere existence of dual or triple missions would distinguish the university situation from the corporate one.

On the business administration side of the university, parallels with the corporation are much closer. Perhaps three distinctions should be noted: (1) the university is seldom in as good a position as the corporation to bid, in dollars, for talent; (2) it cannot offer the same wide-open career ladders to its people that corporations offer; and (3) it must perpetually live with the academic fraternity's demands for things its administrative brothers cannot provide, through no fault of their own. The general goals of excellence in the university are not fully adequate substitutes for the unifying goal of profits in the corporation.

In summary, the personnel assignment of a university president and his vice-presidents and provosts is much more difficult than that of a corporate president and his top officers. It requires more leadership motivation as a substitute for the more tangible motivation available to business. It also requires more finesse and flexibility in personnel relations because of the disparate groups and missions involved. And it must be made in a way that achieves substantial endorsement from students, faculty, nonacademic employees (and their unions), alumni, donors, and various segments of the public. No two of these groups think wholly alike.

One distinction in the traditional attitudes of professional people seeking employment with a university and those seeking employment with a business corporation is interesting. Scholarly talent of a very high level is attracted by a university in large part because of the relatively free and unregimented work patterns that have historically typified the university professor. Executive talent is attracted to the business corporation with a full recognition of the control, regimentation, and drive inherent in successful performance. Both groups of talent are aware of the differences in earning potential that accompany these two life-work styles. It would be rash to conclude that these widely varying approaches have not, over a long period of time, attracted people with the attitudes and talents that best suit the objectives.

PHYSICAL FACILITIES The acquisition and use of physical facilities is another interesting area for comparison. Here again the business corporation has many management advantages not available to the university.

Most business building is not only functional but also cost-justified. Need is distinguished from desire. Optimal costs in the light of construction expenditures, use efficiency, and maintenance charges are sought. The use factor is carefully studied. The overhead cost increment is analyzed. The price impact on the end-use product or service is calculated. And alternative uses of the money required are weighed. Thus capital expenditures of a business corporation tend to be justified either by cost reductions or by profit additions. Theoretically, a university should follow a somewhat comparable course, but a number of variants intervene.

First there is the dictate of a donor who gives substantial sums. He can and often does insist on quite impractical features for which he pays the capital cost with no thought at all about the operational cost for the next hundred years. An influential donor may force a change in priorities or he may insist on impractical locations or excessive heights of ceilings and width of hallways.

This is compounded by the traditional view, sometimes called the "edifice complex," that a campus is an architectural display case on which no cost should be spared. Society benefits aesthetically from this view, but it is the university that must somehow bear the financial burden associated with the construction of these monuments. And yet it is unfair to blame university administrators totally for the end result. They are not in control in the same way that corporate managers are. The demands of their many publics, including those who furnish the money, must be considered.

Item three in the university building problem is a common disjunction between planning for capital expenditures and provision for costs of operation. The university is something like a utility; it must meet certain needs whether provisions for future operational costs have been made or not. This is especially true of the state universities, where something akin to open admissions exists in many places, removing control over the basic factor in expansion. However, physical expansion to meet the need is not caused by increased numbers of students alone. A variety of other factors has thrust building programs upon the campus, especially among the great universities. During the last 15 years, one of these factors was the tremendous growth of foundation and federally supported research. It was unreasonable to expect the research universities to reject this support; yet when the funds for such research were cut back, they were left with buildings, staff, and overhead costs that have contributed substantially to their deficits.

Another force that has pushed building expansion on campuses has been growth of campus facilities such as student centers, drama centers, computer centers, swimming pools, stadiums, and faculty clubs; the publications explosion; and the introduction of new types of laboratory equipment, teaching aids, visual aids, etc. Modern universities have quite a different standard of living in and out of the classroom than they had 20 years ago. Expansion has been compelled by competition, student and faculty demands, alumni pride, and, in many cases, quality requirements. The operating costs attendant on such expansion have seldom been offset by additional fees and tuition increases. So great has been the demand for dollars for this kind of facility expansion that there has been only minimal effort to increase endowments to support the additional costs such facilities engender. The result is a financial paradox: not uncommonly, the greater the performance of the university in recent years, the greater its deficit today. Thus, from a management point of view, the business corporation that adds buildings and equipment to increase its profits is an inadequate model for the university, where building and facility additions merely increase costs. Nevertheless, the university has had its lesson and better control will emerge in the future with some aid from business practice.

The business corporation also has more control over the use of facilities than the university. When demand is heavy, three shifts, inconceivable on a campus, are common in a manufacturing plant. In huge cities, where universities have great numbers of part-time students, a very high use factor is possible. On most campuses, however, use of facilities tends to be inefficient. Significant improvement could be made in building and facility use at universities if faculty and student bodies were driven by financial stringency to explore the possibilities. There is no other segment of the adult world where facilities that could be used until 5 P.M. are not so used or where they are voluntarily closed during a quarter of the year. It is difficult to understand why good use requirements should not be imposed on students and faculty at a university campus, especially when the alternative is deficit financing.

A university can profit in other respects by studying the cost-control guides of business corporations in the scheduling of students and faculty, the size of classes, the amount of work that can be done out of the classroom on the student's own initiative, and the use of examinations to give credit for independent studies. Greater use of television and computers should result in much lower costs. The academic world is only beginning to stir in these fields and will certainly be prodded to innovation by the lack of adequate operating funds.

The business model of tight cost analysis and cost control is not fully transferable to the campus, but its success in the business world suggests that better methods of cost control could be developed in the university if more attention were given to the subject. At present many universities have utterly inadequate information about either the cost or the productivity of the activities their administrations are charged with managing. Certainly the information patterns of the business corporation can be adopted by university administrators. The computer makes this easy, but the use of the data will require some change of attitude and the acquisition of application skills.

ECONOMIES OF SCALE Size of institution is still another facet for comparison. With the exception of a few unwieldy giants or unduly complex conglomerates, business has generally profited from the economy of scale. The bigger the corporation, the lower the cost of the end product or the greater the return on the invested dollar, all other things being equal. Thus business continually strives for growth. It is not at all clear that the same course is advantageous to the university either in terms of cost or quality. Only in recent years have studies begun to emerge in this field. It seems clear that many of the four-year colleges of the country are too small for financial viability, and it is becoming increasingly clear that some large universities are much too big for quality control. Optimum size is hard to determine and may not be the same at all types of institutions. The subject needs much detailed attention, but the corporate model will probably be of little help. College consortia may be an alternative to the economies of scale for medium-sized colleges and universities—but this approach has little application to the very large institutions.

Another important area of management control in any institution is the price charged for the end product or service. With business corporations, this is largely a competitive matter. In the free market the better operator wins. He fixes the price that will obtain the optimum profits, and his competitor must either produce better quality, sell more efficiently, or manufacture more efficiently. A university, however, has quite a different pricing problem. No university can charge its students enough to cover the costs of their education. The private university attempts to cover the difference by use of endowment income and by gifts and grants. The state university covers the difference largely by appropriation from tax funds. Currently the makeup available to the state university tends to be substantially more than that available to the independent university. As the financial problems of the independent universities have grown, they have been forced to increase tuition to achieve a balanced budget. This has driven many students to the state universities, where the tax subsidy is great enough to permit much lower tuition rates. New students are not being found to fill the vacant stations in the independent universities.

Business offers no parallel to this. Even the tax-subsidized publicly owned utility operates for the most part in territory that is not served by the privately owned tax-paying utility. Customers cannot choose subsidized service as students can. Consequently, the private university, in looking to its students to cover its higher costs, is faced with a formula of diminishing returns that cannot be remedied by any normal principle of business operation.

**THE MANAGE-
MENT OF
STUDENTS**
One final element of university management should be mentioned
the management of students. Never a simple area of management, it
has been made vastly more difficult and complicated by the modern
student protest movements. Even the term *management* is inappro
priate, for students are not employees. They do not receive salary
payments from the institution. They consider their out-of-classroom
life strictly their own business and yet often reside in facilitie
owned by the university on campus. Basically their objective or
campus is to help themselves, not to help the university. It is reason
ably clear that the principles governing personnel relationships o
universities with students are almost unrelated to the principle
governing a corporation's personnel relationships with employees

Because students make payments to the institution, one i
tempted to compare them to the customers of a business corpora
tion. To some extent students are the consumers and purchasers o
a service or "product"—i.e., knowledge and skills—offered by the
university. But the comparison must end here, for unlike customer
students are themselves one of the "products" that the university
offers. There is no parallel to this group in business, just as there is
no parallel in business for the tenuous control of university manage
ment over its faculty.

We may conclude from these comparisons that the management
techniques of business corporations have sufficient transferabilit
to university operations to justify careful study by university admin
istrators. But the suggestion that universities would all be better of
if they were managed as businesses are is a half-truth at best, appli
cable to only a few of the functions that must be managed in a
university.

7. A Comparison of the University with a Government Bureau

by Stephen K. Bailey

An assignment to compare a government bureau with a university is not far removed, in terms of generic splay, from a request to compare a fish and a mammal without designating in advance what kind of fish and which mammal. Government bureaus include the Pentagon, state highway departments, and local dog pounds; universities include the large and complex multicampus institution as well as the small single campus, and, now, the "no-campus" "external degree" campus.

With this dilemma in mind, what, if anything, can be usefully said about the generic similarities of universities and colleges, on the one hand, and, on the other, government bureaus (defined to include all operating divisions of government)?

The first thing to note is that in many cases they are identical: state universities, for example, are "operating divisions of government." For purposes of this analysis, we shall pretend that they are not, but this is a dangerous pretense, as politically naïve state university chancellors have discovered to their chagrin and sorrow.

GENERIC SIMILARITIES Assuming that institutions of higher learning, whether public or private, are somehow different types of organizations from the ordinary government bureau (whatever that fuzzy term conveys), are there nonetheless areas of similarity in generic administrative and political processes? A moment's reflection produces at least a tentative yes.

Both types of organizations are constrained to formulate and supervise budgets; both are faced with the necessity of hiring, sustaining, firing, and retiring personnel; both must worry about organizational design and about the management of space and facilities; both are induced by events, leadership, or external threats to indulge in spurts of planning; both must pay lip-service, and sometimes more, to the monitoring of performance.

As administration phases imperceptibly into politics, both kinds of institutions must build consent among those upon whom they depend for financial support; they must compete for scarce resources with other organizations and purposes; they must devote considerable time and attention to rule making (standard setting) and adjudicating; they must make bargains, manage conflict, co-opt talent, and develop systems of internal and external accountability.

Perhaps especially, government bureaus and universities as defined above have structural identities. Both are multidivisional organizations; both have superordinate structures (boards, hierarchial supervisors, legislatures, stock- or franchise-holders); both have subordinate structures (divisions, branches, departments, units) and differentiated personnel (professional and scientific, managerial, clerical, manual); both have external clientele who help to shape purposes, procedures, and structures (farm groups, labor unions, manufacturers' associations; alumni, parents, professional societies). Most organizations of both kinds have internal and external bureaucratic structures that are competitive (e.g., institutions within a single state's public higher education system competing for funds or government bureaus competing for programmatic jurisdiction or money).

It is little wonder that Charles Hitch, a key man in the top management staff of the Department of Defense under Robert McNamara, moved without changing his gait into the management of the University of California.

To ensure that some of these structural similarities will hold, it is necessary once again to identify the importance of size. For example, to move an Albert Bowker, lately chancellor of the City University of New York, into managing the highway department of a rural county, would be, to paraphrase the late E. E. Schattschneider,[1] using a cyclotron to warm a cup of coffee.

CONTEXTUAL SIMILARITIES

If universities and government bureaus share generic administrative, political, and structural similarities, they are equally subject to the vagaries of context. This generalization is important, for it suggests the ubiquity of cultural and economic pressures and perversities over time. This in turn has meaning for the training of institutional leaders and managers, who often enter into new responsi-

---

[1] At one time president of the American Political Science Association.

sibilities with little understanding of changing management environments.

A few examples may serve to make the point. Few would have predicted that the spirit of internal trust and external outreach that characterized the Department of State under George Marshall in the middle 1940s would be followed by the international and internal paranoia of the McCarthy-Dulles era. Similarly, few would have predicted that the docility of student life in the 1950s would be followed by the irreverence and violence on campuses of the late 1960s. Both of these changes in cultural context from the forties to the fifties and from the fifties to the sixties had the effect of diminishing the sovereign rights of individuals and thereby threatened our civil freedoms. One would have to be morally obtuse not to recognize the ethical differences in the respective provocations; but one would have to be intellectually obtuse not to recognize the similarities of effect upon cherished and essential democratic freedoms produced by the two crusades. A context of moral simplifications and self-righteous passions has constraining effects upon both governmental and academic institutions.

Similarly, both government agencies and academic institutions suffer the ebb and flow of financial largesse and changing leadership styles — and with similar manifestations of exuberance and trauma. Those who remember the bouncing ebullience of James Webb and his NASA cohorts in the mid-sixties would find it hard to recognize the decremental-budgeting anguish of faceless NASA leaders five short years later. The "Stassenization"[2] of the Mutual Security Agency in the early 1950s finds its spiritual and administrative counterparts in the harsh retrenchments of colleges and universities in the early 1970s. Engineering professors who, in the heyday of sponsored research, looked with superciliousness or pity upon department chairmen, deans, and provosts have more recently developed a becoming humility, encouraged in part by letters from unemployed protégés.

If there are periods of painful decrements, there are also periods of painful increments. Both academic and governmental agencies in the past two generations have known the excruciating discomforts of metastatic growth. The New Deal and World War II were the

[2] Harold Stassen, director of the Mutual Security Agency under President Eisenhower, was accused of ruthlessly decimating the foreign aid staff — especially Democrats — in the name of efficiency.

most dramatic illustrations of this phenomenon for federal govern
ment agencies; the 1960s were the runaway growth years for highe
education, especially for state colleges and community colleges

The pains have been similar: the mad search to "staff up"; th
elusive pursuit of definitions and devices for making general legis
lation or programmatic mandates specific; the phasing of discret
development plans so that they mesh in time and place; the making
of teams out of raw recruits; the pains accompanying personne
shakedowns when the bright-eyed and bushy-tailed, who are alway
attracted to the new, turn out to be shallow and bumptious; th
anguish of competition or collision with the entrenched in olde
agencies or units.

And recently both government bureaus and universities hav
faced the context of changing views about the legitimacy of author
ity. The American Revolution and the Jeffersonian era produce
far-reaching antipathies to elitist and centralized notions of au
thority. But until recently, these forces were to some extent counter
balanced by the presumed hierarchical efficiencies of large-scal
industry and the deferential mores of the young, the oppressed, an
the subordinate within most formal institutional contexts.

A seller's market in academia, the political awakening of th
American Black, the anguish of the draft and the Indochina War
the growing impersonality of bureaucracies and technologies—thes
and other forces during the 1960s triggered a massive questionin
of traditional authority—political, administrative, and academic
Even large government departments were not spared. During th
final weeks of the incumbency of Robert Finch as Secretary of th
Department of Health, Education and Welfare in 1970, subordin
ates within the agency treated the secretary to "university-type"
confrontations. And Finch was not alone among government ad
ministrators suffering this kind of scene. The military—in the field
in headquarters, in ROTC units on campuses—has had a substan
tial dose of what in earlier times would have been considered ran
insubordination. The dilution of authority in the halls of academ
since 1964, of course, has been newsworthy and upsetting in bot
positive and negative terms. In short, traditional patterns of author
ity have been substantially eroded in both public and academi
administration, and a great demand has emerged to decentraliz
large enterprises.

Finally, in recent decades government bureaus and universitie
have shared similar problems in the care and feeding of scientifi

and professional personnel who seem to be particularly loath to live within administrative constraints set by tradition or by others. This theme has been touched upon earlier. In certain government agencies, notably those devoted to scientific research and development (e.g., Oak Ridge, Argonne, Brookhaven, National Institutes of Health, Bureau of Standards), the struggle, usually successful, to exempt personnel policies from the normal constraints of civil service laws and regulations has had its counterpart in the proliferation of special institutes and programs associated with universities. Often such institutes or programs have been designed to free "productive" and financially patronized scholars from the limitations that have normally applied to academic mortals.

Attempts to explain such discrepancies to the less favored have made both governmental and academic administrators seem harsher and more unfeeling than most of them actually are.

It would be wrong to suggest that these various contextual similarities have produced identical reactions in all government agencies and universities. It would be instructive to discover when, and under what circumstances, reactions have been parallel or generally similar. But societal forces—the drifts and changing moods of public and private opinions—have different impacts upon various types of institutions and leaders. What is clear is that no important institutions in our society are immune to such common pressures.

To this point we have looked at structural, procedural, and contextual similarities between government bureaus on the one hand and universities on the other. It is clear to anyone who has worked in both environments, however, that whatever the similarities, there are also differences. In a perceptive essay on this subject written a decade ago, Harlan Cleveland (1960, pp. 22–27) noted some of the most basic and persistent of these differences. His insights have been confirmed by the common-sense reflections of hosts of academics who have had tours of duty with governmental agencies.

DISTINCTIVE FEATURES OF THE GOVERNMENT BUREAU

Divided accountability

Within the American constitutional and political system, government agencies find themselves subject to the overarching pulls of the two great political branches of government. Elected political executives (presidents, governors, mayors) on the one hand and legislators (congressmen, state assemblymen, local councilmen) on the other have fiscal, programmatic, surveillance, and often

personnel prerogatives vis-à-vis particular government depar
ments. The late E. E. Schattschneider contended that the entir
history of the American government could be written in terms of th
struggle between the President and parts of the Congress to con
trol the bureaucracy. In many cases, this tug-of-war has tended t
make government administrators wall-eyed. In other cases, hov
ever, the source of preeminent power has become so clear as to fo:
ter substantial administrative relaxation. In still other cases (th
independent regulatory commissions come to mind), the exercis
of both presidential and congressional authority is so weak that
invites inordinate influence from the very targets being regulatec

But the generalization is fair that most government bureaus liv
under a dynamic tension caused by executive-legislative compet
tion. This leads to a divided but running accountability traditiona
ly quite foreign to the world of academia.

Overlapping powers
Beyond the question of accountability, however, governmer
agencies necessarily conduct their business within the constitu
tional context of federalism and overlapping powers. In areas c
substantive policy (education, welfare, health, highways, transpo:
tation, housing, environmental control, and conservation), federa
state, and local governments alternately cooperate and compet
in tense rhythms. As though this vertical competition were nc
complex enough, agencies frequently overlap horizontally in sut
stantive jurisdiction. Representative Edith Green discovered a fe\
years ago that 42 federal agencies had some kind of responsibilit
in the field of education. Such overlaps, and consequent jurisdi«
tional struggles, are often exacerbated by committee and subcon
mittee rivalries within the Congress. All of this tends to create
"field of force" unlike that which has surrounded traditional admir
istrative arrangements in American higher education.

Publicity
Another peculiarity of government bureaus vis-à-vis universitie
has been their subjection to the glare of publicity. A large propo:
tion of daily headlines refer to the activities of government. It i
true that much of this news is made by the President and by majc
figures in Congress. But any measure of column inches in majc
newspapers devoted to the business of bureaucracies as agains
the business of universities would fall heavily on the side of th

public agencies. The fourth estate is a major instrument in keeping public agencies responsive and honest.

Impact of elections

Beyond the surveillance of the press, government bureaus are often mightily influenced by the impact of elections. It is true that some agencies seem to be impervious to the ballot, but most are affected by the changing political fortunes of chief executives and legislators. Princeton University has had only three presidents in 30 years. Syracuse University had one chancellor for 25 years. Such environments are far removed from the drumbeat of elections every two, four, or six years in the public sector.

Powers of coercion

Governments, by definition, have ultimate sanctions of force. Governments can employ force not only to protect their people against external threats but also for purposes of maintaining internal tranquility or for the simple carrying out of public policy. The coercive and regulatory powers of government agencies extend far beyond those normally allowed to, or needed by, academic institutions.

Multiple goals

Finally, the ultimate goals of government bureaus go far beyond the acquisition, refinement, and transmission of knowledge. The Preamble to the United States Constitution suggests the diversity and complexity of governmental responsibilities.

DISTINCTIVE FEATURES OF THE UNIVERSITY

Autonomy

The tradition of university autonomy and academic freedom has had a profound effect upon the style and structure of university governance. The notions that a professor should be careful about his tone of voice or should clear a tendentious paper with the top administrative officials of a university before publication are not acceptable patterns of behavior in a collegiate setting. Put in its purest form, one job of the academic is to "think otherwise." Theoretically, at least, the main job of the government official is to implement the constitutionally sanctioned mandates of politically accountable officials and legislators. What is accepted and protected in one context may be considered disloyal and even treasonable in the other. To paraphrase Emerson, a university is a kind of "standing insurrection." In a perverse way, its legitimacy is a fu tion of its heresies.

Government bureaus, on the other hand, operate on the assum tion that hierarchical loyalties, or even divided loyalties to exe tives and legislators, take precedence over individual autonom when issues of public moment are at stake. The bureaucra "leak" may be a protection and safety valve in a democratic socie but it is not acceptable as normal bureaucratic behavior. In university, however, it is difficult to conceive of the meaning of t term *leak*—at least on matters of substantive policy. A profess on a presidential search committee may break a news story abc candidates prematurely. Even without tenure, however, he unlikely to be sacked or even disciplined for such an indiscretic Similar behavior in a government bureau would be treated far mc harshly.

The great symbol and protection of academic freedom is, course, tenure. But tenure regulations could not stand withc widespread public acceptance of the idea that university autonom is socially desirable. Over the years possibly no speech has be given more regularly to university boards of trustees than the c that emphasizes the role of a lay board in interpreting to the wic community the peculiar immunities of academia. This world changing, but it has had a long and significant history.

Flattened organizational pyramid

Another generally accepted characteristic of the university is "flat" organizational pyramid. By "flat" is meant loose cont from the top and, generally, a bottom-heavy locus of effecti power over important matters. The story is told of General Eise hower's first faculty meeting after he became president of Columb University. In outlining some directions for the future, he referr to "my plans for Columbia University." A senior faculty memb rose to his feet and solemnly informed Mr. Eisenhower that t faculty, not the president, was "Columbia University." Clark Ke coined the term "multiversity" to suggest the vast agglomerati of academic baronies that constitutes most large institutions higher education in the United States. Even the presidents of sm colleges often find the power of faculty senates and of division and departmental interests too substantial to be ruled by admin trative fiat. And, of course, the recent awakening of student clair for academic power has not simplified the matter.

The managerial pyramid in academia may be flatter for some purposes than it is for others. One and the same institution may have a firm, towering management pyramid for "buildings and grounds" and an imperceptible pyramid for handling curricular matters and tenure questions. And all administrative pyramids tend to sharpen during financially lean years. But in general, most institutions of higher education have enjoyed a flatter management pyramid than have most government bureaus.

One important extension of this general observation is that universities conduct an enormous amount of their business through councils and committees. Not only is power decentralized in universities, but the reconciliation of differences and divergences among individuals or separate blocks of power is frequently "managed" by committees rather than by single administrators. College and university administrators occasionally enjoy the protection of conciliar movements; equally occasionally, committees become maddeningly inefficient and ponderous instruments of procrastination.

Limited accountability

The consequence of this administrative looseness is that substantial areas of collegiate activity are effectively immune to accepted standards of accountability. In such circumstances, accountability is an exercise in obfuscation by collectivities. Why was Assistant Professor Jones not promoted? Because the "senior members of his department" voted against him. Or, because the "Liberal Arts Promotions Committee" decided against promotion. Why was troublemaker Mary Smith admitted to graduate school and given a fellowship? Because the "admissions committee" of the Department of History so recommended to the "admissions committee of the Graduate School of Arts and Sciences."

No individual can be held accountable under such a system. Few academic administrators would try to hold an entire committee accountable. Some trustee-businessmen take a look at the fuzziness of the academic accountability structure and throw up their hands.

All this is within the context of widespread confusion about the goals of the university. Cardinal Newman may have set standards and goals for the university world of the nineteenth century—at least in Great Britain. But Newman's view in *The Idea of a University Defined and Illustrated* bears little relationship to the land-

grant, professional-school, extension-service, skill-centered com
plexes of twentieth-century America. It is the plethora of objective
as well as the complexity of structure that makes accountability
difficult to define or to achieve in American higher education.

Clientele and purposes

Two other peculiarities of the university should be noted. First
in terms of numbers, the overwhelming clientele is youth; second
the institutional product, however impossible it is to define it
precise objectives, basically relates to the discovery, refinement
and transmission of knowledge—knowledge defined in terms o
skills as well as ideas.

These twin realities give to universities a distinctive flavor
With few exceptions, the life of a government agency is conditione
by a random distribution of age cohorts throughout its system
Furthermore, the young are not paying the old for serving withi
the government agency framework. And in only a few governmen
agencies is the discovery, refinement, and transmission of know
edge a major function. Where exceptions exist (e.g., the Burea
of Standards, the Coast and Geodetic Survey, Oak Ridge Nationa
Laboratory), the young and relatively untutored do not dominat
the corridors and laboratories.

These then are some of the traditional differences that hav
marked the structure and environment of universities on the on
hand and government agencies on the other.

REAL VERSUS
APPARENT
DIFFERENCES

How valid and how significant are these distinctions as we observ
the present scene and look ahead? The first useful generalizatio
may be that many of the distinctions have been more apparent tha
real, and that in any case they are disappearing.

Locus of power

Surely flat administrative pyramids are not reserved to unive
sities alone. Many who have studied the Washington scene, fo
example, conclude that government agencies are, if not bottom
heavy, at least middle-heavy. Real power is generally found not a
the level of the department secretary or even of the President, bu
at the bureau level. It is at the bureau level that stability is s
frequently supported by the tripod of bureau–lobby–congressiona
subcommittee symbiosis. Such a tripod is not likely to be seriousl
upset by a very distant President, by realpolitik Executive Offic

staff, by understaffed and preoccupied agency heads, or by assistant secretaries who have come to Washington for one social season. It is at the bureau level that the continuities of seniority accrue (witness J. Edgar Hoover), that programmatic expertise resides, that what the British call "old-boy" networks are spun.

Is this picture really so different from an accurate portrait of the loci of power within many universities? Are not academic departments and professional schools the bureaus of the university? Are not the legs of the academic tripod — schools or departments, professional associations, and external donors — often quite as supportive of autonomies in relation to top managerial controls as corresponding tripods in HEW or the Department of Justice?

Personnel

And with the growing professionalization and unionization of white-collar workers, are not government bureaus and universities equally enmeshed in problems related to the care and feeding of personnel? Increasingly, both government agencies and institutions of higher education are part of a knowledge industry that requires highly skilled and highly independent labor. The job market for brains, of course, affects both bureaus and universities. But when the market is tight, as it was from the late forties to the late sixties, and when categorical funding spigots are open and are directed into the laboratories of selected "names," the reverse deference patterns in both universities and government agencies are patent. The shift from a seller's to a buyer's market in many professional and scientific fields may temper the authority of specialization; generalist administrations now have a large enough pool of talent from which to draw to ensure that arrogant specialists are not hired. But white-collar collective bargaining, long since a practice in government, is now beginning to move into the professional as well as blue-collar ranks of American universities. The administrative consequences of substituting the adversary proceeding of bargaining for the less structured interactions associated with the permeable membranes of academic senates have not been calculated. The likely consequences are that universities will resemble government agencies even more closely than in the past as far as personnel policies are concerned.

Protective civil service codes have often been compared with academic tenure as dual examples of rigid personnel systems. Too often this has been a superficial, cracker-barrel allegation. Academic administrators have rarely enjoyed tenure in job, even if they have enjoyed tenure in academic (as distinguished from administrative) rank. And even the most imposing career civil service systems of the government have exempted political appointees and have had loopholes that have made many individual career employees the victims of tight budgets and partisan vendettas. The only point here is that collective bargaining in both government and higher education is bound to move both types of enterprise further in the direction of the traditional stereotypes ("you can't get rid of them") governing academic tenure and civil service job security.

Grants

There are areas of activity in which universities and government agencies are not only indistinguishable but inseparable as well. For example, government grants to universities and to individual scholars may be based upon statutory authority; in reality, most of them are allocated according to recommendations made by academic panels whose centers of gravity are the prestigious Association of American Universities and the National Academy of Sciences.

Publicity

On the matter of publicity and public relations, how real is the relative immunity of universities from the constant glare of publicity? From the standpoint of a public agency's public relations office fighting for two column inches in the *New York Times,* the collegiate command of the sports page must be viewed with envy — as must the university scholar's publication outlets in learned (and not so learned) journals. Many a college president would have given his ceremonial mace in exchange for a little less glare of publicity in recent years.

Overlapping powers

And are universities really immune to the pulls and tugs of overlapping governmental powers and of federalism? More than one state university or college has been mouse-trapped by the competing interests of governors and legislators. Private as well as public universities have struggled long and hard with grants-in-aid and with contracts emanating from the federal government. How different really is the struggle of a university to maintain its academic freedom under a federal contract from the attempts of state and local governments to use categorical federal money for locally determined priorities? There may be differences, but there are certainly similarities. And as state and federal money bails out the sinking treasuries of private higher educational institutions, will not the present distinctions between public and private universities, and between universities and government bureaus, be fuzzed even further?

CONCLUSIONS This brings us to our final point. In times of great stress, when values are up for grabs and when an increasing number of allocative decisions in society are made at more complex levels than simple consumer choice, the great symbolic institutions of our past stabilities are bound to be challenged from within and without. Governmental institutions and universities are symbols of power and status associated with inertia in the minds of confused publics. For the timid and the conservative, the behavior of government agencies and of universities that seem to cut away from fixed moorings, and at increasing financial cost, seems to deserve attack and not to merit support. For the young and the politically restive generally, it is the very ponderousness of government bureaucracies and of universities—their unwillingness or inability to relate to present and future needs—that makes them undeserving of loyalty or support.

Whiplashed by those who fear change and by those who crave it, our great institutions of governance and education find it difficult to define their goals or save their souls. And forced exercises in decremental budgeting do not normally promote farsighted vision.

Only the woefully naïve contend that the real problem is efficiency—that government bureaus and universities will receive votes of confidence in new dollars when they can master PPB (program planning budgeting) and related cost-benefit techniques and thereby can be held accountable. The basic issue is political and psychological—a growing belief that what government bureaus and universities do is not worth the cost: that governments reduce freedom too much, and that universities foster too much license. The absence of sophisticated systems of accountability simply adds to the already substantive frustration of politicians and publics.

The perverse reality is that, although government bureaus need some degree of autonomy in order to be fair and universities need some degree of autonomy in order to pursue truth, it is these very autonomies that make both institutions suspect and, in the present historical context, vulnerable. "You can't beat City Hall" is a pejorative cry when addressed to governmental insensitivity and officiousness; it is a noble cry when it suggests that a small group of vested petitioners cannot win unfair concessions. Similarly academic immunities buttressed by tenure can protect the lazy and the irresponsible, but they are also the necessary conditions for inducing sensitive minds to reexamine stultifying traditions and ancient truths.

As private universities become more dependent upon public resources, as public universities become increasingly a part of the political processes affecting all government agencies, and as many government bureaus take on more and more of the attributes traditionally associated with universities, a basic paradox emerges. That paradox is that government bureaus and universities must go far beyond PPB in developing new modes and structures of accountability if they are to acquire the resources to enjoy the autonomies that allow them to perform what they believe to be their socially necessary roles. Yet accountability can be the enemy of autonomy, and autonomy can be accountability's mortal foe.

Until some grand political design is worked out to ensure universities both new public resources and old academic autonomy, university administrators might well turn to selected government bureaus that have for decades mastered this trick, at least in tactical and practical terms. The Corps of Engineers, the FBI, the Atomic Energy Commission, selected regulatory commissions—these have learned the art of attracting appropriations while preserving an astounding independence from political surveillance.[3]

Whether their success has been totally in the public interest is a question too complex and too pregnant with possible implications for the halls of academe (as well as the author's own delightful immunities) to warrant further consideration—at least in this essay.

One final note. Universities and colleges across the nation are undergoing a period of deep introspection; they are upset and frightened by the on-campus turmoil of recent years and are responding to new claims by faculty and students for more authority in university affairs. University constitutional conventions are

---

[3] For a recent comprehensive summary of the problems of accountability in government agencies, see Smith & Hague, 1971.

various reform commissions are springing up like dandelions. Some of them may come up with sensible revisions of archaic and authoritarian structures. Many, unfortunately, will go beyond correction of imbalances and will attempt to enthrone a legislature of student and faculty representatives arrogating to itself supreme power over president and trustees. This will be the tendency especially where past executive leadership in universities has been harsh and insensitive to changing community sentiment.

Alas, the cure may be fatal. The pages of history are strewn with examples of experiments in government by legislative bodies. The results have been uniformly disastrous—from the last days of the Roman Republic to the sullen history of the French Republic after World War I and until the Gaullist Revolution in the 1950s. Of all the weaknesses of the American Articles of Confederation, none was more forcibly or persuasively hit in *The Federalist Papers* than the total subjection of the executive to changing coalitions within the Continental Congress. As to those who believe that faculty-student governance councils can run universities, it is proper to remind them that legislatures of necessity break into committees, and that committees are ipso facto irresponsible in the sense that they are unaccountable. This issue was put with great eloquence in *Federalist* 15 (Hamilton, Madison, & Jay, 1901):

Why has government been instituted at all? Because the passions of men will not conform to the dictates of reason and justice, without constraint. Has it been found that bodies of men act with more rectitude or greater disinterestedness than individuals? The contrary of this has been inferred by all accurate observers of the conduct of mankind; and the inference is founded upon obvious reasons. Regard to reputations has a less active influence, when the infamy of a bad action is to be divided among a number, than when it is to fall singly upon one. A spirit of faction, which is apt to mingle its poison in the deliberations of all bodies of men, will often hurry the persons of whom they are composed into improprieties and excesses, for which they would blush in a private capacity.

The alternatives in university governance are not to make either a body or a person supreme. The dilemma is resolved only by the development of circularities of responsibility, where various bodies and functions—faculty, students, staff, administrators, and trustees—have their own areas of preeminent responsibility and are thereby made conscious of the necessary ambiguities of residual power relationships. In such circumstances, mutual dependence becomes clear and there are motivations to seek not power but consent.

In years when budgets are bound to be tight, when pain must be given, when the very life of an institution may depend upon skillful executive leadership, the move to enthrone legislatures in university governance can only be viewed with singular foreboding.

8. A Comparison of the University with a Large Foundation

by W. Mc Neil Lowry

It has been almost four decades since Frederick Keppel made the judgment that foundations lived behind their good works. In the era that produced Keppel and witnessed the Carnegie Corporation's contributions to higher education, universities also might have been said to live behind their works, good or bad. For both foundations and universities, isolation, privilege, even indifference are positions that can no longer be occupied. Change has come most publicly to universities, less publicly to foundations only because their existence has little importance to the man in the street. It is difficult to foresee the ultimate effect of the forces from within and from without that are taking the American university through perhaps the swiftest evolution in the history of higher education. On the other front, since World War II, foundations, first by choice but later prodded by political or public interest, abandoned the principles or affectations of humility and anonymity. In the last few years they have been provoked into public accounting and public defense to a degree that men like Keppel, Raymond Fosdick, or even Beardsley Ruml would have considered neither tasteful nor necessary. Universities and foundations emerged from the sixties adorned with new problems, shorn of a few old ones, and asked to trade powers and freedoms with new claimants. The total effect of these confrontations is not clear. For the university, the effect already is sharp enough to have begun to influence organizational structure. But to compare this structure to that of a large foundation one must assume that both the university and the foundation are what meets the eye—in other words, are what they have largely been instead of the swiftly evolving institutions one knows them to be.

To put this into perspective will prove troubling. First, however, we need to compare the missions of the two institutions. Over the past few decades highly generalized comparisons between universities and foundations in organizational terms have often been made, many of which are only superficially apt. But beneath the stereotype is a very real and a very important fact of action and reaction between a large foundation and a university, with consequences affecting the organization of the university and, to a limited extent, that of a foundation itself. The action and reaction concerns common missions addressed by both foundation and academic entrepreneurs.

**APPARENT
SIMILARITIES**

Common missions

The traditional comparison of missions is based on the fact that a large foundation supports research, the dissemination of knowledge, the application of knowledge, and the development of skilled personnel. The primacy of these objectives in the university is of course obvious. However, similarities of mission do not inevitably produce similarities in organization. The different ways in which a foundation attacks the three objectives further strain meaningful comparisons when one tries to relate mission to structure.

Large foundations are in the main philanthropies organized with general purposes but keeping nevertheless a great emphasis on a timely and defensible picture of up-to-date disciplinary and intellectual currents and within which scholars are in the vanguard. It is probable that as many as one-third of the principal officers of the 12 to 15 large, general-purpose foundations have had their most recent employment in an academic institution. In broad or specialized foundation program areas (let us say from higher education itself to the technical pursuit of medicine, agriculture, or the social sciences) one easily gains the impression that professional staff themselves constitute a community of scholars, permitting general officers and trustees to carry out objectives of which they have only a layman's grasp. Even the semantics is borrowed from the academy. The professional staff have not only "meetings" but "dialogues" or even "seminars." The impression is cultivated that the foundation officer lives in an intellectual community and that cerebration defines his species.

Structure

This generalization has for many years led foundation persons from the inside and academic persons from the outside to imagine a collegiate structure for a large foundation. The president corresponds, of course, to the president; the vice-presidents or directors of par ticular program areas to the deans; and the program officers and advisors—the persons most directly associated in the field—to the faculty. There have been periods in the history of the Carnegie and Rockefeller Foundations when such a supposed structure was tacitly accepted or at least not strenuously denied. There have been particular programs in the Ford Foundation, at certain periods in its short history, that employed the same rubric for want of a more exact one.

Universities and foundations do have some similarities in organizational structure in that each has to find a way of dealing with particular segments of knowledge—disciplinary, problem-oriented, subject-matter concentrated, or geographically or culturally divided. In university departments, disciplinary fiefs are often rigidly maintained, so that even interdisciplinary programs of research and education require baronial treaties. When certain disciplines, subject matter areas, or geographical divisions are delegated to particular programs in a large foundation, these delegations are sometimes defended with the ferocity traditionally associated with that of the head of an academic department. Furthermore, the review of program or divisional initiatives may at first glance appear similar to collegial evaluations before the president makes final recommendations to the governing board. The foundation professional, like the university faculty member, often succeeds in wresting a degree of autonomy not always enjoyed by mere academic deans or general foundation officers.

But this easy if somewhat plausible comparison either breaks down or reveals many gaps when the actual practice of the large foundation is analyzed. Admittedly, the traditional university organization can also be radically shifted by historical or personal accident, most frequently by the latter. A cadre of scholars with a highly developed entrepreneurial sense often produces a center of power that cannot be explained by traditional structure or by the normal processes of budgetary and resource allocations. Less frequently a new president with his own compulsive sense of direction or change creates circumstances that even the Byzantine powers and skills of departmental chairmen or the de jure fiscal control of the governing board can only partially restrain. These phenomena may appear even more frequently in a large foundation, though they are fairly easily dissipated in those foundations whose traditional and specialized program interests have had a long opportunity for entrenchment.

Decision making

One primary and dynamic fact about the structure of a foundation taken by itself strongly mars its comparability with a university Paradoxically enough it is found squarely in the collegial and cor porate response by which a foundation reacts to appeals for it benefactions. Of all the ancient axioms of organized philanthropy many of which over the past 20 years have been regularly and sys tematically breached, there is one with the greatest survival value in a foundation anyone can say no but it takes everyone to say yes Assaults on the diffused right to say no have frequently been made not only by powerful unsuccessful applicants to a foundation but b its own trustees. The assaults from outside will exist perennially indeed, they are intrinsic to the existence of large amounts of mone of which many people wish a considerable share. Assaults by trus tees on the ability of their own staff to say no have regularly bee controlled, though at times not without wounds to both foundation programs and the careers of foundation officers. In basic terms were the trustees to revoke the power of foundation staff member to turn down proposals, they themselves would be required to as sume staff functions, which they could not do without drastic re vision of their roles. (This is not, of course, true in either small c donor-dominated foundations where persons who are actually trust ees in effect constitute the only staff and the one staff person is kind of executive secretary to the governing board.)

If the autonomy of foundation staff to say no is accepted as it is then, from directors of program areas, divisional officers, or th president and the trustees, there is also in part a consequen autonomy of the staff person to say yes, though by no means s absolute as the right to say no. If a staff officer justifies his recom mendations against particular proposals, he already earns in som measure respect for his affirmative recommendation. At least i lends caution to the general officers when they find themselves i disagreement with the recommendation, even prior to the point a which they may have to identify themselves with it before the gov erning board. If, in addition to the position the professional office has earned as a result of his labors, he is also a person of judgment discrimination, and tact and is given to consulting expert opinior the caution with which his judgment is listened to can affect th institutional decision-making process.

All this is true in general and not confined to that rarer founda tion staff person who either has or seizes the opportunity to prov himself the right person to operate in the right program area at a time which both for the foundation and the society is meaningful and conclusive. Admittedly, even these few easily identifiable foundation persons in the fifties and sixties have their counterparts in greater numbers on the academic scene. Such men are not found among the most thorough and respected scholars even in their own fields, and it is noteworthy that with few exceptions they have not carried off Nobel or other prizes for scientific or scholarly distinction. They have distinguished themselves largely for their ability not to acquire or to preserve knowledge but to apply it — particularly to the material, political, industrial, military, and economic issues of the times. As such they were quite close in their orientation to what foundation officers traditionally meant about the application of knowledge and the development of skilled personnel to "solve" the problems of the society. In the last 20 years such men became more typical on the university scene, an enclave more difficult to fold within the structure, the most visible links between the university on the one hand and government and industry on the other. They were for a time most prized, but more recently most disprized, as the means by which the university converted both education and scholarship to the needs of the corporate state. With the most conspicuous of senior faculty engaged in good or bad ways (depending upon the critic) in serving the government and the military-industrial complex, the development of institutions and resources at home and abroad, the problems of the cities, and so on, each succeeding college generation believed that career symbols and career patterns had little to do with either the education of the young or the maintenance of the community of scholars.

INTERACTION BETWEEN FOUNDATIONS AND UNIVERSITIES

This is not the place to weigh these developments but only to understand them for any comparison of the university with the large foundation. The distance is not far to go. If there is responsibility to be shared, the foundation entrepreneur and the professorial entrepreneur share it completely. The removal of the scholar from the classroom or the intrusion of the institute or laboratory on the campus scene depended for its critical mass upon industry and government, but foundations seeking to help the society "solve" problems either led the way, proved very apt students of government adaptations, or imitated governments in their own programs of economic and social development. Their motives for these activities were presented as neutral and public spirited. And academics did not resist the seduction. Sartre and Gide, from their separate vantage points, can really be read as saying that there is no truly gratuitous act. Aldous Huxley said that for every thug there must be a thugee. But even with this defense, many foundations from the fifties in fact tended to ignore the basic integrity of the academic mission whenever they found willing entrepreneurs for their problem-oriented objectives. Had not many universities—for example, the large land-grant institutions—already seen an expanded mission for the university in services to the states, the regions, and the national and international communities? Did not the constituted heads of the universities, the presidents themselves, endorse what the professor-entrepreneur wanted to do for the foundations? But the foundations ought themselves to have kept in balance the primeval missions of education and scholarship. The tempter is equally responsible with the tempted, and in Eden it was the serpent who was condemned to go on his belly rather than upon his feet.

Until the 1920s large foundations included in their programs general endowment of universities and other institutions. Then they moved mainly to the direct support of research, except for continuing endowments by some foundations to specialized academic institutions such as colleges for blacks, medical schools, and others. When, in the fifties, institutions of higher education were overwhelmed by college-bound students, those that were not tax supported had vastly inflated needs and greater difficulties in meeting them. The Ford Foundation in 1956 moved on two of the most basic functions of a university, the improvement of faculty salaries and the support of scholarships and fellowships throughout the disciplines, as in the programs of the National Merit Scholarship Corporation and of the Woodrow Wilson Foundation. In the early sixties the Ford Foundation moved to cover the broadest needs, the whole institutional base, in hundreds of millions of dollars directed to special capital programs for universities and colleges. At the same time Ford continued to use universities for problem-oriented and special national and international ends, as in the vast support of area studies initiated by the Carnegie and Rockefeller Foundations, the training of advanced students and faculty in these areas, the provision of economists and business managers to both the developed and underdeveloped areas of the world, the cultivation of the behavioral sciences for problem-oriented enterprises across a broad spectrum, the development of agricultural tech nology in company with the Rockefeller and other foundations, and in many other ways in which both the training of personnel and the support and application of research were largely specialized.

These actions of the Ford Foundation are cited because the author is more familiar with them than with similar manifestations in other foundations, but not at all because the Ford Foundation constituted a model in its influence on the university. In the first place, it is easier for a foundation with very large financial resources to keep, in its impact on universities, some balance between the basic institutional functions of higher education and the use of academic personnel and resources to serve national and international policy. But without availing oneself of this special circumstance, one would have to say that the dominant tone and milieu of even this largest of foundations was a product not of the magnitude of its investments in the basic educational mission of a university but of its initiative and dexterity in converting academic personnel and scholarly resources to the service of national needs and international policy.

Impact on University Structure What has this to do with a comparison of the structure of the university with the structure of a large foundation? Are we not considering more specifically the political and social thrusts of Americans in the second half of the twentieth century and the perhaps inevitable partnership between an institution with both skills and skilled personnel on the one hand and an institution with financial resources on the other? The point is more relevant to structure than at first glance it may appear, particularly since the structure of an institution is affected by its governance and in turn conditions how it is governed.

Though the conversion of the university into a contractor or an entrepreneur in the service of government and industry was not underwritten by foundations, the foundations found themselves at many key points in the arrangements, whether at their own initiative, the initiative of government, or the initiative of scholars or the universities themselves. Despite the recognition foundation officers might give and did give to the basic historical functions of institutions of higher education, they gave strength, leadership, and public defense to academic entrepreneurs, singly or in teams, who for good or bad altered not only the mission but also the shape of the university. To many vocal segments in the younger generation, this twentieth-century brand of academic entrepreneurship helped to depersonalize and dehumanize professorial relations with undergraduates and to emphasize career patterns that had less to do with a community of scholars than with service to the corporate state and the perquisites and powers pertaining thereto.

With the creation of specialized centers and institutes outside the regular departmental and college structure, the university organization grew more complex. Center and institute directors often dealt directly with top administrative officers without having their programs evaluated by their peers in a faculty meeting. In fact, the funds that a well-connected faculty entrepreneur could bring to the university gave him a bargaining power often disproportionate to the actual contribution his projects might make to the total university community. Thus the governance of the institution became more and more difficult and even at times uncontrolled. At the very heart of the academic fraternity continued to stand the all-powerful department, making recommendations for appointment in the light of its own particular interests and jealously guarding its own jurisdiction.

Impact on Foundation Structure

The structure of the foundation cooperating in the use of the university for national and international ends was also affected, but in far less important and less obvious ways. In the context of this analysis of the university structure compared to that of the foundation, the point is tangential but worthy of brief attention. When a large foundation has entered into contracts with major educational institutions for sustained development in foreign countries of other educational institutions, planning and management commissions, and rural and village development, those contracts are by their very nature long-term. Moreover, these are contracts not only with foreign governments or with foreign academic institutions but with particular American universities, requiring the presence both in the American institutions and abroad of scholars and administrators who see their own careers in terms of the success or failure of what a foundation has agreed to attempt. For effective control, the various stages of these projects are in the hands of the field representative, who under these circumstances exists not only in the person of the foundation's local executive but also in the university specialist who may, for two, three, or five years, operate far from his home institution. Back home in the headquarters of the sponsoring foundation, every stage in the funding of the continuing project goes through the normal collegial evaluation, the formal recommendation of general officers including the president, and the frequent review and endorsement of the trustees. But these long-range projects in Asia, Latin America, the Middle East, and elsewhere are pipeline projects. Once into them, the officers and budget makers back home must depend very heavily on the conviction and the momentum, or sometimes simply the moving bureaucratic commitment, of the foundation's field representative. If one wanted to exaggerate the dynamics in this situation, he might conclude that the imperator at home found that the proconsuls abroad were out of control. Though on paper a chief representative of the foundation in a foreign capital might have neither the status of a general officer nor a singular autonomy over project recommendations, his de facto autonomy might affect both the approval authority at home and, more importantly, the planning and budget allocations controlling the course of projects for which he was responsible. At least a part of the background is his commitment to the American academics who contribute the skills of their specialties and the administrative functions necessary to his success. Thus, just as the utilization of the university for international and national goals changes the balance of authorities and resources on the campus, so does the provision of funds for such diversion subtly shift control in the foundation itself.

By a circuitous route, the structure of a university has been compared with that of a large foundation at one level of the philanthropic institution, that occupied by professional staff. Traditionally, foundation officers on this level have often been compared to faculty and department heads seeking to push forward, through deans and other administrators, initiatives and proposals that would affect collegiate and corporate policy and influence the allocation of institutional resources. The analogy has probably been strained at this level of comparison between the two institutions. A large foundation engages in the support of research and its dissemination, in the application of knowledge, and in the training of skilled persons. A university does all these things directly and then does other things, some more basic, in addition. But if the subject is organizational structure, these joint objectives, with the university operating chiefly directly and the foundation chiefly indirectly, are of only marginal influence. What is far more pervasive, and indeed inevitable, is the common traffic of university specialists and technologists with foundation officers to a point at which the interests and even the roles of the two become blurred or identical. The effect of the foundation officer on the structure of the university, as has been pointed out, is far greater than the effect of the faculty member on the structure of the foundation. But what occasions all the generalizations about hierarchical, functional, and role similarities between university faculty and foundation professionals is their intimate associations, their effect on one another, and the fact that frequently the foundation professional was formerly identified as an administrator or scholar in a university.

Influence of the president

We found the comparison between the two structures to be actually either marginal or complex at the professional staff level in both institutions. We now turn to comparisons at the level of the president and of other general officers and at the level of the governing board. In their influences on structure and in their ways and means of influencing policy and governance, how do foundation presidents compare with university presidents? In this analysis we must bear in mind not only the cardinal fact that foundations have no students but also—and of equal importance—the fact that the scale of a university in terms of staffs and echelons is far weightier and far more stratified than that of even a very large foundation. It is obvious that the president and the governing board can more quickly influence the course of a foundation than that of a major university.

Comparing the roles of foundation and university presidents is a fruitful subject inhibited only by one's inability to separate what a president says from what he does. On one level this means attempting to look behind the president as spokesman for every policy initiative in the institution, wherever originated, and at the president as initiator of a policy stratagem that is uniquely his own contribution and reflective of his own leadership. Since both a large foundation and a large university are traditionally institutions that make pronouncements in the president's name, the separation between the symbol and the man is more difficult perhaps than when pronouncements are made by large industrial corporations, state governments, or mayoralties. Another difficulty arises from another tradition common to both universities and large foundations. In an important crisis, or in one that has accidentally become publicly known even if not important, the president is expected to represent the corporation even when he has not been directly in volved in the situation. As chief executive officer of a complex institution, he must necessarily support any action or policy taken by one of his subordinates. To do otherwise would be to expose either accident or internal conflict. As the last court of appeal between the staff and the governing board, he is the public witness that the organization both knows what it is doing and means to do so.

It is easy, therefore, for outside observers to gain an inaccurate or incomplete impression of the influence of the president on the structure of the institution. This has undoubtedly been a more recurrent syndrome for the university president in recent years than for his counterpart in a foundation. One reason is, of course, that there are more examples of the large university than of the large foundation on the national scene and, except in rare instances, these are more visible and more interesting to the public than are the large foundations.

But admitting the difficulties of identifying personal causation and separating it from the president's role as symbolic spokesman, we can yet conclude that even such large and ingrained institutions as great universities and foundations are heavily affected in their structure by the philosophy and temperament of chief executive officers from one period in their history to another. We can also conclude that at this level of structure, at least, the university and the large foundation appear to be similar. Organized foundations on the scale of those we have described are less than a century old even as a type. There is nowhere within them a long-prepared jurisdictional enclave comparable to that in a university department. The nearest example is one or two highly specialized staffs of the older foundations. As long as a university or a foundation does not terminate its program in biological sciences or agricultural technology, any new president will have difficulty in changing affairs, no matter how new the broom he brought with him.

But these are exceptions. In the main the president of a university is more influenced by entrenched departments than is a president of a foundation by particular program staffs. New incumbents in both institutions can exert influence upon the structure. But the president of even a large foundation can exert a great deal more of such influence than can the president of an established university with a large and complex staff. The foundation president may not even be conscious that his own way of administering the foundation will inevitably have profound effects on its structure. He may, in fact, retain most of the defined positions and echelons on the tabl of organization that he found when he came in, adding only on or two to administrative levels below his own to carry out nev functions of which he is enamored. But by his method of relating t the entire staff he will, in effect, change the structure, whether o not he changes the labels, and the staff is not so large that he cannо relate with all the key members.

Arrangements of structure and efforts to shift them can affec executive administrations, and action and reaction between th chief executive and organizational jurisdictions can be crucial t his control. Since 1966 examples of this interplay between a presi dency and conflicts influenced by changes in the power structur have been, of course, far more numerous on the university scen than within organized philanthropy. There is not space to elaborat on them and the writer is not ideally equipped to do so, but varie cases could obviously be drawn from the recent histories of Berke ley, San Francisco State College, Wisconsin, Harvard, Johns Hop kins, and other important institutions.

Effects of personal style   These intraorganizational changes an conflicts are, of course, the products in toto of multiple cause from within and from without the institution. The influence by o on the president is the most visible to the public but not mor important than those involving the institution's governing boar and its constituents. The confrontations are in a sense transitory o evolutionary in their number and in their severity, and they ar therefore not perennial, as is the steady influence on an institutioı of the personal style and approach of an individual chief executive A great deal has been written about the styles of American uni versity presidents, and the subject has proved particularly attrac tive when it has concerned successive presidents of the most stabl or encrusted universities. Harvard College is the most obviou example. A somewhat different but equally attractive example ha been the University of Chicago, with emphases ranging across th idiosyncrasies and the particular elements in its origin and forma tion, the highly visible and experimental administration of youn; Robert M. Hutchins, and the attempts at stability made by his les; flamboyant successors. Charity and secrecy combine to draw a veil over personal styles of those more embattled presidents of th sixties, and we leave the record where at least one or two chose t make public their own cases or their own woes.

The personal styles of chief executives of large foundations hav been of great and continuing interest within a special circle, but far less has been written about them and far less attention has been paid by any significant segment of the public. History has caught up to this point only with a few, including Frederick T. Gates, Frederick Keppel, Raymond Fosdick, Beardsley Ruml, and, through the annals of journalism but to a lesser extent, John Gardner and Paul Hoffman. All these except Hoffman were the lore givers and rule makers of the profession of organized philanthropy, but, except for Gates and Ruml, presidents were often overshadowed by colorful associates or consultants—men like Abraham Flexner, Wickliffe Rose, Robert M. Hutchins, and Warren Weaver. A few persons of great influence on the structure and evolution of foundations after midcentury were even more anonymous than the precepts of the older generation required. One was William W. McPeak who, within the staff of the Gaither study group planning the Ford Foundation, most distilled the experience of older foundations and through two administrations served Ford either de facto or de jure for policy and planning. At the other extreme, after foundations had inevitably moved from the Keppel position nearer the center of public attention, one president, McGeorge Bundy, revealed a personal style that in its influence exceeded any since those of Gates and Ruml.

The intrinsic nature of both a large foundation and a large university makes any treatment of the influence of a chief executive incomplete until one has disposed of the role of the trustees. (Indeed, if one looks deeply enough, the same can be said of any treatment of the role of key staff officers below the level of the president or even of the general officers.) As previously noted, the university president feels more pressure from his departments than does a foundation president from his particular program staffs. Nevertheless, at times not only the foundation president but the trustees themselves find occasion to worry about the control of staff, just as in even the most established university (or perhaps most of all in the most established) both the president and the overseers may regularly feel themselves controlled by tenured professors fiercely contending for departmental budgets. We shall see this more clearly when discussing the constituents of universities and foundations.

Role of trustees

The spirit may often be bruised by the letter, but the spirit of foundation governance is that trustees are representatives of the general public interest in deciding how a foundation may best serve society. The public itself until recently had only to decide whether actions by a foundation appeared generally reasonable. Special publics—for example, elite institutions in higher education or bodies of scholars with special interests—fluctuate extremely in their views as to the reasonableness of a foundation's course almost exactly in terms of whether or not the foundation lets the special group dispose of a large quantity of its funds. Congress and the press may eventually enforce their own concepts of the public interest on foundations, and they began to do so extensively in 1969. But at the moment the reflections of public interest and control with which foundation officers must deal exist very importantly in the organization's trustees. Trustees may or may not at any one time truly reflect the general public interest, with results that in consequence can range from good to bad. They can in one time or in one action either defend the institution from unthinking, unhelpful, or reactionary public influence or deliver the institution to the currents of public doctrine or public fashion. A president can do the same if he has a majority of his trustees with him.

As long as the affairs of a university are going along normally, its board of governors is less important in influence on the organization than are the trustees of a foundation. When affairs are not going along normally and more especially when they are subject to turmoil caused by the university's constituents, the quality and courage of the trustees are crucial. On this point the analogy with the foundation as an institution exists, if in lesser degree. If a large foundation has continuity and tradition and pursues particular lines of research and action motivated by long-range interests in science, scholarship, or education, then the character of the trustees is of less consequence than in a foundation working in experimental and controversial ways on short-range and complex public issues.

But the role of trustees in large foundations breaks sharply from that of university overseers in a crucial way, though one not generally understood. Universities have constituents, both within and without the structure. In particular, universities have students. Foundations have only clients. In the strict sense, foundations have no constituencies with one exception: trustees of foundations control broad policies, represent the public interest, and *at the same time* are the only true constituents such institutions have. It is this paradox that escapes general attention. From time to time even foundation trustees themselves may see the picture quite differently. They anticipate (and they are right to do so) the risk of seeing the institution captured by special cadres, ranging from a particular staff within the foundation itself to the practitioners representing special interests. But trustees can largely control or even avoid these risks, if sometimes at the cost of colliding with a president or an important staff officer or of confronting and restraining the influences of outside special interests. Indeed, only in their role as constituents can foundation trustees also properly execute their other function, representation of the general public interest.

The constituent role of the trustees may even have been strengthened in the second half of the century, since general public interest in organized philanthropic institutions was a flagging one. Except for the traditional know-nothing segment of the American public that distrusted both knowledge and its professors, even the universities experienced little more than stereotyped public acceptance of their instrumental role with the young. Even in the early fifties, when man's right to knowledge and the free use thereof were under special attack, the blows aimed at universities may have helped solidify their privileged position through providing cause for a vigorous counterattack. The scholar with tenure in a university had more weapons at his disposal in combatting McCarthyism than did the civil servant in a government bureau, and his defenders on the campus did not have to go to the electorate to conserve their positions. To probe the foundations, McCarthyism produced both the Cox and Reece investigations, which missed their targets widely by both the extremity and the carelessness of their charges. Even after these small Indian wars, the foundations continued to treat appeals to the general public and, in large part, the exchange of information as subjects of little importance.

Throughout this period, the true constituents of the foundations were as always their trustees. By this nothing so crude is meant as that foundation officers and staff promulgated recommendations only in terms of their appeal to a trustee majority. The testimony of trustees in more than one foundation could be taken to prove the contrary, if proof were necessary. In truth, the image of public interests and public issues reflected by trustees of large foundations in this period was identical and interchangeable with that of a large number among professional staffs. In all but actuality, staff and trustees were conceived of as peers, in a way not unlike the accepted image of relationships between scholars and governors on the university scene. (One reason for this has already been discussed, namely the emergence of the university professor as an independent entrepreneur and a diminishing of his role as a tutor of undergraduates.) In this same spirit, over the past two decades the image, and to some extent the practice, in both foundations and universities were of movable parts exchanging themselves among professorial or professional chairs in foundations, universities, institutional governing boards, and key spots in the structure of government.

OTHER RELATIONSHIPS BETWEEN UNIVERSITY AND FOUNDATION

This discussion would not be complete without incidental and obvious reference to other ways in which the structure of foundations and universities relate and to ways in which the foundation influences the organization and function of a university. In both institutions, intraorganizational communication is seen on the surface as the development of a consensus. In actual practice the ways in which actions emerge vary greatly even in the same foundation or in the same university in terms of the administrative style of chief executives or the compulsion of trustees to fraternize with key staff.

There are other less general and less important examples. Some concern direct efforts by foundations to alter or insert in universities their emphases on particular subject matters or the rearrangement of service or power centers in the interests of social, national, or international policy. An obvious illustration was in the great swing toward specialized studies and the training of specialists in areas and cultures foreign to the American initiated by the Carnegie and Rockefeller Foundations and developed by multimillion-dollar investments by the Ford Foundation. In truth, the initiative for this development originated on the campus (as did scores of foundation professionals), but little would have come from this initiative without a large commitment to it by foundation staffs, a commitment completely shared by important trustees. Many other examples akin to this one exist, often in a similar way resulting in interdisciplinary programs at the universities and the creation of interdisciplinary centers and institutes. Over a 20-year period, working together, foundation officers and university professors moved to emphasize "studies" rather than branches of study.

More functional influences are found in experiments by foundations in the support of new management processes in universities, changes in fiscal policies, changes in arrangements for the governance of universities, and even in models of universities or colleges presumed to be unlike existing ones in their total structure.

CONCLUSIONS This discussion has centered on similarities, differences, and interactions between large, general-purpose foundations and the major universities in the United States. Only by exclusion has it treated the smaller or donor-controlled foundation in which trustees in effect occupy the positions of staff and (with only a few, if conspicuous, exceptions) restrict themselves to traditional or personalized giving.

The discussion accepts the existence of a popular view of a close resemblance between the structure of a foundation and that of a university, a similarly collegial process within, each moving toward a consensus, and a comparable influence on each by a board of governors. The writer takes issue with this view by seeking to focus attention on a more real and more pervasive interchange between foundations and universities. At bottom that interchange is found in the development in the United States since World War II of concepts and techniques for converting human and material resources to the purposes of social and economic development. The verdict on the effects produced is not yet in, though it is being vigorously and even violently argued from vantage points ranging from quite old to brand new. Neither foundations nor universities will ever again contribute to this development in anything approaching privacy.

9. Perspectives on the University Compared with Other Institutions

by John J. Corson

If one studies those descriptive materials—charts, manuals, and sections of catalogs—that universities use to explain what their organizations are like, one may conclude that the university organization is substantially similar to that of the corporation, the government agency, or the foundation. Place the organization of each before you, and you will see similar hierarchies pictured: a governing board on top, a chief executive, several levels of subordinate officers, and in the background—unpictured—customers, investors, bankers, and suppliers for each. The titles of the participants vary, but the similarity in structure simply makes it clear that organization charts, while highly useful in depicting the skeleton of an organization, do little to show how a group of people, banded together to achieve common objectives, are related in their day-by-day efforts.

That there are differences between the Virginia State Highway Department, the International Paper Company, the United States Army, the Protestant Episcopal Church, the Danforth Foundation, and the University of South Carolina is obvious to anyone who has been exposed to such organizations. But are these differences substantial? Where do they stem from?

The comparisons made in the three preceding chapters confirm the uniqueness of the university as an organization and emphasize the substantiality of differences that obtain between the university and other institutions. The purpose of this chapter is to identify the root causes of the differences that have been noted and to spell out the implications of these causes in terms of how the university is structured and how it operates. We will consider in turn the:

1   Charter of the organization: Not the formal wording of a musty document but what in fact a university exists to do.

2 Activities of the organization: How and to what extent the university's activities relate, or fail to relate, the individuals who make up the organization.

3 Character of the organization: The kind of a world the university provides for those who are part of its structure.

4 Membership of the organization: What distinguishes the individuals and groups that make up the university.

5 Bonds of organization: The ties that hold the members of the university together and with what degree of consanguinity (Bakke, 1959).

CHARTER, PURPOSE, AND GUIDANCE Organizationally, the significance of the charter of an institution — be it a business enterprise, a government bureau, a foundation, or a university — lies in its capacity to provide a guiding and unifying concept for all members of the organization. For most business enterprises the articles of incorporation serve this function.[1] The statutes that establish governmental agencies define the purpose of each more precisely and make it known more generally to members of the organization. Since these statutory purposes are often enforced by the legislatures and sometimes by the courts, they tend to constrain each agency and its members. To obtain the benefits of prevailing legislation, the philanthropic foundation is required to state clearly its reason for being, and while this may be stated in general terms, law specifies increasingly what the foundation may do, on whom it may bestow its largesse, and how it should operate.

Lack of clearly stated purposes in the university charter
In contrast, the university's charter states its purpose so vacuously as to provide little guidance to the members of the organization. William C. Fels pointed up, in a delightful tongue-in-cheek essay, the varied and intangible purposes colleges and universities claim for themselves in what they say to prospective students and their parents in catalogs: for example, "to develop the individual," "to develop the well-rounded man," or "to give students the greatest possible opportunity to develop their individual capacities" (Fels, 1959). Fels's point is affirmed if one looks at the basic charters in

---

[1] For that limited number of business enterprises that operate as "partnerships," the articles of partnership tend to state the purpose of the enterprise and the role of each partner more precisely than the more generally phrased language of articles of incorporation.

which the founding fathers stated the purposes of particular institutions. Typical of statements in the charters are: "to produce ornaments of the church and the state" or "the advancement of knowledge and the education of young men."

A central reason for such generality of purpose is that the discovery and transmission of knowledge is achieved by many and varied approaches, and the search for new knowledge is often directed toward unspecifiable goals. The individuals who research, teach, and learn have many interests and their concerns are related only in a very general fashion. When one cannot articulate ends that claim the interests of many, it is difficult to plan collegial ways of achieving them.

A second reason for such generalities, as reflected in the day-to-day operations of the college or university, lies in the even more varied concerns of the several factions that make up the university: faculty, students, trustees and administrators, alumni, and, last but not least, the university's clients—particularly the government agencies that look to it to perform research or provide services, and the professions (medicine, law, engineering) and semiprofessions (business administration, social work, and teaching) that look to it to guard their gates of entry. Only the most broadly stated purpose—one encompassing the objectives of each faction—will be generally acceptable.

But organizations—with the exception of governmental agencies—seldom look to historically stated purposes to guide and interrelate the activities of individual members. In the well-managed business enterprise, original purpose is translated into operating plans that specify for the here and now, in quantifiable terms, what is to be accomplished and when. A government bureau's activities are specified from year to year by a legislatively approved budget; where the appropriation process works well that budget spells out, in conformity with the originally legislated purpose, what is to be accomplished within a specified fiscal period. A philanthropic foundation with a known annual revenue can and often does plan in advance what proportion of its funds will be used in each of several program fields—for example, research in the natural sciences or in early learning, archeological exploration, or experimentation in public health.

Planning for the college or university—and particularly for its core activities of teaching and research—is less feasible and, despite the noble efforts of some proponents of academic "management," less often practiced than in the business enterprise, the govern-ment bureau, or the foundation. Plans can be and are developed for the physical facilities of the college or university (the development of the campus), for the institution's financing (the raising of funds, expenditures, and the investment of endowments), and for its busi-ness affairs (housing and feeding of students, purchasing, mainte nance of grounds and buildings, keeping of accounts, and construc tion). But the teaching and research activities are so inadequately quantifiable and so subject to the varying approaches of different teachers and scholars that institutionwide plans can seldom be formulated. Departmental plans—of a sort—are formulated but in general represent only the planning of incremental additions to the work of the department, for example, the addition of an assistant professor in a field not covered by the teaching of the several members of the department.

In summary then, for reasons that stem from the basic nature of an institution of higher learning, the college or university functions with only the most general understandings of goals to guide the individuals who carry out its activities.[2] In this respect the uni-versity differs significantly as an organization from its counterparts discussed in the three preceding chapters.

ACTIVITIES, STRUCTURE, AND PROCESS   Even as the organization and functioning of a multiproduct manu facturing company differ from those of a chain of retail grocery markets or from those of a technically oriented consulting firm, so the organization and functioning of the business enterprise differ from those of the government bureau, the foundation, and the uni versity. The activities to be performed dictate the kinds of personnel required and the roles and influence accorded different categories of personnel (e.g., the production executive in the manufacturing company, the buyer in the retail grocery chain, and the scientist in the consulting firm). Together the nature of the activities to be per formed and the personnel mobilized to carry them out shape the organization and modes of functioning.

To achieve the general purposes for which colleges were created (for example, "to develop the individual"), these institutions tra

---

[2] There are notable exceptions. A few colleges, usually of modest size, have estab lished a distinctive purpose that is generally accepted by faculty, students administration, board, and alumni. Perhaps the best-known examples are Antioch, Reed, and Swarthmore.

ditionally carried on two avowed activities and two implied activities. The core activity was and is, of course, teaching. Research has been, in theory if not in fact, integrally related to the teaching activity. The less explicitly recognized activities of the college and university are the socialization of youth and the certification of individuals for entry into, traditionally, the professions, and, more recently, a wide variety of semiprofessions and occupations.

Society, as well as individual institutions, has recognized the large importance of these activities and has accorded to those who perform them certain protections that influence the structure and processes of the college and university. Those protections are customarily summed up in the term *academic freedom.* This term means in practice the guarantee to the teacher of the freedom of expression (to interpret in his teaching the knowledge accumulated as he sees it) and to the researcher the freedom of inquiry (the right to pursue his research wherever it may lead him). To assure these protections for those who perform these roles, the college and university have traditionally claimed, and society has generally granted, autonomy — the right of the institution to govern its internal affairs without interference by the state or by any powerful group within the society.

Moreover, as knowledge has accumulated, the individual teacher or researcher has gained an additional dimension of freedom. This freedom flows from his possession of so specialized an understanding of a particular field of knowledge as to make impracticable or impossible the direction or control of his activities by others.[3] A further consequence of this high degree of specialization is of prime organizational significance: much of what the individual does in his teaching and his research is unrelated to what his fellow members in the organization do.

Impact of activities on structure
The reflection of the nature of these activities, their social importance, and the protections consequently accorded the institution, its teachers, and researchers can be seen in three aspects of the college and university structure. The lay board (with broad powers

---

[3] Talcott Parsons (1971, p. 489) writes, "[I]n a sense probably not true of most bureaucratic organizations, it is not possible for academic men, competent as they may be in their own fields, to understand each other's specialties at a very high level."

of governance in theory and limited powers in fact) exists to repre-sent the concerns of society in the autonomous institution and to see that teachers and researchers are assured of the freedoms essen-tial for the performance of their functions. The existence of two internal structures within the college or university—the academic structure, made up of departments, schools, and colleges, and the administrative structure, responsible for supporting services and business affairs—reflects the self-governance granted the teaching and research staffs. And the relatively flat organization of the aca-demic structure reflects the relative independence accorded the individual teacher and researcher.

The nature of these activities simultaneously conditions the internal processes of governance. The processes by which the all-important resource—i.e., personnel qualified to teach and to carry on scholarly research—is acquired, evaluated, promoted, retained and retired are distinctive. The processes of academic decision making are highly diffused. Decisions about who shall teach are made by each department; about what shall be taught, largely by the individual teacher in concert with his departmental colleagues about how it shall be taught, predominantly by the teacher; and about what research shall be undertaken, almost exclusively by the individual researcher. The processes of control—of seeing to it that classes meet and are taught effectively, and that research undertaken is carried out competently and as scheduled—are sub-stantially self-administered. The conscience of the individual teacher and researcher and his desire to gain the esteem of his peers constitute the primary bases for control.

Uniqueness of university structure

In these aspects of organizational structure and processes of gover-nance the university differs markedly from the business enterprise the government bureau, and the foundation. And these difference flow directly from the nature of the activities the university carrie on. Stephen Bailey (see Chap. 7) has raised the pregnant question for students of organization: Will these differences persist or dis-appear? As the business enterprise performs an increasing array of functions important to the society (e.g., employing the hard-core unemployed, producing drugs on which many individuals depend for the maintenance of life itself) and as the business enterprise the government bureau, and the foundation utilize increasing proportions of highly specialized workers who claim for themselves substantial self-determination of what they shall do and how, the uniqueness of university structure and the processes will be less apparent.

The character of organizations—the kind of environment they provide for their members—flows from the purpose for which they exist and the nature of the activities they carry on. While leadership may markedly influence the character of an individual organization, for categories of organizations—business firms, governmental agencies, philanthrophic foundations, and institutions of higher learning—it is the basic purpose and the activities involved in achieving that purpose that mold the organizational character.

The purposes for which colleges and universities exist—the transmission of knowledge to the young (and, incidentally, the shaping of the values of a major segment of the oncoming generation), the discovery of new knowledge and its application to the ills and problems of society—are purposes that claim relatively great social approbation. The approbation has been reflected in the financial support accorded these institutions and in the willingness of individuals of better than average talent to devote themselves to academic life despite alternative opportunities. The academic world provides an environment in which faculty members may enjoy ego satisfactions greater than those enjoyed by the manager of the Avis Rent-a-Car station, the engineer in the public highway department, or the foundation staff member engaged in dispensing the funds of a dead philanthropist. That social approbation rests on the presumed contribution to the prevailing culture and not on such tangible payoffs as may be discernible for the bank, the municipal water works, or the foundation that supports medical discoveries. It is based on the presumption that the education of people and research findings are, in the long run, of great benefit to the society. And the intangibility of that presumption makes the college and university vulnerable when happenings on campus run counter to the conventions of society.

Traditionally, it has been held that the college or university should enjoy not only autonomy—a freedom from external interference that would ensure the academic freedom of individuals— but also a degree of physical detachment from the rest of the society. (The typical location of the college or university in a rural community, removed from the workaday world, and the physical separation of the campus from that community emphasize this detachment.)

When entry into employment is increasingly dependent on the holding of a degree, the college and the university perform a function that is increasingly essential to the individual and to employers generally. Hence, we see the institution assuming some of the social obligations of a public utility and losing some of the autonomy it has deemed essential. This autonomy has also been eroded as the institution of higher learning has become involved in the study of, and the application of knowledge to, problems of business, government, and the community. The teacher and researcher have more and more recognized their need for interaction with society, and institutional autonomy has been reduced.

One characteristic of the college and university associated with this earlier detachment persists, though in lessened fashion. The institution of higher learning has been (and to a degree still is) a "total institution."[4] That is, it tends to encompass for many of its members (faculty and principally students) not only the work-associated aspects of their lives but the social and recreational aspects of their lives as well. In this respect, the residential college or university located in rural areas did provide for many of its members an environment more akin to the monastery, the convent, the prison, or the asylum than to the business enterprise.[5] In the "total institution" all aspects of life are conducted in the same place, in association with the same individuals, and under the same authority; the work, social, and recreational phases of the individual's life are, in varying degrees, scheduled in relation to one another in an overall plan purported to accomplish the purpose of the organization. Obviously an organization of this kind strives to maintain a different relationship and interdependency among its members than obtains between the employees, customers, and executives of the business firm or the government bureau and between the foundation staff and the grantees who are accorded their support.

Yet within the college or university organization is found a notably loose kind of social organization. The individual faculty member — and, more and more, the student — is relatively free to

---

[4] See Goffman (1961, pp. 3–124).
[5] See "The Man from Mars" (1971, p. 41).

determine his own activities, without supervision and direction. He is also freer of evaluative controls than is his counterpart in other kinds of organizations. And that freedom tends to build in the kinds of individuals that make up institutions of higher learning a great capacity to resist change in what they do and how they do it.

MEMBERSHIP AND ORGANIZATION

At least seven distinguishable categories of individuals are found in most institutions of higher learning: trustees, administrators, faculty members (tenured and nontenured), the emerging semi-professional staff (e.g., librarians, computer operators, laboratory directors), nonacademic staff (the accounting, purchasing, building operation, and maintenance staffs as well as others), students, and alumni.

The university is, in economic language, a "labor intensive" enterprise. It is dependent on the caliber, the effectiveness, and the zeal of the human resources it assembles. So too are many businesses (e.g., high-technology firms such as IBM and Polaroid), professional enterprises (a hospital or a law firm), government bureaus (such as the Federal Council of Economic Advisers), and foundations.

It was Chester Barnard (1948) who pointed out a quarter of a century ago that to be effective an organization must persuade the individual member that his personal interests are in accord with, and will be furthered by, the interests and objectives of the employing organization. By this yardstick the university lacks an important organizational strength. The zeal of the semiprofessional staff and the nonacademic staff can be and usually is enlisted in principal part by compensation and the prospect of permanent association. The alumni hold a continuing emotional attachment to what the institution was. But the key categories of personnel that make up the college or university are not as integrally identified with the institution as Barnard indicates is ideal.

Degree of Allegiance to the University

Trustees are, in major proportion, attracted to their posts by the social status the role of trustee grants, a desire to contribute to the public good, or their emotional attachment as alumni. Their interests and zeal are not unrelated to the objectives of the college or university but, in most instances, neither are the objectives of the institution as central to the individual's concerns as are the objectives of the corporate director or the elected legislator who oversees government agencies.

Most academic administrators (from departmental chairmen t
presidents) divide their allegiances between the academic disciplin
in which they have been trained, their fellow scholars, and th
institution they serve.

Faculty members' interests and zeal are more related to thei
academic disciplines. They see their futures more in terms c
advancement as physicists or historians than as members of th
XYZ institution. This is less true, however, for faculty members c
prestigious institutions and for those long associated with a partic
ular institution.

Students' identification with the objectives of the residentia
college or university may be close and deep yet necessarily of limite
duration; as more and more students commute to the large, urba
universities, their allegiance to the institution competes with thei
family life and in many instances with employment.

Role of Faculty and Students in Decision Making Despite their lesser concern with the interests and objectives of th
institution, faculty members and students claim a greater part i
its governance than do their counterparts in other organizations
The faculty claims, in increasing measure, a voice in decisions abou
their compensation and working conditions, and in addition the
claim the right to select their colleagues. Increasingly, students ar
claiming the right to determine the individual course of study an
their own living patterns. And both claim the right to participate i
shaping the policies of the whole institution. The question arise
concerning their capabilities for these roles.

The faculty member has been trained over many years for servic
as a scholar. During that period he endures financial stringency an
rigorous and persistent application of his mind and time to a steac
ily narrowing range of problems. "The personality that eventuall
emerges . . . is," in the opinion of one observer, "typically underlai
with a deep sense of inferiority, fear and maladjustment, yet ovei
lain by an almost frantic sense of superiority . . . a latent hostilit
to that which is non-bookish and non-intellectual . . . a fluttery ir
security" and a single mindedness (Williams, 1958; see also Cari
ter, 1970–71). In addition, in comparison with his counterpart i
other institutions, the professor is more likely to hold as importar
for organizational decisions such choices as absolutism versus rela
tivism, objectivity versus commitment, freedom versus authority
and sacred versus secular (Corson, 1960, p. 115). Concern wit
such fundamental values may limit the individual's capacity to cor

tribute to the making of decisions on practical matters central to the institution's needs at the moment.[6]

Those faculty members who succeed to administrative posts, particularly at the rank of dean and above, often possess the personal qualities required. But they may lack any experience in educational programming (e.g., curriculum design), in educational policy (e.g., admissions policy, professionalism versus general scholarship), or the capacity for institutional leadership rather than peer-group representation. Yet the present structure of colleges and universities offers no alternative to the selection of academics for such administrative posts, for the core business of the college or university is education and there is no other source of potential administrators. Moreover, the academic who succeeds to an administrative post cannot look to the trustees, most of whom lack any significant understanding of higher education, for counsel on issues of educational programming or policy.

In comparison with other organizations, the role in governance claimed by students within the past decade is a unique phenomenon. Students come and go, bringing little in the way of experience or accumulated wisdom and having, perhaps, little time to devote to matters of governance. Yet their right to participate in governance has been recognized by many institutions (Hearn & Thompson, 1970, pp. 132–135). Why? Because most decisions of the institution affect them; because students believe that if education is of fateful significance to them, they should have a voice in its character and quality; because students today have strong social and educational motivations and have demonstrated that they can provoke desirable educational change; because participation in governance is preparation for responsible citizenship in the larger society; and because students can play a refreshing role in the improvement of institutions (McGrath, 1970, pp. 51–62). In considerable part, students have won their right to participate by the demonstration of the raw power to close the institution. The stimulus to the exercise of that power is the general revulsion to paternalism in the Ameri-

---

[6] The late Mrs. Ewart K. Lewis presented a supplementary point of view in a Phi Beta Kappa address at Oberlin College in 1956: "For it is also characteristic of those who are steeped in *philosophia* that they are always disagreeing on its significance; if they agree on a principle, they disagree on methods. In an academic community, the love of wisdom seems scarcely distinguishable from the love of argument. An academic community is in a perpetual condition of war. . . ."

can society, but in no other organization has this rejection of pater nalism (or authoritarianism) taken the form that student participa tion constitutes in the college and university.

THE BONDS OF ORGANIZATION What ties hold the college or university together? "Sociologist commonly conceive," Burton Clark (1971, p. 499) has written, "o two broad dimensions of social bonding: the structural, consistin of patterns of relation and interaction of persons and groups; an the normative, consisting of shared beliefs, attitudes and values.

It is unnecessary to emphasize that the business enterprise, th government bureau, and the foundation (perhaps to a lesser degree because the unit is normally smaller) are held together as organiza tions by structure. Each has as its organizational skeleton a hierar chy that relates one unit to another and establishes clear lines o authority. Each has a supplementary system of superordination an subordination that is reflected in the vital processes by which de cisions are made about the allocation of resources, the appointment promotion, and evaluation of personnel, and the control of perfor mance. And in each, as size grows and as the power of the apex c the hierarchy to direct and control the whole declines (whethe because of unionization or geographical dispersion), rules an procedures are developed to constitute a system of due process tha ensures the articulation of each unit within the whole.

Decline of Shared Values in the University Traditionally the college was held together as an organization b normative values: the individuals who made it up—particularly th faculty and, less cognitively and more emotionally, the students— had "shared beliefs, attitudes, and values." Those beliefs had to d with the importance of learning for learning's sake. Those attitude had to do with the responsibility of the scholar to his academi discipline, to his peers, and to his students. And those values inclu ed the worthiness of the academic way of life, of a life devoted t the conservation and discovery of knowledge and to the develop ment of youth. Analogous beliefs, attitudes, and values have cor tributed to the integration of some government bureaus for period of time (e.g., the Social Security Board, 1936-1939; the Economi Cooperation Administration, 1945-1959; and the Peace Corps 1960-1963), some foundations when launched on a new missior and a few business enterprises. But in the college—particularly college that has hammered out a distinctive and respected purpos (e.g., Antioch)—this form of "social cement" links department emphasizes the whole, and commits the individual to the college. In those colleges where no distinctive purpose was achieved or where common beliefs, attitudes, and values were not cultivated by a more authoritative president, this form of "social cement" was replaced by greater emphasis on hierarchical structure and by a system of superordination and subordination.

Over the past five decades, we have moved in this country from the small college (less than a thousand students) to the medium-sized university (3,000 to 5,000 students) to the multiversity (10,000 to 100,000 students). As institutions have grown larger, the normative basis for governance has slowly but implacably been replaced by increasing emphasis on hierarchical structure, on refined processes of superordination-subordination, and on rules and procedures that would ensure due process for the individual or for the subunit.

The larger the enterprise, the more difficult it is to maintain a set of beliefs that will claim the interest and zeal of the faculties and students of several schools and many departments. On most campuses it is found only in the departments, and only in those departments that can claim some standing in their particular disciplines. The maintenance of common beliefs is even more difficult when both faculties and student bodies are subdivided into political factions. And a normative system of governance is substantially negated whenever the institution is a part of a state system in which governance decisions are made by an authority removed from the educational process on the campus (e.g., the state coordinating board).

The furor that has been experienced on many campuses in recent years is, in substantial part, a consequence of the effort to find a mode of governance that will effectively interrelate several schools, many departments, the factions found within the faculty and students of each, and the increasing power of external agencies, particularly the state government.

A PRESCRIPTION FOR UNIVERSITY ORGANIZATION The Assembly on University Goals and Governance, in the forty-ninth of the 85 "theses" it presented in February 1971 as an agenda for the reform of higher education, stated that:

For too long, colleges and universities have borrowed their governance models from business and public administration. Neither is appropriate for most functions of academic institutions.

The foregoing analysis of five basic elements of the universit organization validates that conclusion. Unlike other institution colleges and universities lack clear, unified, and tangible purposes. The activities of the university differ not only in substance (e.g the transmission of knowledge versus the manufacture of a produc but also in emotional quality, in degree of social approval, and i the degree to which they relate individuals in a common effort. I character has been distinguished by the extent to which the institu tion involved not only the work but also the social and recreation aspects of the lives of its principal members and the extent to whic the institution allowed its members—the individual teach researcher and student—such relative freedom as to create a ve loose social organization and one substantially resistant to chang That character is being remolded as the institution has lost t autonomy and even the physical isolation it once deemed essenti and has acquired increasingly the status of a public utility. T membership of the university is marked by the limited degree which the members manifest attachment and loyalty to the insti tion and the extent to which the dominant groups—faculty a students—claim a part in the governance of the whole institutic Finally, the bonds that traditionally held the college together a functioning organization—shared beliefs, attitudes, and values have been disintegrating. In the larger university these are gradua being supplemented or replaced by more formal structure and rules and procedures.

This analysis, moreover, highlights the logic of five proposals the reform of university organization that seem to be gain consensus.

1   The university must be recognized as being made up of groups that each relatively independent of the institution and of each other and that simultaneously more capable of exercising power over the institution t are the staffs of the corporation, the government bureau, or the foundat

2   The governance of such a community requires structure and processes will facilitate the engineering of consensus: such a community canno governed with the structure and processes that rely on authorit command.

3   A communitywide agency (such as the Council of the Princeton Comm

---

[7] In Chap. 6, Ralph Besse makes a related point in terms of the lack of a "cl defined common interest group" comparable to the shareholders.

ty, the Twin Cities Assembly of the University of Minnesota, or the Senate of the University of New Hampshire) that includes representatives of all seven elements of the membership of the university is needed as a mechanism through which the president and the board can build essential consensus.

4 The authority of the president to lead what is a large and complex enterprise needs to be strengthened and reaffirmed. This redefinition of authority must encompass not only that of the president (and his principal staff) but simultaneously the precise definition of the evolving authority of the faculty, students, and board. The aim of such a redefinition is to authorize the president to make promptly those decisions that are essential to the efficient functioning of the institution while permitting the democratic participation of each constituency in the formulation of institutional policies by which the president will be guided.

5 A system of accountability must be (and gradually is being) established. Such a system constitutes the quid pro quo for *(a)* the redefinition, enlargement, and affirmation of the president's authority for executive leadership; *(b)* the freedom of the individual faculty members; and *(c)* the abandonment of institutional regulation of the social lives of students and the reduction of proscriptions on the academic path that they will follow.

For the president, this will mean periodic evaluation of his services by the whole university community and an invitation to continue or to leave. Such evaluation might take place every five or seven years. For the faculty it will mean more extensive and better-designed evaluation of teachers and courses and perforce the modification of the institution of tenure. And for students it will mean the increasing assumption by civil authorities, by private operators of dormitories and dining halls, and by student organizations of responsibility for the governance of personal conduct, living arrangements, and relationships with the academic enterprise.

Part Three
Corporate Authority: Trustees and Regents

10. Higher Education and the Law

by Lyman A. Glenny and Thomas K. Dalglish

In recent years there has been a proliferation of laws relating to higher education which, coming from a number of sources and in innumerable forms, conjures up the image of the law as the proverbial "seamless web." Much of the law has been beneficial. The interests of students and minorities are finally receiving the protection they deserve. On the other hand, a number of scholars concerned with the future of the university perceive in the evanescent mists over the campus "a legal octopus about to strangle the academic community with its tentacles of insensitivity, conflict, obtuseness, technicality, wrangling, inflexibility, expense, and delay" (Byse, 1968, p. 144).[1]

Whether the effects of law on the university are good or bad, whether the fears and apprehensions of some are well-placed or not is conjectural. Arguments can be found on all sides. As never before, law is reshaping the university—forcing new roles, new organizational designs and relationships, and new concerns. On two critical dimensions—the autonomy of the university and the academic freedom of its faculty and students—the law is causing a dilution of the first and establishing the second as a last probable redoubt for the protection of academic values.

The sources of law are many; so are its forms (e.g., statutes, court decisions, administrative rules, and regulations).[2] Furthermore, law

---

[1] Clark Byse was actually characterizing the reaction of some to "due process" and judicial review. Byse, it should be noted, regards due process "not as an enemy, but as an old an trusted friend."

[2] For our purposes, the term *law* includes state and federal constitutional provisions, statutes or legislation passed at the state or federal level, local ordinances, court decisions at all levels, and rules and regulations of state and federal administrative agencies. The last category includes not just those rules and regulations of federal agencies such as HUD (Housing and Urban Development)

173

has a differential impact on the university. Law affects the environment within which the university operates. It articulates the powers and structural relationships of the state and federal governments with respect to the university. It defines the legal status of the institution and its governing board. It describes the range of permissible activities and duties. It affects the nature of authority and, indirectly, the internal organization of the university. It affects the relationships between the university and students, faculty, and staff. Law is also the mode by which broad issues of social policy (e.g., access to education, race and labor-management relations) are pursued, often with far-reaching consequences for the university.

LEGAL ENVIRONMENT OF THE UNIVERSITY The legal environment of the university is determined largely by the confirmation in law that education is important to society and to the individual. The fundamental role of education in the United States is perhaps best reflected in the provisions of most state constitutions, in which education is identified as one of the primary missions of government. Such provisions often link the stability and preservation of government with the education of the electorate — goals reflected in the compulsory school attendance laws. Although, by virtue of the Tenth Amendment to the United States Constitution, education has been conceived of as primarily a state function, the federal government has been instrumental in promoting educational development through a variety of its constitutionally prescribed powers and obligations relating to the general welfare, national defense, equal protection, and interstate commerce.

Just as governmental or societal interests in education have been advanced and given importance by law, individual interests, too, have recently achieved recognition. Chief among these has been the

---

or HEW (Health, Education and Welfare) or state budgetary or construction agencies, but, in the case of public universities, internally generated rules and regulations adopted by the governing body as an exercise of its rule-making powers (e.g., in connection with faculty or student conduct). Administrative rules and regulations are often referred to as *sublegislation*. Also included in the definition of *law* are a variety of contractual or associational relationships, sanctioned or entered into by the university (e.g., collective bargaining agreements, accreditation schemes, athletic associations, corporate charters). Although contracts are not law in the same sense as statutes or court decisions are, they are a frequent and often unavoidable formal constraining influence on the university.

conception of higher education not merely as a privilege but as a significant private interest or opportunity which, once possessed by an individual, cannot be taken away without due process. In a case involving the expulsion, without due process, of a number of students from Alabama State College for Negroes, the U.S. Fifth Circuit Court of Appeals in 1961 stated:

> The precise nature of the private interest involved in this case is the right to remain at a public institution of higher learning in which the plaintiffs were students in good standing. It requires no argument to demonstrate that education is vital and, indeed, basic to civilized society. Without sufficient education, the plaintiffs would not be able to earn an adequate livelihood, to enjoy life to the fullest, or to fulfill as completely as possible the duties and responsibilities of good citizens *(Dixon v. Alabama State Board of Education, 1961).*

For similar reasons, an even earlier decision by the Washington State Supreme Court held that a college education was a "necessity," and ruled that a divorce decree could be modified to require the father to provide an allowance for the educational expenses of his college-age child *(Esteb v. Esteb, 1926).*

A description of the legal environment of the university would be incomplete without citing laws that have an indirect effect on higher education, such as those pertaining to selective service, professional licensing and accreditation, or foundations. One cannot ignore the impact of such laws on university enrollments, both graduate and undergraduate, on programs and curricula, and on the availability of funding from nongovernmental sources.

LEGAL STATUS OF THE UNIVERSITY Of immediate significance to the university are the legal status of the institution itself and the effect of law directly on its organizational structure, its relationships with both state and federal government, and its constituencies inside the institution and out.

Almost without exception in the United States, the legal status of the university is vested in the governing body. In a strictly legal sense the board of trustees, regents, curators, or whatever the governing body might be called, *is* the institution. The governing board is said to be legally responsible as well as accountable and to possess certain powers delegated by the legal instrument creating the institution. Some of these powers may in turn be delegated by the board to others within the institution. Although pluralists assert that the university speaks with many voices and that the institution per se is ephemeral, most lawyers would say that governing boards alone are legally responsible for final institutional decisions. This is so for two reasons. First, a board has certain legal duties that cannot lawfully be delegated—a decision on the selection of a president, for example. Second, even in those matters where the board may delegate authority to institutional officials, the board's ultimate responsibility is in no way abrogated.

Constitutional Status While the legal status of the university is nearly always vested in the governing board, the precise legal character of that status varies among institutions. First, there are those public universities or university systems that possess *constitutional status* (or *constitutional autonomy*) as a result of having been especially created and provided for in the state constitution. Such constitutional provisions purport to vest almost exclusive powers of governance, control, and management in the governing boards of the respective institution. In theory, constitutional status removes the institution from the vagaries of legislative and gubernatorial politics. In fact, actual control by the governing bodies of these institutions is not exclusive, as will be shown later. Even so, such institutions are often viewed as fourth branches of government, coequal with the legislative, executive, and judicial branches. As the Supreme Court of the State of Minnesota declared in 1928 of the constitutional status enjoyed by the University of Minnesota:

> . . . the purpose of the Constitution remains clear. It was to put the management of the greatest state educational institution beyond the dangers of vacillating policy, ill-informed or careless meddling and partisan ambition that would be possible in the case of management by either Legislature or executive, chosen at frequent intervals and for functions and because of qualities and activities vastly different from those which would qualify for the management of an institution of higher education *(State v. Chase,* 1928).

Constitutional status does not mean that identical status is conferred on all such institutions. Some institutions are created as "constitutional corporations." State constitutions often prescribe the geographical location of such institutions and the composition and manner of selection of the governing body, and they vest extensive power in the boards. How much autonomy universities with constitutional status actually enjoy is difficult to assess. At least the following states confer such status on universities: California, Colorado, Michigan, Minnesota, Idaho, Georgia, and Oklahoma (Moos & Rourke, 1959, p. 22; Hicks, 1963). Missouri and Utah are unique, for in both states, it can be argued, the leading universities at one time possessed or came close to possessing constitutional status, which was lost or negated through constitutional amendment or court decisions.[3] In addition, some claims to constitutional status may also be made by universities in Alabama, Arizona, and Nevada.

Statutory Status A second class of public universities or university systems consists of those which, whether or not referred to in state constitutions, are clearly deemed to be subject to laws enacted by the legislature and to be part of state government (Moos & Rourke, 1959, p. 22). Such universities and their governing bodies are created and vested with powers by statutes. They are legally on a par with general state administrative agencies also created by statute. Universities in this class, which also includes most state colleges and community colleges, are often referred to as agencies of the state or creatures of statute, denoting their subordinate status with respect to the legislative body. Occasionally, statutory universities are created as public corporations, but the legal advantage of being so characterized is often marginal. As much as anything each state's own traditions are determinative, some (e.g., Illinois) attaching more importance to corporate status than others. Universities with statutory status are commonly thought to be subject to far more political and governmental pressures from legislatures, governors, and other state administrative agencies than those with constitutional status. At least one state (Maryland) has conferred "autonomy" on its univer-

---

[3] In *University of Utah v. Board of Examiners,* 1956, the court decided that the University of Utah, which might have enjoyed constitutional status similar to that of the University of Minnesota, had for years submitted to legislative "interference" without objection or challenge, and that such acquiescence constitutes subsummation to legislative control (see Hicks, 1963, pp. 249–281).

It should be noted that the degree of autonomy enjoyed by leading institutions in Georgia and Colorado by virtue of such "constitutional status" as they possess under their respective constitutions is not exactly clear. Some observers might equate Georgia and Colorado with Michigan, Minnesota, and California. In addition, Oklahoma might be dropped from the list altogether. The authors are currently engaged in a research project with the Center for Research and Development in Higher Education designed to calculate both the legal and operational meaning and effectiveness of constitutional status.

sity by statute, which seems to have been fairly effective thus far, though it could be repealed at any time.

Private Status Third, there are the private universities which are by nature charitable or nonprofit corporations. The status of these institutions is embraced in a corporate charter—meaning in law a "contract" between the state and the original incorporators and their successors. Private universities are normally organized under state laws pertaining to charitable or nonprofit corporations. Created for an indefinite duration, such universities are traditionally protected against state interference[4] except that state and federal legislation enacted for the general health, safety, and welfare of the people usually applies to them (e.g., laws relating to nondiscrimination, construction and safety standards, pollution control, and campus disorders). What independence the private university has from governmental and political pressure is more directly a function of its legal status than is the case with the public universities with statutory or even constitutional status. Public tax support to private higher institutions may bring about a change of this legal status.

Other Legal Status The three classes described above reflect the major differences in legal status among universities. Several other kinds of institutions of higher education are differentiated by their legal status. A number of institutions exist under federal statute—for example, the service academies. Some institutions, among them a large number of community or junior colleges, are municipal corporations governed locally and supported primarily by locally generated taxes. These are not subject, except by general legislation, to state legislative interference. Some colleges are wholly owned by large corporations or exist as separate profit-making enterprises. Some of these institutions receive public funds, by contract or regular appropriation, for certain programs, activities, or schools.

EFFECT OF LAW ON THE UNIVERSITY The differential effects of law on the university are a function of the source of laws and their intended purposes. The source may be the constitution, the legislature and the courts or a state administrative

---

[4] The reader is referred to *Dartmouth College v. Woodward* (1819), 17 U.S. 518 (4 Wheaton 518).

agency, the governing body of the institution, or even a voluntarily assumed contractual obligation. The purpose of a law may be to establish government structures (e.g., creation of budget agencies, planning agencies), to accomplish broad social goals (e.g., collective bargaining, minimum wages), to create new functions for a university or governmental agency (e.g., power to grant new degrees, start a new campus, or centralize data processing), or to protect an individual's rights. Some effects of law are remote and not very apparent, as, for example, a change in authority relationships in the university, in internal organization, or in processes of decision making. It is often difficult or impossible to determine cause and effect relationships between the law and certain phenomena concerning the university. The law may be the cause of a university problem; it may be a result of a university problem; it may be an utterly neutral reflection of social change; or it may be all of these at different times.

Legislation at the state level constitutes by far the most significant source of law currently affecting the university. Federal law, however, is fast becoming as influential. Legislative activity reflects the increasing costs of higher education, the numbers of people involved, the complexity of state and federal government, and the changing individual and societal expectations of higher education. In years past, elected representatives may not have understood or known what to do about the university; the recent wave of legislation indicates that they are catching on to higher education and its more Byzantine traditions. As Robert M. O'Neil noted in a speech given at the Assembly on University Goals and Governance (1971):

The evidence is mounting that legislators do know just what to do, or at least that they are learning about higher education much faster than the educators are learning about legislation.

State Legislation Much recent state legislation has created new state agencies or vested additional powers in existing agencies. This activity is consistent with a trend beginning in the 1920s to create new executive agencies and to strengthen the role of the governor in state governments. The powers vested in planning agencies, coordinating boards, civil service agencies, management information centers, purchasing and construction agencies, and budgeting and auditing agencies have considerable impact on the university.

Of the several state agencies that control aspects of public university activity, two stand out as extraordinarily powerful: the state wide coordinating board and the state budget office.

Statewide coordinating boards

Prior to 1941, 13 states had placed the governance of all their public four-year colleges and universities under a single statewide governing board. In 1972 state governing boards numbered 21, and while they are no more or less powerful than a governing board for a single university campus, they often apply their rules, formulas, and directions to many kinds of institutions. In 1941, Oklahoma created by constitutional amendment a statewide board to coordinate (not to govern) the budgets and programs of the public higher institutions in the state. The 1941 amendment left all the existing governing boards intact but with modified powers. Other states followed the Oklahoma model during the 1950s and 1960s; today 27 such boards exist, all except for Oklahoma's created by statute.

The amount and scope of power vested by law and exercised by these statewide coordinating boards vary considerably from state to state. The statutes creating them delineate specific powers. In some cases such powers have been taken away from the institutional governing boards. In others specific functions (e.g., budget review, program review) formerly exercised directly by the legislature, governor, or their immediate staffs have been delegated to coordinating boards. A few boards are limited to giving advice and making recommendations, while others have a great array of powers ranging from those of recommendation to final management and review. In some situations coordinating boards are in a position legally superior to that of the governing boards of the institutions. Their powers to develop master plans and to approve all new majors, degrees, departments, schools, and campuses determine in large part the role and function of each institution in the state system. The exercise of these powers may protect the university role in graduate education and research but also circumscribe the university's power to create new campuses or to determine enrollment levels. Budgets are often generated by formulas established by these boards.

This new legal entity—the statewide coordinating board—seeks its legitimate role between the institutional governing boards and the executive and legislative arms of state government without being an advocate for either. In theory, the statewide board promotes or mediates the "public interest," assuming it to be neither the collective aspirations and goals of the institutions nor the political desires of the governor or legislature. In practice, most statewide coordinating boards have difficulty achieving this precarious balance of interests: by strongly advocating one interest, a board can cause a loss of confidence and cooperation by another interest and thereby impair its long-run stability and effectiveness.

Despite their precarious position between powerful, often competing interests, statewide coordinating boards have considerable influence over university policy. Two responses are discernible. First, as more powers are given to these coordinating boards, the governors and legislatures expect them to act more and more like governing boards. Some states are considering the desirability of the abolition of the coordinating board and all public institutional governing boards in order to establish a new omnipotent governing board (Berdahl, 1971; Glenny, Berdahl, Palola, & Paltridge, 1971). This action would centralize all legal power and responsibility in a single agency, making it fully accountable for the activities of all public higher education (and in some cases public elementary and secondary education, too).

The second response is that of the scholars, who believe that, considering the growing complexity of educational agencies and the need for a diversity of substantive educational activities, one governing board for higher education is simplistic. They doubt that a single board is capable of developing and controlling all institutions and their activities. The scholars opt for a looser structure, which would allow most specialized tasks to be continued under separate boards or councils, but they prefer a central board with coordinating power sufficient to bring some rationality to state planning and resource allocation.

A number of states are fundamentally reevaluating the roles of both governing and coordinating boards and are assessing alternatives which range from a single governing board for all education to a coordinating board or to a more decentralized system, with each campus having a governing board along with a stronger coordinating board.

State budget office

The impact of state executive or legislative budgeting agencies on higher education is frequently underestimated. State political leaders, particularly as they fail to satisfy their demands for control and accountability by other means (substantive legislation, political influence, coordinating boards and governing boards), increasingl: resort to the budgeting process to exert influence on higher educa tion. Budget offices, of course, have existed for some time. Th transition, yet to be fully accomplished in most states, from incre mental, line-item budgeting to something akin to a planning-prc gramming-budgeting system has encouraged or at least allowe state budgeting officers and politicians to challenge not just certai items (e.g., stationery, travel, equipment) but entire programs Newly instituted techniques for evaluation (cost-benefit analysis performance auditing) combined with an improved technology fo data gathering (management information systems) and sophisti cated professional staffs in the various executive agencies or legisla tive committees have all vastly enhanced the capacity of state gov ernments to deal with the university. Nearly all the new budgetin procedures and approaches are sanctioned by statute or by rule c regulation. Universities have little choice but to comply.

The results of such a complex budgeting process are significan In some states budget reviews are so thorough that, in reality, un: versity governing bodies and coordinating boards perform only broad advisory function. The formulas and criteria used for predic tion and analysis by the state may be different from those employe by the various boards concerned with higher education. Mor important, a complicated budgeting process which correlates fund ing with policy objectives and programs exposes the university t greater risk of legislative conditions being attached to appropria tions. As a result of the new analytic techniques, a legislature, aide perhaps by its own staff and that of the executive budget agency may prescribe in the appropriations bill student-faculty ratios, fac ulty workloads, ratios of out-of-state students to in-state students and so on, as the University of Michigan discovered between 196 and 1970 and as have universities in many other states since then

Most of these newly developed techniques, procedures, criteria and conditional appropriations are unchallengeable on lega grounds, since they are authorized by statute or fall well within th rule-making powers of the budgeting agency and the constitutiona powers of the governor and the legislature. Moreover, a universit that chooses to battle in the courts may well lose more politicall than it could ever gain. Only universities with constitutional statu stand any chance of successfully challenging a conditional appropr: ation as an incursion by the legislature on the constitutional power of self-governance of the university. And risks for a constitutiona university are severe. Any challenge may tread on sensitive political feelings, while no challenge at all results in acceptance of the undesirable condition and a chance that a future legal challenge will be weakened by prior acquiescence (see footnote 3). A not uncommon alternative for the university is to accept the funds and ignore the condition, which places the legislature and its staff in the awkward position of having to seek enforcement after the fact (which, in actuality, may mean the next legislative session).

State scholarship and loan agencies
State scholarship or loan commissions also have an obvious impact on the university. In 1972, more than 30 states had such agencies. These agencies may control the distribution of many millions of dollars of state and, at times, federal funds. State enabling laws ordinarily provide wide latitude in the rule-making power of scholarship and loan agencies. Thus the funds they control may be distributed in various ways—to aid the private or the public institution, or one type of institution rather than another (e.g., the university, not the community college). The agencies may be able to administer their funds by dealing directly with the students rather than through the institutions. As more and more funds are administered, these agencies can substantially influence the rate of college going and the flow of students into different types of institutions. Since they exercise no direct controls over the university, their operations would probably not be subject to challenge by private universities or by those public universities with constitutional status. Scholarship and loan agencies have become so important in some states that they are being placed under the direction of statewide coordinating boards in order to subject them to the states' master planning constraints and goals.

Other state agencies
In addition to the statewide coordinating agency and the state budget offices, other state agencies endowed with rule-making powers may have control over activities or operations of the university. There is wide variation from state to state in the existence of such agencies and the degree to which universities are included in their jurisdictions. A few states require that all nonacademic employees be subjected to the state merit (civil service) system. State building commissions, state architects, and public works departments may design, build, and accept for the university all

academic (and, in a few states, nonacademic) buildings. Other issue revenue bonds and then rent the buildings to the universit until the bonded indebtedness is retired. State central purchasin; agencies appear to annoy university administrators more than man: other state offices exercising more substantive powers. Here, toc practices vary widely among the states. Occasionally universitie are exempted entirely or at least in part for purchases of scientifi or instructional equipment but are required to purchase all offic equipment and stationery supplies through the state agency. A computers and new record management systems make the stat agencies more efficient—and perhaps also more effective—th purchasing of office equipment and commodities seems destined fc more, rather than less, state control. Further, centralization of stat computer and data-processing facilities, equipment, and service increasingly threatens university efforts to go it alone.

As planning-programming-budgeting systems come into use, th practice of subjecting expenditures to a pre-audit is likely to wane On the other hand, post-audits for determining the legality of ex penditures already made are likely to be as thorough as ever Nevertheless, the really effective audit will be the auditing of pro grams (performance auditing), which will occur at the time o budget reviews when unit costs, program productivity (degrees o: credit hours), and cost-benefit analyses are made. Such progran reviews may eliminate total programs, whereas audits of the legalit of line-item expenditures rarely cause more than a few embarrass ing moments on even the most marginal of purchases.

Finally, a variety of other agencies in some states have exercise(their statutory powers or adopted rules that affect universities These include state printing agencies, economic development agen cies, various advisory councils (e.g., on the arts, government organi zation, computer management), attorneys general's offices, nationa guard and state police, recreation departments, agencies responsi ble for state forest management (including lands set aside fo university purposes), the state treasurer, state boards against dis crimination, the state department or official responsible for educa tion from kindergarten through the twelfth grade (and often teache certification), and professional licensing agencies.

State government and the universities

Some general observations may be made about state governmen and the universities. With the exception of statewide coordinatin;

agencies, most state agencies exercise their lawful powers over all other state agencies or citizens and only incidentally encompass universities within their jurisdictions. Unless specifically exempted or specially endowed with private or constitutional status, universities can expect no general exclusion from the sweep of a state agency's powers. Further, the new state agencies and the old agencies with new powers have generated a shift in the locus of decision making. In numerous matters, decisions once made by the university are now the province of a variety of state government agencies. This trend may not constitute centralization of decision making in the classic sense so much as diffusion of the process by which decisions are made. The framework for decision making has expanded.

Besides creating new agencies and new functions for government to perform, state legislation often attempts to implement broad social policy which affects the university and with which it is expected to comply. Examples are laws dealing with discrimination, collective bargaining, drugs, and voter residency. Some legislation deals specifically with the university—e.g., laws relating to campus disorders, the hiring and dismissal of faculty and staff, and suspension of students.[5] In many states general administrative procedures acts are, unbeknown to many, applicable to state institutions of higher education. Legislative processes, such as committee hearings, investigations, and interim activities, in subtle but very influential ways also affect the universities.

Federal Legislation

Rapidly gaining central importance in American higher education is federal law in all its forms—the Constitution, statutes, rules and regulations, and the strings that attach to funding.

The United States Constitution has no provisions clearly sanctioning federal legislation dealing directly with the nation's universities. Higher education is seen as a state responsibility. Neverthe-

---

[5] Ohio now has a law that vests an attorney in the county in which an institution is located, by special regent appointment, to serve as a referee and make decisions on immediate suspensions from the institutions of faculty, students, or staff charged with violation of certain laws (*Page's Ohio Revised Code;* Sec. 3342.22, effective Sept. 6, 1970). The decision in such situations is *not* made by anyone connected with the particular institution. In the spring of 1971, California passed a new tenure law for community colleges which calls for a hearing officer (an individual not associated with the institution) to hear appeals in cases of tenured faculty dismissed from their positions.

less, federal legislation—especially civil rights acts, laws pertainin
to capital construction on the nation's campuses, laws relating t
the establishment of new programs and to student aid, and ac
providing funds for research—has had an historic impact on highe
education and particularly on the larger universities. Legislation c
this sort is clearly defensible under Congress's powers to provic
for the general welfare of the nation as a whole (or the nation
defense, viz., the National Defense Education Act).

Federal legislative influence on the universities falls into tw
general categories. First, a range of conditions, rules, and regul
tions may accompany federal funds which universities are free t
accept or reject "voluntarily." Second, a federal grant may call int
effect some general federal legislation dealing with such matters
fair labor standards, minimum wages, labor-management relation
and campus disorders. Laws such as those on patents, copyright
and taxes may have an obvious but incidental effect on the univers
ties.

Federal funds for higher education are subject to conditions ir
posed by law in a variety of ways—by federal statute, by rule
regulation of a federal agency, by rule or regulation of a state agenc
through which the funds pass, or by conditions established in
contract with the recipient. In all cases, however, the acceptan
of federal funds is in a legal sense voluntary on the part of tl
recipient. There are five methods by which federal funds for high
educational purposes may be awarded:

1   The funds may come in the form of a grant to the university based upon
    contract or letter of agreement about the purposes and conditions of
    penditure. The purposes and conditions are usually established at the fed
    al level by statute and rules and regulations of the granting agency, and t
    contract may incorporate by reference other agency rules and regulatior

2   The funds may be channeled through a state agency which has nothi
    more than ministerial power over their disbursement (a noninterveni
    state agency). The conditions established follow some formula contained
    federal statute or regulation.

3   The funds may pass through a state agency which has extensive power
    interject its own (or the state's) plans, objectives, and means for fund d
    tribution (an intervening state agency). Either the funds are allocated to t
    state agency directly for reallocation to institutions (e.g., Title I, Higl
    Education Act, 1965, Community Service and Continuing Educatio
    or the federal office keeps the funds for final dispensation but authoriz
    the state to establish the priority among projects or institutions witl

the state (e.g., Title I, Higher Education Facilities Act, 1963). Under such programs, the state agency submits a plan to the controlling federal office in which local rules, regulations, criteria, and conditions are set forth for allocating the funds to institutions. Within general federal guidelines, all these conditions can be made to support state master planning efforts of coordinating boards or other planning agencies. All such federal laws require that the state make no categorical restrictions based on the status of the institution as public or nonpublic.

4   Faculty members may receive grants directly to provide some service to a federal agency from which the university may skim a percentage for its overhead costs. The grant may be on a contractual basis with the faculty member (but through the university), enabling the faculty member to take the grant and the overhead with him as he moves from one institution to another.

5   The funds may go directly to students in the form of grants, work-study programs, scholarships, or loans. By far the most historic student support program thus far has been the GI Bill. Of all the methods of disbursement of federal funds, aid directly to students has the least predictable consequences for the university, the uncertainty being attributable to the vagaries of student choice.

As higher education enters an era of scarce resources, the federal government, chiefly through its financial support, is bound to exert considerable influence on the university. The government will assert national priorities, national criteria for evaluation of programs, and its own statutes, rules, regulations, and guidelines for distribution of funds and reporting of expenditures. The fundamental fact is that universities are not self-sufficient. As long as government provides the funds, expenditures are bound to be controlled through law, which is historically the way our governments articulate and apply policy.

Administrative Agency Rules and Regulations   At both the federal and state levels, administrative agencies are responsible for the implementation of the various statutes. Indeed, the statutes typically establish the broad policy intended by Congress or the state legislatures and delegate to the agencies the responsibility for putting their intent into operation. This process results in a wide variety of specific guidelines, policies, rules, regulations, and contract forms generated by the agency, sometimes with and sometimes without consultation with concerned groups or organizations. Obviously, what administrative agencies do and the sublegislation they produce can have an enormous and concrete (sometimes constraining) effect on the university. In some respects administrative agencies, with their rules and regulations, can reach further inside the university and have far more influence on university activities and relationships than can Congress or state legislatures with their more general laws and levels of operation.

University rules and regulations themselves often constitute law, although the university, unlike many government agencies, is not thought of as having general powers to regulate actions of other state agencies or at least does not attempt to exercise its own powers in such ways. Except for admissions, parking regulations, and use of property by nonuniversity individuals, university rules are thought to be confined to "internal" matters. Those state administrative agencies that share in state government responsibilities for public higher education are far more likely to have influence over the university than are federal agencies (such as Housing and Urban Development; the Department of Health, Education and Welfare, Office of Education; the Department of Defense; the National Science Foundation; and so on) with which university relationships are voluntary and tied to specific funds or projects.

Court Decisions   In the courts, both state and federal, the cases of greatest consequence for the university have turned on constitutional issues relating to due process, academic freedom, tenure, admissions, privacy, speech, association, religion, political activities, the press, and similar concerns. Usually at stake has been an institutional decision or the applicability of a statute to an individual (e.g., a loyalty oath law). Under the state and United States constitutions, students, faculty, and staff are considered as citizens, entitled to no more or less protection of their constitutional rights than other citizens *(Tinker v. Des Moines Independent Community School District,* 1969*).*

Yet at the same time that its members are protected as citizens, the university community as a polity is much more prone than the citizenry at large to exercise constitutional rights, especially those under the First Amendment.

Some have argued that the courts have been extremely solicitous of university prerogatives, denying jurisdiction or upholding university decisions when the issue seems to touch on academic matters. The sheer increase in the number of cases litigated and the number of issues with legal implications arising from within the university has expanded the university's consciousness of judicial attitudes and approaches to problem solving. This has caused what some have called the judicialization of the university. The obvious drawbacks in resorting to the courts are the expense, the strain on personal relationships, the delays, and the insensitivity of courts to academic issues. But there are other more subtle costs: the abrogation of independent university judgment either by not making a decision at all and thus avoiding a challenge or by passing the buck to the courts for final decision; the substitution of a strictly legal or constitutional decision for a desirable or wise one; and "creeping legalism," that is, the transformation of educational decisions into "judicial" decisions.

Contractual Relationships The university enters a wide variety of contractual relationships. The university-student relationship is said to be contractual, as is the faculty member's association with the university. The athletic conference or compact is an association that has its basis in contract, with the conference setting standards for such matters as recruitment and imposing penalties for their violation. University relationships with the federal government are essentially contractual. Most significant, perhaps, have been the variety of consortia, compacts, associations, and accrediting bodies, each constituting a slightly different organizational form designed to achieve specific objectives. Many of these contractual arrangements have led over the years to the development of a kind of canon law for higher education (e.g., tenure and accreditation).

Consortia

The institutional trend toward forming consortia is relatively recent. Historically, universities have done little to cooperate with one another in sharing facilities or resources, even in public systems in which several campuses or institutions are governed by the same board. The trend started slowly within the nonpublic sector, took several different forms, and focused on a variety of matters including the exchange of guest speakers, the hiring of joint faculty, the exchange of students in high-cost or highly specialized programs, and even the creation of entirely new institutions through joint participation of several existing ones.

A 1965 report noted the existence of over a thousand consortia, and the number has since increased rapidly (Moore, 1967; Burnett, 1969). Some increases can be attributed to federal grant programs, such as the Special Opportunity Grants of the Higher Education

Facilities Act and the Model Cities Act, both of which favor inter
institutional cooperation in matters affecting certain of their gran
programs. The greatest motivating force for consortia is the nee
to make the best use of resources in the face of steeply rising cost
in both nonpublic and public institutions. Federal grant program
and financial pressures have caused institutions to view their auton
omy less cautiously and to attempt the strengthening of their educa
tional offerings and management practices.

Consortium agreements are often formal, written contracts i
which the objectives, rights, and duties of the parties are spelle
out. Other arrangements are no more than loose, informal verba
agreements between administrators or other persons associate
with different institutions. It is doubtful that even governin
boards are entirely aware of the informal working arrangement
that exist among their institutions.[6]

Accrediting agencies
Perhaps the most influential of all the voluntary bodies establishe
by institutions of higher education are the accrediting agencie
The purposes of accreditation initially arose from concern ov
"diploma mills" and the need to facilitate the transfer of studen
among institutions. According to their statements of purpose, a
crediting agencies also typically promote and maintain high sta
dards of education and preparation for the professions, prote
society at large from incompetent professional practitioners, e
courage self-evaluation and experimentation, and protect instit
tions from undue political interference and society from educ
tional frauds (Burns, 1960, pp. 11–15; *Accredited Institutions* . .
1970).

Accrediting agencies fall into three types: state government age
cies with rule-making powers regarding standards (e.g., for teac
ers, lab technicians, pharmacists, chiropractors); voluntary region
associations concerned primarily with accreditation of institution
and national professional associations concerned with accreditati
in more than 40 professional fields. (In many states, standar

---

[6] Representative consortia are The Big Ten's Committee on Institutional Coop
ation, Associated Colleges of the Midwest, Atlanta University Center Corpo
tion, The Claremont Colleges, College Center of the Finger Lakes, The Fi
Colleges, Inc., and San Francisco Consortium.

are also provided by law for the training of doctors, dentists, and lawyers.)

Lack of accreditation of an institution or a professional field at one time meant only that the student pursuing such a program was heavily penalized in transferring to another institution. Today the lack of accreditation has more drastic implications: federal aid for categorical purposes as well as for student assistance may be withheld for lack of accreditation; students may not take a federal or state scholarship, grant, or loan to an unaccredited institution; and states which aid nonpublic institutions prohibit such aid to unaccredited institutions *(Marjorie Webster Junior College, Inc. v. Middle States Association of Colleges and Secondary Schools, Inc., 1969).*

As categorical grants for training and for construction of facilities for certain professional fields increase, pressure mounts for all institutions to become and stay accredited. The complex university is especially vulnerable to the demands of numerous accrediting agencies. Not only does the number of professions that want to accredit increase, but the demands of professionals upon the university to conform to higher and more elaborate standards of organization, administration, curriculum, and financing become more strident.

The six regional accrediting agencies and the many professional ones are, at least in form, voluntary. The institutions themselves, however, organize and control the regional agencies and from them obtain consultative services as well as standards for quality of operation. Professional associations, on the other hand, are formed by practitioners in the field and the university professors who prepare the practitioners. The institutions have little control over such associations, which, though dominated numerically by the field practitioners, seem to act as internal self-interest groups for the professional school or department. An institution may be subject to the demands of 20 or more of these influential professional groups.

Recent studies of accrediting reflect the concern of institutions for reducing the number of different bodies with whom they must work and for encouraging better coordination of the agencies themselves (Burns, 1960, pp. 11–15). Some states are even considering the possibility of reasserting old powers to set standards by establishing their own accrediting machinery and removing their public institutions from all regional and professional accrediting practices.

The federal government would then, the thinking goes, recognize state accreditation for its funding purposes, as would the state itself. Moreover, some agency heads in the federal government are suggesting that the federal government itself establish a comprehensive accrediting commission.

Institutional associations

To further their common interests, institutions usually join national associations, which often function as lobbies.[7] The Washington, D.C., "secretariat" for higher education consists of more than a dozen of these associations under the umbrella of the American Council on Education (ACE). The Association of American Universities (AAU) is considered the most elite and prestigious, since universities may become members only on invitation, and the membership includes the nation's largest and greatest universities. Until 1948 the AAU also provided the nation with a list of its own accredited institutions. The National Association of State Universities and Land-Grant Colleges and the American Association of State Colleges and Universities have overlapping memberships with each other and the AAU. Together these three associations hold the memberships of most of the universities in the nation.

These national associations act individually and at times in concert through the ACE to influence public policy, particularly at the national level, and to suggest approaches to broad educational problems. The policy positions adopted by such associations reflect a high level of commitment to them by the member institutions but their policies, only morally binding, are not legally enforceable against the members.

Regional and national compacts

Another kind of voluntary association for higher education is the regional compact, which is an association of states, not of institutions. Examples are the Southern Regional Education Board formed in 1948; the Western Interstate Commission on Higher Education, formed in 1950; and the New England Board of Higher Education, formed in 1954. In the Midwest, in lieu of a compact, the Council of State Governments has established a loose confederation of institutions and state agencies.

The compacts are formal, legal agreements to which the state

[7] See Bloland, 1969.

government, through action of the governor or the legislature, subscribes on a voluntary basis. State governments provide the operating funds for these boards, whose membership consists of representatives from each state and includes university presidents, other educators, legislators, and laymen. Some governors are also members of the Southern Regional Education Board.

Regional compact boards promote the interstate exchange of students for enrollment in special education programs, the collection and dissemination of data ("fact books"), awareness of needs in graduate and professional education, and improvement in state planning. Much current activity is focused on training for health care needs, including mental health. Regional compact boards also produce many publications and periodically hold workshops to acquaint legislators and other public officials with problems, attitudes, and data concerning higher education. Each compact board has considerable prestige among state officials. While boards have stimulated regional and state planning, they have no legal power to effect plans except through action of the state governments or the institutions in the states. The boards exercise no legal controls over individual institutions or the state systems of education.

Of potentially great influence in higher education is the Education Commission of the States (ECS), which arose out of the National Governors' Conference in 1966–67 (also under the aegis of the Council of State Governments). ECS received its authorization by legislative action in each state. A voluntary organization, its membership is similar to that of the regional compacts, with the difference that the governor is the chief member from each state. The commission has held numerous conferences, including some dealing with accreditation and statewide planning, and it has adopted policy statements resulting from extensive task force work on student assistance, community and junior colleges, statewide planning, and vocational education in higher education. The commission has also formed a Council of State Higher Education Agencies, which includes the several state councils and boards administering physical facilities, student scholarships and loans, community services and continuing education, and the state higher education executive officers of statewide coordinating and governing boards.

While neither the regional compacts nor the Education Commission of the States has legal power or authority over any matter within the states or over the institutions, the intimate involvement of legislators and governors in the operations of these agencies makes them influential in the development of state policy affecting universities. Beyond these organizations, the Council of State Governments also sponsors national conferences of state budget officers, state planners, and other officials who, as noted previously, have extensive power to intervene in public higher educational matters at the state level.

IMPLICATIONS FOR THE UNIVERSITY The long-range implications for the university of the law and its effects are uncertain. Considering the role and functions of the university in our society, by far the most significant trends concern the relative autonomy of the institution and the academic freedom of the individuals—notably the faculty and students—associated with it.

Diffusion of Authority Decision-making power in the "academic community" is increasingly shared by a variety of interests both inside and outside the university. Constituencies and groups within the institution—faculty, students, departments, administrators, nonacademic staff—are atomized as the differential interests of each are pursued. Whether this phenomenon has been caused or merely reflected by the law, it has certainly been made more permanent by law. At the same time, state and federal agencies created by statute and endowed with rule-making powers have blossomed forth, each with a highly specialized interest in and contribution to policy in the university. Accrediting associations also apply their standards and conditions. All these interests seek to share in decision making for the university; some are required to by law, others are merely permitted. In any event, the nature of authority in the university is dispersed among a variety of agencies "outside" the institution and among groups or interests "inside." Decision making now proceeds incrementally, each agency or interest contributing its special expertise or perspective to the whole, though not always in a neat, linear, or precisely quantifiable fashion. As Roger Heyns (1971) has remarked, decision making "is an uneven and complicated partnership among many groups."

Interdependence of the University and Society The "disintegration," as T. R. McConnell (1971, pp. 2–3) has called it, of the "academic community," whatever its immediate causes— campus disorders, size of the institutions, costs, numbers of people involved—reflects a growing interdependence between the university and society as a whole. This interdependence is reflected in a variety of statutes, rules, court decisions, and other laws dealing with relationships and activities between the various constituencies on campus. "Perhaps there has never been a time," says Robert M. O'Neil (1971), "when the capacity of campus constituencies to shape and direct their own destiny was so severely circumscribed from without." Historically, academicians were content to perform what they considered the purely educational function, broadly conceived to include teaching, research, and public service, without much concerning themselves with legal relationships between the university and the general community and other social institutions. This neglect, according to O'Neil, is in part

... the result of a failure to develop, articulate and promulgate a posture for the university within the system of public institutions of which it is a part — whether publicly or privately supported. Other administrative agencies have this relationship defined for them, typically by statutes embellished by court decisions on judicial review and delegation. The university must do the job for itself (O'Neil, 1969, p. 17).

The failure of the university to define and to regulate itself, the argument goes, has left the way open for others outside the institution to do so (indeed has given them ammunition for doing so) in ways that are perhaps harsher and less acceptable to the university than if self-regulation had been attempted (ibid., p. 58).

Self-regulation may be an impossible and unrealistic goal if the university is as interdependent with society as some scholars seem to think it is. The central role of the production, storage, and transmittal of knowledge and information in a complex, technological society has resulted in the university's being properly regarded as a public institution, as Dwight Waldo has noted, and by definition the university is potentially or by implication "within the ambit of the political" (1970, p. 108). The university, says Waldo, "is already an instrument of government and will become more so" (ibid., p. 111). The effect of this alliance between the university and the government is notable:

... there is a pervasive belief and powerful sentiment that the university ought to be independent. It is inconceivable that short of becoming *the* governing power of society, the university will ever be as independent as it would like. As the university "pushes outward" it is wholly predictable that other institutions, those of formal government and others, are going to "push inward" more insistently in reaction . . . (Waldo, 1970, p. 111)

The "push inward" by governmental agencies will find law the natural medium for expression. Whether because of the university's central knowledge function, disorders on campus, or the costs and numbers of people involved, one major effect of the recent plethora of laws is a gradual erasure of distinctions between universities with constitutional status and those that are merely statutory and between those that are public and those that are private. The independence of constitutional universities fades as state budget agencies and legislatures ignore their special status and force on them controls that the universities may ignore only at the probable cost of losing all or part of their appropriations. Private institutions become subject to the same constraints as public universities as they accept public funds and the restrictions and conditions that accompany those funds.

Inflexibility   The "legalization" of the university—the establishment of structures, policies, and relationships by law—tends to result in rigidity and inflexibility. Law becomes the exclusive means for accomplishing change or reform. And if change and reform must proceed through legislatures, governors' offices, and state and federal government agencies, as it must if law is the medium, the result is bound to be a politicization of the process of university reform, a possibility many parties associated with university affairs neither favor nor like to admit.

In addition, the new agencies and boards created by law have assembled a whole new set of specialists and bureaucrats (e.g. budget and systems analysts, lawyers, management information systems specialists, educational planners, researchers, developers, architects, public relations and legislative liaison officers) to operate the university. These specialists are naturally interested in self-preservation if not advancement and, if history is properly recorded, they are likely to resist change. Further, as a force for conservatism, if law articulates policy and structures authority, and if authority then identifies itself with policy, the preservation of policy becomes confused with the preservation of authority and with law. Conflict is inevitable unless means are established for criticism and change. Finally, inflexibility induced by law subjects the university to vestiges of the past. Tradition, of course, has its place among the conserving functions of the university. But the university may not independently respond to changing conditions because of its "legalization." In a sense, it is a prisoner of the law, chained to the past.

Promotion of Hierarchical Structure The formal organization of the university (and of various governmental agencies for that matter) is very much affected by the laws that create the institution and vest its governing body with a variety of delegated powers, which in turn are described, limited, or subdelegated by rules and regulations. The cascade of delegation and subdelegation of powers (more true for statutory universities than for private or constitutional universities) tends to forge a hierarchy in the university:

> ... modern universities are also "formal" organizations, chartered by the state for the "efficient" achievement of special purposes upon the regular allocation of public funds. This fact has tended to produce a hierarchic administrative structure, and demands for central responsiveness to the public's view of those functions (Lunsford, 1970, p. 610).

The rationalistic bias with which laws operate facilitates what the laws expect: clear, unambiguous delegations and subdelegations of authority, power, and accountability. The pressure, then, is to conform the behavior of individuals in the university to legally prescribed objectives, at a pace determined or fueled by a prescribed amount of funds, always with the expectation of holding people accountable. The result may be a model system of rules and laws which, when all is said and done, may not accomplish specific educational objectives but appears reasonable from an administrative perspective.

Max Weber long ago pointed out that the growth of "legal-rational" regulation in human affairs carried with it disadvantages for the handling of particular cases. He saw that the growing "formality" of Western European law, with bureaucracy as the "pure" form of its administration, sacrificed "substantive rationality" in specific cases for the "legal certainty" that detailed and unambiguous rules make possible (Lunsford, 1970, p. 608).

One study has shown that governing bodies of institutions of higher education favor a hierarchical structure, though they rely on the president and his administrative colleagues for decision making. The governing bodies of private institutions, it was shown, are less hesitant to involve faculty and students in decision making than are their counterparts in public institutions (Hartnett, 1968, pp. 57, 59). Even if one argues that the power of faculty and administrators has increased relative to that of governing bodies in the last 25 years or so, as T. R. McConnell has observed (without condoning):

. . . there is reason to believe that boards of trustees may reclaim elements of their legal authority which they had formerly delegated to faculties and administrative officers or entrusted to them by custom and informal understanding (1971, p. 13).

If hierarchical tendencies are observed in the university or in governmental agencies, it ought not to be concluded that the results are necessarily bad. Indeed, some argue that the unity and solidarity of purpose a hierarchy can achieve may have facilitated the university's protection of its interests against a variety of hostile pressures outside the institution, and that such a hierarchy could respond more effectively to future outside pressures than could the collegial model. On the other hand, there may be inherent deficiencies in a hierarchical organization, whether in a university or governmental agency:

It [the formal hierarchical organization] is an instrument of great effectiveness; it offers great economies over unorganized effort; it achieves great unity and compliance. We must face up to its deficiencies, however. These include great waste of human potential for innovation and creativity and great psychological cost to the members, many of whom spend their lives in organizations without caring much either for the system (except its extrinsic rewards and accidental interpersonal relationships) or for the goal toward which the system effort is directed. The modification of hierarchical organization to meet these criticisms is one of the great needs of human life (Katz & Kahn, 1966, p. 222).

However great or slight the pressures are for a hierarchy and however one views the result, strong countervailing traditions exist within the university, as differentiated from other institutions, to the tendencies towards hierarchy. These traditions are often referred to by theorists as characteristics of the informal organization. They include consensual governance, the hope of arriving at decisions through reason, the existence of expertise and professionalism within the various academic disciplines, a resistance to institutional paternalism, and the range of competing values of the constituencies in the university (Lunsford, 1970 pp. 610–611). University rules often embrace and seek to enforce these values and traditions.

Conflict The inherent conflict between government and the individual, whose rights are protected by the Constitution, is carried by law into the heart of the university. Laws (including university rules) are seen to serve a more negative than positive function. They become necessary to control or prescribe conduct or activities previously unregulated and uncontrolled as well as to promote some social policy.

Because of the formal structure of authority (already established by law), the governing bodies of the universities provide the internal law. The aura of negativism with which governing bodies necessarily come to be associated arises from board action in implementing laws that infringe on real or alleged individual constitutional rights (including conceptions of academic freedom); examples are university laws concerning student and faculty conduct and discipline, cancellation of classes, recognition of student organizations, presentation of student grievances, student newspapers, privacy in the dormitory, discrimination against women, and admissions requirements. Individual constitutional rights are asserted in opposition to board action. This conflict, both sides of which are sanctioned by law (the one by statute law and rules and regulations, the other by the Constitution and its protection of the individual), illustrates the dual premises for decision making and the split in the nature of authority within the university.

Decline of Autonomy The relative importance and function of institutional autonomy and the role of academic freedom have both been greatly influenced by the "legalization" of the university. Autonomy is often confused with academic freedom. The former is a characteristic sought or claimed by the university per se, and is considered "the relative ability of a university's governing body to run the university without any outside controls" (Hurtubise & Rowat, 1970, p. 67). Academic freedom, on the other hand, is a right possessed and assertable only by individuals, whether students or faculty. It has been defined as "liberty to pursue and teach relevant knowledge and to discuss it freely without restriction from school or public officials or from other sources of influence" (*American Heritage Dictionary* . . . , 1969).

Institutional autonomy, at least as traditionally conceived, is fast disappearing. The reasons for this have already been noted: the dispersion of the academic community, the diffusion of the decision-making process, the interdependence of the university and government, and the "legalization" of the university. The factors that have contributed to the decline of autonomy have been hardened into law by the creation of new governmental agencies vested with powers to regulate and make policy with and for the university. Indeed, it is possible to argue that there is an inherent inconsistency in the position of the governing board. Such autonomy as the university has, in a strictly legal sense, is directly synonomous with the autonomy of the governing board. Yet the board is responsible for implementing and enforcing laws made by others to which the university is subject. The governing body cannot be autonomous and at the same time subject to law and the responsibilities law entails. Paradoxically, "the autonomy so vigorously defended is deposited in a body whose very purpose and justification is to keep an eye on the academics" (Hurtubise & Rowat, 1970, p. 65).

With the decline in autonomy, distinctions between institutions as defined by their legal status are gradually erased as well. Institutions with constitutional status, which are theoretically beyond the reach of legislatures and executives, find the value of such status seriously eroded (Epstein, 1970). The distinction between public and private universities may be extinguished by the courts, particularly if the issue involves the protection of constitutional rights—e.g., academic freedom, speech, and due process (*Report of the American Bar Association* . . . , 1970, p. 10; *Coleman v. Wagner College,* 1970). And, as previously noted, as private universities accept public funds and accompanying rules and regulations, they become more like public institutions.

Emphasis on Academic Freedom

In part because the relative autonomy of the institution has declined, emphasis on the role of "academic freedom" has increased. First, it has come to be conceived as something students, not just faculty, are entitled to. Second, not just academic freedom but a congeries of individual constitutional rights (speech, association, petition, privacy, etc.) has found protection in the university setting. Third, the decline in university autonomy has rendered the institution less capable (or desirous) of protecting the faculty and students from pressures from "outside" the university. Often, individuals must now protect themselves (and their academic values), and self-defense can be expensive: viz., publicity, costs of litigation, time and energy, necessity of proceeding case by case. No doubt legitimate societal interests, as expressed through laws, rules, and regulations of governmental agencies, are at stake. The dividing line (some would call it a battle line) between societal interests and the academic interests of faculty and students to think and speak freely and to pursue truth openly and creatively has not yet been clearly drawn. As the university loses autonomy and "community," it is less able than ever before to interpose itself between these two competing interests.

The battle has begun under the guise of "accountability." Thus far, the concept of accountability has tended to imply an interest by governmental agencies and legislatures in accounting for funds, faculty load, faculty performance, and student and faculty conduct. Even students demand more teaching from faculty. Less, however, is heard from the remainder of the university community calling for accountability from governing bodies and others in protecting academic values from intrusion by political bodies. Less, too, has been heard from scholars (except from those on the Left) calling upon their colleagues to account for the ethics of their research and the degree to which humanitarian goals are satisfied or striven for.

Collective Bargaining   All the implications noted thus far lead to a situation ripe for the process of collective bargaining as an essential part of the policy-making process. The advent of collective bargaining in the university may invite a mutual calling to account, which would be beneficial to both sides. Although some are concerned about the introduction of an adversary relationship in the university and the possibility of marked changes in traditional patterns of governance (McConnell, 1971, p. 18), a bargaining process leading to a contract may well be the most effective and enforceable way to reconcile the tradition of academic freedom (and an accompanying host of academic values) with the values of the legally evoked hierarchy and its values of accountability. Younger faculty support unionism more than older faculty (Trow, 1970). Students may also demand a part in the bargaining process, which may lead to the emergence of three-way bargaining (McConnell, 1971, p. 19).

One qualification to the fruitfulness of bargaining over academic values (rather than, say, salary increases) is that generally the management of an agency of government does not bargain with its staff members over the agency's public policy role, and yet faculty are likely to insist on bargaining over matters of educational policy (Epstein, 1970, p. 19). If they do not, will faculty allow an erosion of academic values and a limit to expression on controversial issues in return for greater material benefits? Though in theory individuals cannot bargain away their constitutional rights, they may in fact be asked to do so or they may unwittingly do so. But the courts generally will not uphold an agreement insofar as it impinges upon an individual's rights.

Collective bargaining, in short, is a logical outcome of the legalization of the university. A collective bargaining agreement may be detailed, constraining, and legalistic in its own right, but it may be a solution of sorts to the rigidity of the law. It may, indeed, be the paradigm of a temporary society of scholars linked together for the duration of a negotiated collective bargaining agreement.

11. Conflicting Responsibilities of Governing Boards

by James A. Perkins

The complex way in which university governance has had to adjust to the accumulation of missions on the one hand and constituencies on the other is especially visible in the operations of governing boards. The board room itself is an arena for the external and internal forces that influence the purpose, structure, and administration of the university.

Just as the university has suffered as an organization in its attempt to embrace a variety of missions with conflicting requirements, the board has been dislocated by its assumption of new roles without paring away the features of older ones. The board today has not one but three major roles to play, and the requirements of each of these roles are in conflict. A board that has assumed three conflicting responsibilities for a university that has assumed four conflicting missions is a board caught in an entanglement.

The board's original role was that of *agent* of its creator—the church or the state. To this was added the role of *bridge* between society and the university. In recent years the board has begun to act in its third role—as agent for the university community and particularly as *court of last resort* for the ultimate resolution of conflicts between the internal constituencies of the university.

The board's evolution, like that of other organisms, has not been tidy. Thus we must paint the stages in its development in broad brushstrokes rather than in fine detail. We should also note that though the board has followed a similar evolution in different countries, change has taken place at different times—often in different centuries. Our analysis of the board is concerned mainly with its development in the United States, although it was by no means an American invention. Its roots are in the medieval university.

The board's first and primary role was that of agent for the legal parent of the university—whether church or state.

In the earliest universities there was no board of governors and no need for one. Teachers and students came together informally; the only charter that was required was their agreement on the importance of learning. The dynastic system of the Middle Ages left a great deal of elbow room to the private sector and, in the absence of a public structure to confer legitimacy, these loose associations were considered legitimate by the nature of their mission (the advancement of learning), not by their establishment as formal institutions.

Gradually, as Western civilization evolved more formal structures for the conduct of public and private business, universities became formalized. The first step in this process was the acquisition of a charter. As the size and range of interests of universities grew, local bishops as well as townspeople began to take an interest in the fledgling institution and, as is commonly the case, interest was quickly translated into interference. To protect the university and ensure its independence, teachers and sometimes even students appealed to the Pope or bishop for letters of privilege or papal charters. The strategy worked. Universities were granted status as corporations—legal entities with legal rights; and this new status served as a shield against many unwelcome interventions.

As the adoptive parent of the university, the church had to see that the institution adhered to the church's purposes. Consequently the church appointed a chancellor to oversee the institution and to act as its representative or agent. Just as the corporate form became typical of the way in which universities were certified and protected under the law, so too the idea of an agent for the church became embodied in the office of chancellor—the progenitor of the board.

We see in this development the beginnings of an organizational complexity that has persisted to this day. As universities sought independence through papal decrees, they acknowledged that their legitimacy and autonomy rested upon the affirmative support of an outside body rather than in their status as free associations. To achieve independence from some, they had to surrender it to others. Students of the current scene are not unfamiliar with this intriguing paradox.

With the decline of feudalism and the rise of nation-states, the Roman conception—that government holds exclusive legal power to legitimize organizations and their actions—prevailed. This notion was superimposed on an earlier idea that has never died out—that organizations are legitimate by the fact of their existence as free associations of persons with common aims. The board, in its role as agent, reflects the notion that legitimacy must be conferred; the faculty reflects the earlier idea that legitimacy is inherent. Here is the root of much current ambivalence about who can speak for the university: the faculty, as a community of scholars, or the administration and board, who receive their powers from the state? Each claims to be the legitimate voice, but each appeals to different concepts of legitimacy.

It did not take long for the medieval contest between church and state, Pope and emperor, to manifest itself in interest by kings and princes in the university centers that were being born. With the increased secular authority that accompanied the growth of the nation-state, charters for universities were obtained from kings as well as Pope and Holy Roman Emperor. Centuries later, of course, the state displaced the church as chartering authority, and in academic processions the mace replaced the mitre.

Logically enough, greater secular authority was reflected in shifts in the membership of boards. Those concerned with statecraft began to take the places of those concerned with religion. But though the composition of the board changed, its basic function did not. It was still to act as agent, to oversee the institution, and to ensure that the purposes of the institution were compatible with those of its founders.

Boards of United States Universities— Private and Public   The university in the United States evolved forms similar to those of the medieval English institution, though it also developed the unique pattern of lay boards of trustees. Because of the diversity of institutions—religious, public, and private—that flourished in the United States, the board's role as agent took on a different cast in different types of institutions.

In religious institutions, the boards were agents of a dual set of interests, those of the founding church, which made the appointments to the board, and those of the state, which granted the charter. In other private institutions, the board's role as agent was complicated because such trustees were in fact "owners" of the institution; these institutions were linked to the state through their charters. In public universities, on the other hand, the board's role

of agent for the state is clear. The board of regents is the legal re
pository of the power, granted by the state, to manage the univer
sity.

The use of the terms *trustee* and *regent* needs a comment. Trust
ees of private institutions receive charters from the state to form
universities and to acquire and administer property. The term i
appropriate because a trustee is "a person to whom property i
legally committed in trust." It is, however, a fine point whether th
charter is granted *because* the university (or board of trustees) i
inherently legitimate or is granted to *confer* legitimacy. If the appl
cation for a charter is properly prepared, must the charter b
granted? If legitimacy is inherent in the purpose and activity of th
university (the early medieval notion), then the state retains th
right only to ensure that the institution is, in fact, functioning as
university and that it conforms to the specifications of its charte

Do laws of the state follow the charter into the university?
legitimacy is inherent and the charter only a recognition of tha
legitimacy by the state, then the answer would seem to be no. Th
Dartmouth College case (1819) supported the independence of th
private university by reference to this doctrine. But if the chart
confers contingent power, the answer might be yes. Is tax exemp
tion an act of grace on the part of the state, or is it an inherent righ
of the university? Clearly an effort is under way to interpret ta
exemption as an act of grace, which can be rescinded — the recent.
imposed tax on foundation income (after decades of exemption)
a striking case in point. The right to tax exemption is increasing
judged by the extent to which the university performs in accordanc
with the public interest as defined by the government.

Thus far, the states have granted charters to universities wit
apparent recognition of the doctrine of inherent right. On the oth
hand, state legislatures are increasingly inclined to use their fisc
controls to ensure that universities dispense public funds :
conformance with and for the discharge of public purposes. B
even here the universities argue their right to receive public funds :
a university qua university and not as an agency whose activiti
happen to coincide with a specific public purpose. In considerab
measure this argument underlies the current debate between ins
tutional versus categorical grants from the federal governmer

The board of trustees of the private university is, therefore, i
agent of the state in a complex way, depending upon the extent
which one interprets the institution's legitimacy as grounded in t

authority granted by the state in the charter. By chartering the private institution the state has created a perpetual agency outside itself.

In public universities, on the other hand, the board's role as agent of the state is clearer. Such boards not only manage the university on behalf of the state but achieve their offices through that political authority. Here the term *regent* is more appropriate than *trustee*. A regent is "one who rules or reigns" or "one who governs a kingdom in the minority, absence, or disability of the sovereign" (*Webster's* . . . , 1971). The regents are openly and avowedly agents of the state, appointed or elected to perform a task for the state.

Whether a university is public or private, religious or secular, the board was and is the supreme legal authority for the university community. As a result, all appointments, all expenditures of funds, and the granting of degrees must be made by the board or by a process (or in accordance with delegations) approved by the board. (It should be noted that faculties have only reluctantly acknowledged that their role is to recommend degrees while the board actually grants them.) Conflicts of jurisdiction between faculties and boards have been resolved by acceptance of the idea that board approval on strictly educational matters is largely *pro forma.* This delicate etiquette is generally observed, and only when it is ignored is its importance understood. The board is both the symbol and the fact of institutional authority.

BOARD AS BRIDGE The expansion and rise of education—particularly higher education —to an almost independent estate has had profound consequences for the board, resulting in its assumption of a new role—as bridge between the university and society.

As we noted in our first chapter, by the end of the nineteenth century the United States university had assumed two large new missions in addition to that of disseminating knowledge. These activities—research and public service—were to thrust the university and particularly the board into a new posture vis-à-vis the state. The assumption of both large-scale research and public service required that the university develop active involvement with other institutions of society. To perform research, the university looked to government, foundations, and industry for funding and other necessary support; to perform public service, the university developed relations with government, agriculture, and industry. As a mature institution with large and complex requirements of its own, the university became a pressure on society as well as an institution of society. Both individually and collectively, universities encouraged public policies that would be supportive of higher education and its institutions. It was this development of a reciprocal relationship with the society that was to bring the board into play increasingly as a bridge—representing the university's interest to society as well as society's interest to the university.

Sometimes the bridge model was replaced with that of the baffle or barrier, in which the board's role became one of protector of the academic community from the incursions of hostile societal interests and protector of society from disruptive university activity. During the McCarthy era of the early fifties, for example, boards functioned very much as barriers against attacks on the university and faculty. The University Grants Committee of Great Britain, though not a board of trustees, also reveals the features of a barrier, protecting the universities and their autonomy from improper interference by the state in university affairs. The board may also function as "protector" of society: the recent firing of a Stanford University professor for disruptive activities may serve as an example.

An interesting question is whether the same body can act as bridge and barrier at the same time. A cynical view might be that the board is called upon to act as bridge when those in one constituency insist that their ideas be carried over to the obdurate on the other side. On the other hand the trustees are called upon to be a barrier when one side is under adverse pressure from the other—be it the university community from society or society from the university. In either case, though, the board in its role as bridge is presumed to be a neutral body.

Perhaps an even more interesting question is how the board maintains its role as agent as well as that of bridge. In some ways the board's assumption of the role of bridge helped solve some of the dilemmas of being an agent. It was the board, after all, that had to deal with the question of how it could function as agent of the state *within* an autonomous institution. If the university is an autonomous body independent of its legal parents, then to whom is it responsible? In state universities the board of regents is, in general, responsible to the governments that created the university and appointed them to their posts. But how does a regent act as an agent of the state and as a member of an autonomous organization at the same time? How does a regent conceive his role when he is appointed by the state to an office designed to protect the institution from the state itself? By assuming the role of bridge, the board expanded its constituency to include not just the state and the public but also the internal constituency of the university.

Protection for the Board As the bridge had to be insulated from those who would use it for one-way traffic or for partisan purposes, built-in protections for the board were in order.

In public universities, long terms of office for regents are such a protective device. Presumably regents could be independent of a particular governor or legislature when their terms of office spanned several election periods. California and New York are examples of such an effort to ensure protection in this manner. Appointments by the executive, as is the case in some states, rather than by the legislature or by popular vote, have also proved of value in protecting regents. The direct election of regents (as in Colorado) makes the role of buffer or bridge especially difficult.

Church-appointed trustees have also gradually become more and more independent of the founding church. The first step toward independence was the appointment to the board of non-church members and alumni who could be expected to take a somewhat independent line. Such changes, incidentally, have only just begun in some church-related institutions. The end of the process would be the complete secularization of trustees with appropriate charter changes to establish their independence from the church that brought them into being. These changes, like those in government-appointed boards, reflect the basic shift in function from that of agency to bridge, which, in turn, reflects the fact that higher education has become more dependent on secular sources of funds, which has required a loosening of church control.

The self-perpetuating board of the private secular university has also undergone changes stemming from the shift to the role of bridge. As alumni have become more important for financial contributions and for recruitment of students, they have begun to insist on the right to *elect* trustees directly (even though the board might be made up entirely of alumni) and have introduced limitations on age and length of term. These ideas reflect the belief that both the general public and the alumni have an interest in seeing that trustees keep abreast of their times. If trustees are to function properly as a bridge—explaining the university to its public constituencies and vice versa—they must be sensitive to changes in public priorities. The concealed major premise is that without these devices, the self-perpetuating board cannot speak for its new constituencies, nor can it understand the new tides shaping the relations of the university and society.

Changing Functions as Bridge

As trustees' relationships to society have changed to reflect this new role of bridge or barrier, so have their relationships with faculty and students. In earlier days trustees, whether of public or private institutions, were generally preoccupied with matters of construction and finance, while the faculty were presumably concerned with managing the educational process. This differentiation of function presented few problems because both trustees and faculty came from the same social stratum and had roughly the same political and social philosophies.

As the educational process became more complex and specialized, a lay trustee could not presume to hold his own in professional arguments with a physicist or philologist. And the faculty concentrated on their scholarly activities, taking little interest in the functioning of trustees. Thus, regardless of whether the trustee was an agent of church or state or even a representative of a general or alumni public, he had a relatively easy relationship with the faculty —namely, little or no relationship at all.

As trustees have moved, however, into the role of bridge and buffer, they have had to become more knowledgeable about the educational process. Even the least virile buffer likes to know what he is buffering; and if he must act as a bridge between the faculty and society, explaining each to the other, then he must know more about the academic business than did his predecessors, who left such matters strictly to the faculty. It is ironic that while in earlier days faculty did not want trustees to concern themselves about educational matters, they have recently insisted that no trustee decision should be made without the fullest investigation of its educational, social, and indeed moral implications.

One thing is clear. Both *bridge* and *baffle* describe entirely different roles from that of agent. Yet boards have not relinquished their first role. Assumption of the more recent function of bridge, necessitated by the new missions of the university, has not so much erased the former responsibilities of boards to church or state as it has attenuated them.

BOARD AS AGENT OF THE UNIVERSITY COMMUNITY The board today, in addition to its roles as agent of external authority and bridge between university and society, has assumed a third role—that of agent of the university community. Primarily a response to a complex change in the university itself—its attempt to become a democratic institution—this new role has two major dimensions.

First, through this role the board has assumed more and more the function of court of last resort for the university's various internal constituencies. Though this role was always implicit in the board's authority, in recent years boards have moved from being the supreme legal authority in principle to being that in fact, and to exercising that authority over a much broader range of issues. The disparate interests of the faculty aided this process, but the primary catalyst for this new function has been the polarization on campus in recent years, which has brought to the attention of the top authority, the board, controversies that could not be settled on lower levels by the disputants.

Second, the board is today responding to the pressures to transform the university into an active instrument for achieving social justice in society. For example, in decisions about the institutional future of the university, the board is called upon to exercise more than financial acumen—it is to weigh its investment policies in light of the social and moral priorities of the society.

Both dimensions of this new role have called for the board (particularly the private board of trustees) to respond to the twin democratic tenets of *representation* and *participation.* If the university community is to be a democratic polis, then its highest authority should be responsible to the internal constituency it serves. And as the board has become the ultimate arbitrator and resolver of internal conflict, there is, naturally enough, insistence that it represent the various viewpoints within the community it controls.

Drive for Representation on Boards When the board was acting simply as agent of state or church, it was in the faculty's interest to encourage a division of responsibility between educational and institutional (primarily financial) interests. But as universities have grown in size and complexity, as research and public service have been added to the mission of instruction, institutional decisions have inevitably affected the heartland of faculty interests. As financial stringency has required reconsideration of educational ambitions, the dividing line betwee the institutional and academic spheres has been blurred.

The dissolution of the implicit division of responsibility betwe boards and faculties has led to faculty interest in board memb ship. Some faculty members wish to participate in board decisio either as members or advisers, although they may be dimly awa that faculty participation in institutional matters may bring abc nonfaculty participation in academic matters. Others are willing forgo participation on the board in order to maintain the purity faculty control over academic concerns, although they may be dim aware that decisions affecting their interests will be made by tl board. Some have tried to resolve this dilemma by asserting t right to protest or veto institutional decisions by boards on whic in principle, they will not serve. All three options have their faul but the last one is perhaps the least graceful.

Another solution has been to have faculty represented on t board, but not the faculty of the institution concerned. Represent tives could be faculty from another institution or faculty who a alumni. This notion fitted into the mission of bridge, whereby t board's membership was to include those who are knowledgeal about the peculiar and unique features of the university communi Faculty expertise was needed, it was agreed, if the university was be interpreted to government and society.

Legitimacy Based on Consensus As the university has turned toward the new major mission attempting to achieve more democratic style and processes with the institution, the notion of authority based on legislative or admi istrative action has been displaced by the idea that authority a legitimacy must be based on the consensus of the community. U der these terms, a legitimate board must be composed of a faithf cross section of the community it serves. The demand has thus f lowed that faculty and students, as well as members of previous neglected groups in the community outside the university, be i cluded in board membership.

As democratic standards were applied to the board as suprer authority of the community, and as rights of representation a participation were asserted, the composition of the board w bound to change. In some places (as at Cornell) faculty membe were already on the board before these standards and rights we applied generally. Now students are demanding representation. / the largest numerical constituency, how could they, particular after most of them acquired the right to vote, be denied? Staff also have asserted the right to representation, for nonacademic employees are a part of the community too. Boards will find participation more attractive than staff unionization; thus the access of staff to the higher councils is being hastened.

Proponents of the democratic precepts of representation and participation were supported in their efforts to achieve board membership for the "new" constituencies by the parallel interests of those members of the community who wished the university to use its institutional powers to press for change in public policies to meet new ideas of public wisdom and social justice. In their traditional composition, boards seemed unlikely to assert these new priorities, so new membership seemed the means to that end.

CONCLUSIONS The newest role of the board would have been complicated enough if it had replaced the roles of agent and bridge. But it did not. As a result, the board has been expected to carry out all three at once. The board must still represent lay authority or the general public interest or the specific interest of the religious or state authority that created the board in the first instance. It must still act as a bridge and buffer between the university and society. If it does not continue to perform these functions, then the university will have lost its greatest shield and defender. One has only to live for a brief spell in the office of the rector or chancellor of a foreign university to discover the limitations of running a university under the white heat of political interests and, therefore, political directives.

But still the three roles are in conflict. How can the board be agent simultaneously for society and for the university community? How can it mesh the functions of neutral bridge with those of unneutral agency? We are asking many of our boards to play dissimilar roles in the same costumes. No wonder both they and their audiences are confused.

Resolution of this dilemma is taking two forms. The first is a lowered profile of the board as the legitimate spokesman for the public interest in the university. As it has become enmeshed in the campus community, the board has lost credibility as society's agent. Power and influence have shifted to public or semipublic bodies that appear to have a greater claim to speak for the public interest. This process has been abetted by the rise of state and regional coordinating bodies that frequently bypass the board of the individual campus and thus reduce further its larger public responsibilities.

The second form of resolution is the establishment of an institutional body that represents faculty, students, administration, and sometimes staff, alumni, and even members of the local community. Frequently called university senates or university assemblies, these bodies are specifically designed to meet the democratic tests of representation and participation.

Here again we find two concepts of legitimacy confronting each other. The board asserts its decision-making rights based upon legal authority while the university assembly asserts its decision-making rights based upon its representation of university constituencies. Both assertions are valid but incomplete. Society does have a legitimate voice through *its* representatives. The university has a legitimate voice through *its* representatives. The two voices will have to be merged into a new and larger notion of public and private interest. Perhaps because of our Anglo-Saxon training in accommodation, we are in for a period of gradual adjustment while the board rearranges its relations with larger public coordinating bodies on the one hand and universitywide representative structures on the other. The task for the board may now be to become the link between the university assembly and the external coordinating body, a task which will require patient statesmanship to succeed.

12. Trustees and the University Community

by Samuel B. Gould

THE IMAGE OF
THE TRUSTEES The term *establishment* has acquired a pejorative sound these days, especially in academic circles. At the very pinnacle of the academic establishment, and therefore attracting a good many of the lightning bolts, stand the trustees of colleges and universities. Hitherto secure in the most absolute sense, trustees are now not only criticized for their alleged attitudes and activities but their very existence is being challenged. Throughout the history of American higher education they have managed to stay in undisputed power; they have been the highest court of appeal and their decisions have been accepted with no more than muted grumblings when there was real or imagined cause for dissatisfaction. Nobody, except perhaps an occasional recalcitrant student editor, dared to raise his voice openly against them, and even this gesture was an empty one. Only rarely did a volatile faculty member or rash administrator challenge the trustees, but the victor in such a clash was always virtually preordained.

The current vogue of disenchantment with authority has begun to reach even into this holiest of sanctuaries. When the hierarchy of major business corporations such as General Motors is made the subject of critical scrutiny, one can certainly expect that the hierarchy of institutions more related to the public interest will similarly receive assiduous attention and examination. Predictably, too, the more positive achievements of trustees of academic institutions, public and private, will be overshadowed by whatever shortcomings or abuses are inevitably uncovered. Unrest and dissatisfaction with life permeate society today; a critical stamp is put on everything. Accordingly, boards of trustees, including those whose services have led to exemplary institutional progress under trying conditions, are already under attack and will continue to be.

Part of the challenge to trustees stems from such factors as the way they are chosen, the time they serve, and the nature of the responsibilities they assume. All these factors, evolved over the past two centuries, have become part of a strong tradition that trustees themselves have long considered immutable. To a large extent, boards are self-perpetuating; they tend to make replacements by electing those with whom they feel they will be comfortable. Members are ordinarily chosen for their business acumen and their ability to assist the university financially either by their own gifts or by those they can attract. While their responsibility is for the entire institution, their attention centers largely on nonacademic matters about which they naturally feel more knowledgeable. They serve for very long periods, even when their single terms may be no more than three years, since reelection is virtually a foregone conclusion. In the case of public universities, where trustees are appointed, the same circumstances seem to apply, with the additional factor of political party relationships.

Obviously a group such as this becomes a race apart in the eyes of the university community. Boards of trustees are clothed in a certain mystery; they have an alien quality since they come from the world outside the campus. Moreover, they function with a sort of absolute authority that can be disquieting to students and threatening to faculty. Individually or collectively, they appear on campus at infrequent intervals and usually with a relatively high degree of pomp. They seem benign, dignified, and concerned, but they are too remote to inspire confidence among those who live within their purview.

Another part of the challenge to trustees is rooted in more specific factors relating to how they function or to the characteristics they exhibit. At one or another time and place, trustees have managed to make themselves unpopular with the university community because of positions they have or have not taken on issues important to the academic world and by unilateral actions or no actions at all. These have occurred often enough to make people forget the eminently positive achievements of so many boards of trustees over the years. Their defense of academic freedom in periods of our country's history when such a defense required extraordinary courage is only one example — possibly the finest — since it preserved the essential basis for a free society. When institutions have been faced with severe financial crises, generous support by individual board members has sometimes meant the difference between solvency and disaster. Trustees have repeatedly defended students, especially when students have been attacked irrationally or used by unscrupulous agitators as instruments to foment violence. At their best, trustees have been superb.

Fine actions, however, are rarely newsworthy; human failings capture the headlines. Thus other and less pleasing characteristics have been associated with trustees, sometimes fairly, sometimes less so. Trustees are all too often felt to be aloof and insensitive, unwilling to mingle with the rest of the university community, and insufficiently aware of the academic world and its role in society. Boards are usually considered bastions of conservatism in an institution whose heart-blood is the untrammeled exploration of ideas. Sometimes trustees are viewed as unwilling to commit their time and energy to the institution and as looking upon their duties as honorific rather than as a most serious responsibility. They are accused of preoccupation with the financial progress of a university to the detriment of its academic progress or with the development of its physical facilities because such development is tangible and can be measured. They are criticized for approaching their responsibilities to academic institutions with the corporate management attitudes they bring to their own businesses or industries. They are deemed to be more concerned about the public relations of their college or university than about the honesty with which it comports itself. And they are attacked for willingness to compromise on all-important issues that to idealistic youth can never be subject to compromise.

A perspective on how trustees are frequently viewed in the university community becomes particularly important when one remembers that trustees represent an important link between the university and the larger world. The academic world is full of peculiarities which the general public finds strange and difficult to understand. Some of these peculiarities are easily identifiable even though they involve complicated concepts. The tradition of tenure for faculty, for example, has good reasons for existence: it protects the faculty member against the punitive actions of the public when he expresses unpopular opinions or explores unorthodox ideas. Though abuses of tenure occasionally occur, the inherent necessity for academic freedom in a democratic society remains. The trustees, coming out of that larger world and closely associated with it, are buffers for academic life when they insist that this feature be preserved and when they take advantage of every possible occasion to interpret it correctly when it is challenged.

Other characteristics of the university similarly require trustee

defense and interpretation: the concept of an academic comm
nity—a world of thought, so to speak—where teacher and learne
work together cooperatively toward the advancement of knowledg
the philosophy that conceives of education as a major investmen
of the people in the future of America and thus legitimizes the eve
growing and increasingly burdensome expenditures called for
achieve educational goals; the unusual and powerful role of th
faculty in academic decision making whereby curricula are fasl
ioned, colleagues chosen or rejected, promotions given, areas
research selected, and funds for academic outlays justified an
allocated. These traditions and practices are sometimes misunde
stood by the layman. Trustees who take the trouble to becom
familiar with these patterns are the logical persons to explain then
When they do so, they cannot be accused of being self-serving.

Just as trustees can be the source of interpretation of the ac
demic life to the outer world, they can also, unfortunately, be th
focal point for controversy within the university. When they me
sure the progress of the institution on the basis of completely pra
matic elements founded in corporate experience or something sim
lar, they create restlessness and even dissension among facult
students, and administration. Many trustees are accustomed
assuming complete direction, since they constitute the top echelc
of authority and see no reason to worry about whether their dire
tives are generally understood and accepted. Some feel that th
growth in numbers of students or in size of the physical campus
the major criterion of success. Some are much too intrigued by pa
terns of cost analysis and other quantitative factors that coul
potentially add to the economy and efficiency of the university
operation. Still others are concerned about research activitie
urging acceptance of any amount that will generate income, emph
sizing the values of applied rather than basic research, and mair
taining that classified research is completely appropriate to th
university function. Some are negative about experimenting wit
innovative methodologies such as the new possibilities offered t
educational technology. And, of course, some still adhere to th
traditional elitist view of higher education that was much mor
prevalent in their own university days; they feel that the increase i
educational opportunity, particularly in the public sector, has ha
and will continue to have a debilitating effect upon the quality
learning.

These issues are subjects of endless debate in a university con munity. Because the trustees are almost always expected to be conservative in their approaches and judgments, the debate can so distort their image that their basic concern for the advancement of education is seriously questioned. Such a circumstance is bound to retard university progress and create a campus atmosphere marked by insecurity and tension. It should be avoided by every possible means, not the least of which is frequent and regular contact between trustees and the rest of the community.

TRUSTEES AS A REPRESENTATIVE BODY Do trustees represent the university? Because their points of view are often contrary to those of faculty or students and because boards are generally top-heavy in conservatism, they are now subject to pressures toward doing away with what is considered an imbalance in their structure. Boards are accused of being chosen undemocratically and of being similarly undemocratic in carrying out their functions. Requests, even demands, are being made that faculty and students be included in board membership. Some colleges and universities have hastened to accede to these requests, but it is too early to tell whether the results have been successful.

The arguments for inclusion of faculty and students are sensible and relatively obvious. Faculty and students should have a voice in decision making since ordinarily they are the ones most affected by the decisions. They are also two-way interpreters for the university community; they bring a special expertise to the trustees' discussions and reflect internal points of view that should be evaluated, and they carry back to their separate constituencies a firsthand or eyewitness report on just how university policies and plans evolve. Both these roles are of vital concern to the community if it is to feel truly and formally represented at the highest level of authority.

But there are equally obvious arguments against formal representation of faculty and students that cause many institutions to hesitate before taking such a step. Some contend that representation would be more a shadow than a reality, especially in the very large universities, because of physical limitations; if boards were enlarged sufficiently to meet this objective, they would be huge, unwieldy, and unproductive. Others question whether any methods of selection, acceptable to all concerned, can be devised that will ensure truly competent and disinterested board members rather than politically expert lobbyists. Some wonder about the degree of real and permanent concern for the institution as a whole faculty or students will reflect. Are faculty as interested in the progress of the university as they are in strengthening their own academic disciplines? Are students as interested in the long-range implications of decisions as they are in immediacy of action?

The basic clash between trustees and the rest of the community, which results in the demand for formal faculty and student representation, originates in a lack of agreement or understanding about the purposes and goals of the institution itself. One must sadly but truthfully admit that not all board members accept their responsibilities on the basis of a deep commitment to the specific objectives of a university. Nor can they be taxed with the total blame for this. All too often, these objectives have never been stated or, if once stated, have not been reexamined in the light of modern circumstances to determine whether they still apply. Before accepting his appointment, the trustee rarely asks himself whether he can wholeheartedly subscribe to the institution's purposes. Indeed, except in a vague way, he rarely knows what they are and is usually too shy or embarrassed to ask his colleagues.

The same lack of understanding and commitment exists among many faculty and students, who choose their institutions for personal reasons that have little or nothing to do with what these institutions are trying to be or to achieve. Their interest in the university is peripheral except when it affects a specific goal of their own.

Trustee decisions, with or without faculty and student representation, which are made against this background of varying interpretations or varying degrees of misunderstanding are bound to increase tensions within the university. All elements of the community, therefore, should come together to fashion a statement of purpose. This can be the starting point, at least, for relieving such tensions. And the president of the university, as chief executive officer of the trustees and as educational leader of the university community, should take the necessary initiatives. He should be on the watch for misinterpretations and evaluate their causes whenever they occur. And he should create the machinery by which tensions caused by misunderstanding may be lessened and even made to disappear. He is the logical and, indeed, the only true liaison between faculty, students, and trustees.

In this capacity the president may soon realize that not enough attention has yet been given to other, less formal ways of providing representation, not only for faculty and students but also for alumni and able, interested citizens. No group of trustees can be expected to have all the expertise necessary for dealing with all matters, even when boards are formally augmented by representation from alumni or faculty or students. They should, therefore, not be limited to their own resources, but should be able to call freely upon any appropriate source.

It is quite possible and perhaps more practical to supplant some of the present trustee standing committees with others organized on an ad hoc basis, each dealing with a specific problem and augmented with talent from outside the board.[1] Much wider representation of faculty, students, alumni, and general citizenry would result. Such a development is particularly important in large institutions to counteract the criticism of inadequate representation and to forge stronger links between the trustees, the university community, and the larger community beyond. The outcome could well be a more unified, broader-based, and more productive effort toward moving the university forward. This procedure is effective not only in providing better solutions but also in easing tensions, educating all concerned to a new understanding of the nature and unique qualities of the university, and taking away much of the mystery that frequently surrounds trustee activities. Most importantly, decisions made in this fashion are more readily acceptable to all and therefore more likely to be followed by effective, cooperative action.

TRUSTEES AS DECISION MAKERS Since trustees are the ultimate decision makers on policy matters in any university, it is important to identify the ways in which they can enhance the quality of their decisions. Hasty, incorrect, or undocumented judgments will lead to a weakening of the institution. They can also lead to antagonism in and out of the university, culminating in a loss of support. A certain amount of human error is inevitable in any enterprise. A preponderance of error, however, quickly destroys the reputation of a board and does irreparable harm to the institution the board legally governs.

It is axiomatic that the quality of board decisions is in direct ratio to that of the staff work provided by the president through his office and other administrative offices under his direction. To begin with, superior quality is more likely to result when one staff member is responsible for coordinating information and analysis for trustee study. This staff member is normally a secretary to the

[1] A fuller treatment of ad hoc committees will be found in Chap. 13, pp. 235–236.

trustees, reporting to them rather than to the president but maintaining a very close relationship with the president.[2] To fulfill such a responsibility effectively, particularly in large and complex universities, the secretary should turn for assistance to other staff members when decisions that relate to their special competencies are pending.

The quality of decisions is further enhanced when staff members make certain that the materials they prepare for trustees are sufficiently detailed to give board members a grasp of the subject and its problems. These materials should be presented clearly, graphically, and in terms understandable to laymen, so that the trustees can assimilate their content with ease. Naturally, no important facts should be withheld. The staff can hardly be expected not to have a point of view; this, however, should be predicated on all the information available and presented fully, honestly, and without prejudice. Subjects of such reports normally include annual budgets, revisions or additions to degree programs, physical expansion, investment changes, problems of campus unrest, or major innovative changes.

Better board decisions will result when the academic philosophy and directions of the university are constantly kept in view by the trustees. In this they need regular reminders from the president, whose task it is to show them how every major move of the university, every change in policy, every new venture, flows out of the institution's efforts to achieve its stated goals more effectively. The president's sense of commitment and his academic vision should be evident to trustees and should inspire them; his enthusiasm should reach out and touch them until they share with him the dreams and hopes for adding to the richness of all academic offerings and the growth of the individual. Describing the president's relationship to the trustees in these terms may sound evangelistic, but the leader who does not inspire is a limited leader, and his limitations will virtually guarantee limitations among the trustees and others who work with him.

Trustees must feel free to seek information from whatever sources they deem appropriate. These may be both inside and outside the university. Under ordinary circumstances, the staff can supply whatever data are needed by the trustees. There is no reason, how-

---

[2] See also the analysis of the role of the secretary and staff work in Chap. 13, pp. 231–232.

ever, why trustees should not augment staff information with their own searches if they remain unconvinced or uncertain about what they have already received. Such searches, however, should be carried on with the president's full knowledge; otherwise, dangerous situations can develop—dangerous in that they destroy normal channels of communications and encourage doubts about the validity of staff work.

It is imperative that trustees meet with relative frequency, are rarely absent from scheduled meetings, and set aside enough of their time to enable them to stay through each meeting. Many poor decisions or whimsical board actions have come to pass because the board did not meet often enough, because members did not appear for meetings, or because they left meetings before important decisions were made. Absence excuses are typically accepted *pro forma,* and regulations calling for the removal of trustees guilty of excessive absences are embarrassing. But the work of the university cannot proceed smoothly and intelligently without the assiduous attention of all the trustees.

The quality of trustee decisions is also dependent upon the degree of independence the trustees insist upon and exert, regardless of political affiliations, professional loyalties or predilections, ethnic or religious ties. Elected trustees are sometimes unduly sensitive to the constituencies that elected them; appointed ones are sometimes equally sensitive to the political figures or bodies responsible for their appointment. Both vitiate their contributions to the progress of the university and endanger the university's integrity when they allow it to be compromised by their own lack of independence.

A trustee inevitably brings to the board a body of valuable knowledge originating in his own experience. He may be a labor union official, a member of a minority group, a banker, a medical doctor, or a social worker. But he should not serve as a representative of any of these groups. His responsibility is rather to make decisions that are in the best interests of the university and that strengthen the educational process. When he does otherwise, he weakens the university and raises doubts about its intentions. When he interprets his role of representation narrowly, he creates an attitude of interference with institutional objectives. Such an attitude often contributes to divisiveness among trustees and sharply limits the scope of their interest and concern.

One can readily understand why trustees would normally be sensitive, sometimes oversensitive, to public criticism of the university. They are bound to be in the public spotlight and are called to account for whatever happens. Their natural desire for campus serenity and happy relationships with the outside world may cause them to forget that at times the university cannot help but be controversial if it is to fulfill its obligations completely. Important ideas are rarely comfortable to deal with. Yet it is entirely possible for trustees to approach controversial issues realistically without giving the impression either of stubbornness on the one hand or of surrender to external and internal pressure on the other. It is possible to admit mistakes candidly without losing integrity. And it is also possible to be adamant in defense of the university when trustees are confident in the rightness of its actions.

Trustees are inevitably the court of last appeal in matters related to university independence and integrity. They must understand that their reactions to external pressure inevitably influence the ability of an institution to function effectively. There is ample documentation in the history of American higher education to support the validity of this point.

Thus, as trustees carry on their role as representatives of the larger community, the strength, clarity, and honesty with which they adhere to the principles of independent action become paramount in importance. And part of this role of advocacy is to interpret academic, social, and structural changes within the university in terms of the independence necessary to bring them about. This is one major way to bring about understanding and acceptance of what the university does. Support of the university, including its continuing financial stability, depends on the success of this kind of interpretation.

TRUSTEES AS THE VOICE OF THE UNIVERSITY The subject of interpretation brings us to another facet of the relationship of trustees to the university community—that of when and under what circumstances trustees should speak out in behalf of the institution.

Just as there are policies relating to all major substantive matters by which the university is guided, so should there be prior agreements and understandings among the trustees about how to conduct themselves vis-à-vis the news media and the university administration. There should also be prior understandings about how the university community is to be informed of trustee decisions and actions. Otherwise, one can expect confusion and error each time a critical situation arises.

Obviously there are times when the trustees as a group, usually with the chairman as spokesman, should make public statements on university matters. These statements, however, should always be related in some way to university policy rather than administrative detail, so that there is never doubt that the trustees are examining matters within their purview. This is important even when dealing with controversial situations. The division of responsibility between administration and policy making should always be completely clear in the public mind, just as it should be clear in the minds of the trustees themselves. Statements of the trustees should either set forth new policies or support administrative actions taken in accordance with already established policy. Nonsupportive statements only divide or weaken the university and confuse or titillate the public. They call unmistakably for a change in administrative leadership. Such matters are not for public airing but should be dealt with privately if the best interests of all concerned are to be served.

When important policy decisions are to be presented by the board to the university community, their announcement should be preceded by appropriate communication and discussion with those groups that will be affected. No major decision for change in policy should come as a surprise. Furthermore, such decisions should reflect not only agreement of the trustees and administration but also the advisory judgments of others and sometimes their actual participation in the decisions. Unfortunately, there are cases in which policy changes have been announced without prior agreement with the president, and divisiveness has inevitably resulted.

In most instances policy decisions should be announced to the university community by the president, although in some cases joint involvement of the trustees will be required. For example, the president would typically announce a major new academic program, while a decision to increase tuition or room and board fees might be presented jointly. In the larger community, press conferences on policy changes should be attended by trustees, and news releases should make clear where the responsibility for such changes rests.

Many communications problems within today's academic world, however, arise from the unrest, confrontations, or occasional violent actions of the university community and are primed with potentially disastrous consequences. These problems offer a much more dramatic set of trustee relationships. At times of campus crisis trustees are strongly tempted to take charge and to initiate whatever actions they consider necessary, stating their reasons to the public. This natural reaction is compounded of many elements: anger, fear, a sense of authority, a desire to be helpful and, most of all, an eagerness to reassure everyone and to return to normality. Yet in this reaction there are dangers that can create havoc in the trustees' relationship to the university community.

Trustees should recognize that a time of crisis on a campus usually calls for swift action under the leadership of the president and his staff. Although the president should be in regular communication with the trustees (either with the chairman or the full board, depending on the nature and seriousness of the crisis), he should take full responsibility for day-to-day or hour-by-hour decisions and actions and should announce such decisions and actions as his own. There are good reasons for this procedure: it clearly identifies and establishes the administrative leadership educationally and in every other way; it makes plain who is in charge and who is, therefore, accountable; and it leaves the board free to serve as a court of appeal if or when there are dissatisfactions within the community over administrative decisions and actions.

It is important also that the trustees make no statements at a time of crisis without prior consultation and agreement with the president. As individuals they will be pressed for their opinions and will sometimes find the opportunity hard to resist. But their role in a crisis is to keep informed, to watch carefully, to assist when they can, and to adhere to the rule of silence until the appropriate and agreed-upon moment arrives. When they do speak, they should do so with one voice, not as individuals. Divisions of opinion among trustees should be settled internally, not aired in individual statements. Nothing destroys confidence in the university more quickly, internally or externally, than an awareness that its trustees are in sharp disagreement among themselves or that they are taking the responsibilities of the administration into their own hands.

THE TRUSTEES AND THE PRESIDENT Probably the most crucial relationship of trustees with the university community is that with the president, who is their executive officer. This is so because their other relationships—those with faculty, students, and employees—will be effective only when the president takes sufficient initiative to make them so. And as he does this, he creates understanding attitudes among the trustees in regard not only to all those within the university but to himself as well.

The initiative of the president in building strong ties with the trustees is a vital part of his educative function. This designated duty is to be their executive officer, but he should be their teacher too. He should never let opportunities pass to make their meeting an experience that increases the trustees' educational understanding. Indeed, he should create such opportunities regularly so that the gap between trustees and the university community steadily narrows. For example, he should arrange for frequent presentations and discussions of matters relating to the academic growth of the institution so that trustees become familiar with the accomplishments and aspirations that are the constant preoccupation of the university community.

The president should remember that the questions in trustees' minds are often the same as those in the minds of the public generally; the more frequently these questions are answered and answered well, the more supportive the trustees become. The president, as the chief interpreter for the whole university, is potentially the major unifying element.

The president is also the major factor in unifying the trustees themselves. It is largely through his efforts that they become a unified body, with pride in their educational obligations and with respect for and enjoyment of one another.

The relationship between the president and trustees should be one of complete truthfulness and full disclosure, lest the atmosphere of meetings be charged with suspicion and clouded by rumor. Trustees should always be able to feel that the president will give them full and frank explanations of whatever is happening or is expected to happen. The president should also make certain that trustees are aware of the competencies and achievements of administrators, faculty, and students, giving credit freely and often. By doing this, he promotes the community effort necessary to the university's achievement and enhances his own relationship with his colleagues.

CONCLUSIONS Like all other problems involving relationships with people, those of the trustees and the university community can be resolved only with painstaking, never-ending care and planning. Solutions to these problems will not ordinarily come about through happenstance or good fortune. Even if they do, the same or similar problems may soon reappear as individual personalities replace one another. These problems can be considerably mitigated, however, when the functions of trustees are thoroughly understood and agreed upon. Although it is probably impossible and perhaps undesirable to draw up a complete bill of particulars and incorporate it into bylaws or regulations, a definite style of operation can evolve no matter how many times the dramatis personae change.

The bases for a sound relationship between trustees and the rest of the university community are a common understanding of educational purposes, a common dedication to those purposes, a deep loyalty to the institution, a realization of what role is appropriate for each constituency, a sensitively fashioned system of sharing ideas when decisions are being reached and, above all, a full commitment to the protection of the independence of the university and its preservation in the face of impending erosions of whatever sort. The concept of trusteeship is sound. What remains to be done is to refine the functions of trusteeship until they more nearly match the concept.

13. Internal Organization of the Board

by Morton A. Rauh

The purpose of structure in a board of trustees is to provide a framework that will support the board's function. It should follow, therefore, that a clear understanding of the board's role must necessarily precede the determination of its internal organization. Unhappily, such understanding is often absent. Most boards are not sure what their true function is, and their internal organization does not stand scrutiny. Too often one finds standing committees that rubberstamp, treasurers who have no real say about finances, and secretaries who read a corporate record written by someone else.

When corporate charters and state legislation established governing boards as the agency of both trust and management, they created a situation that has given rise to acute symptoms of schizophrenia. When a board of trustees is asked to concern itself with the visiting hours in dormitories at one meeting and then finds itself confronted with the issue of open admissions at the next, it is no wonder that there is confusion about its proper mission.

In addition, there is increasing confusion about the relationship of the board to the total governance structure. The classic model of a line structure which placed the trustees at the top and the students at the bottom no longer applies. Indeed, when students lock up trustees in a board room, it would appear that the structure has been turned bottom over top. The concept of the university community as one in which the administrators administrate, the faculty teach, and the students study is hardly contemporary.

The variations in style of board operation fall on a spectrum whose extremes may be described as *working boards* and *policy boards*.

The working board is characterized by its intention to be closely associated with most major institutional decisions. Its model lies in the corporate board of directors which is composed largely of management personnel and major stockholders. Public school boards of education are close to this philosophy of detailed involvement, as are hospital boards.

The policy board, on the other hand, delegates the decision-making process to the full-time management. The board's major role, then, lies in evaluating, cirticizing, and supporting management. It may review, approve, and counsel, but it seldom undertakes the detailed consideration of data that precedes and characterizes the true decision. Its closest model is likely to be the large corporate board of directors, the majority of whose members are not part of the company's management.

The confusion of purpose arises when these contrary styles are intermixed without consistent plan. Then the board is tempted into playacting. It appears to reach decisions when in fact it is only giving *pro forma* assent to a decision made elsewhere in the university.[1]

It should therefore be the aim of any board to clarify its role and to be alert to the ever-present temptation to digress from this central role. Its efforts in these directions can be helped by a sound internal organization.

FORMAL STRUCTURE

The principal formal components of the internal board structure are its officers and committees.

Chairman of the Board

It is taken for granted that a governing board shall have a chairman—so much so that most bylaws are silent on the duties of the office other than to specify presiding at meetings. As a result, the chairman assumes the role of "head trustee" and fills it according to his own inclinations, which are influenced and modified, of course, by the attitude of the president and the traditions of the board itself.

Some chairmen see their position as primarily one of supporting the president. In that role, the chairman helps form the board agenda, supplies a friendly ear and perhaps some advice, and acts as liaison between the president and the rest of the board. It is an

---

[1] It sometimes seems that universities go out of their way to create confusion about the board's function. A sign on a parking lot at the University of California, Berkeley, reads, "Open only to cars with *C* and *D* stickers—By order of the Board of Regents."

important role and, when executed with warmth and sensitivity, it can be a major factor in improving the president's performance.

At the other end of the spectrum is the chairman who so actively involves himself in the affairs of the university that he becomes a "copresident." He almost always lives near the university and thus has frequent personal contact with the president. Since he knows the university structure and the key people in it, he has direct access to information not normally available to other trustees. He probably has the ability to raise money either from private sources or through political activity in the legislature. He is closely involved with the president in key personnel decisions, including the selection of trustees.

When a chairman operates in this style, he may be seen by some as sharing the president's authority. Unless he functions with exceptional skill and sensitivity, the president's role as chief administrative officer becomes clouded. If the chairman does in fact have administrative responsibilities, then it would seem logical to convert the office to a paid position. Although such an organization is common in business corporations, it is little used in universities.

Vice-chairman of the Board

"The Vice-chairman shall serve in the absence of the Chairman." So reads a typical university bylaw. It does not vest much authority in the office or lay upon it very onerous duties. The real determinant of the scope of this office is found not in the bylaws but in the traditions of the board—that is, whether the vice-chairman customarily succeeds the chairman. When this office is seen as the stepping-stone to the chair, it takes on importance and becomes a position for training and indoctrination.

Possibly because so many board chairmen hold office without limit of time in private universities or have little assurance of reappointment or reelection in public universities, the concept of succession is not common in educational institutions. It is much more generally followed by boards of hospitals, museums, and churches. There is much to be said for providing a structure that fosters continuity of board leadership, and the office of vice-chairman could be put to good use in this cause.

Secretary

The secretary's basic duty is to maintain a record of the transactions of the board of trustees. In too many cases that is all he does, and so the importance and potential of the post is lost.

Fortunately, the position is increasingly viewed in larger terms, and at most universities it is held as a full-time job. The days of the trustee who acts as secretary and reads the minutes someone else has prepared are happily drawing to a close.

Increasingly, the secretary provides staff assistance to the board. Whether the board operates with concern for detail or only in terms of broad policy, it will need information. The secretary is in the best position to supply it. In many universities he operates out of the president's office and can thus be the principal channel of communication between the board and the university constituencies.

The secretary's job as custodian of the corporate records also needs to be broadened. A minute book of board transactions is no longer an adequate corporate record. The structure of decision making in the university is now so complex that to single out for the records only those transactions that take place in board meetings (or in meetings of its standing committee) is to create an inadequate and, indeed, a misleading record. Quite obviously an action in a meeting of the faculty senate may be at least as important as a board action, and the time may be at hand when the same can be said of the student council.

It would seem, therefore, that the concept of *secretary of the board* ought to be scrapped in favor of *secretary of the university*. It would then become the duty of the incumbent to create a comprehensive system of institutional records. He would identify the various seats of decision making and devise a system for recording their proceedings. The activities of the governing board would become but one aspect of the record. To the extent that the secretary can create a systematic and unified record, he will also have created the means for communication among the constituencies of the university.

Treasurer Since the clergy who administered the early American colleges were not considered reliable money managers, financial control was vested in an officer chosen from the trustee body itself. The common title for this office was *treasurer*. As the financial affairs of the university have become more complex, it is no longer possible for the trustee-treasurer to carry the actual financial responsibility. Nevertheless, some boards have been reluctant to abandon this symbol of control; a trustee fills the office of treasurer though the actual financial responsibility has passed to a full-time employee known variously as *controller, vice-president,* or *business manager.* As recently as 1968 it was found that of 33 private colleges surveyed, 14 still filled the office of treasurer with a trustee. The same survey showed that this practice had all but disappeared in the public universities.

By whatever name the chief financial officer is known, trustees tend to keep some sort of direct line open to him. For example, it is far more common for the chief business officer to sit regularly with the board than it is for his counterpart in academic matters to do so. What seems to emerge is that trustees don't entirely trust the president in financial matters. However, creating some special tie between trustees and financial personnel is not likely to create confidence. The only reliable means for a board to discharge its financial responsibility is through the president. The board must remember that financial matters are merely the expression of an academic program, and control of the first follows control of the second.

Executive Officers The officers described so far are commonly designated as *officers of the board* in order to specify a direct relationship with the board rather than with the university administration. In addition the university has another set of officers consisting of the president and his senior executive associates, who may or may not carry typical corporate titles. For example, the chief academic officer may be *vice-president* or *provost;* the chief business officer may be *vice-president* or *business manager;* the student personnel officer may be *vice-president for student affairs* or *dean of students.*

Differentiation between officers of the board and officers of the university needlessly confuses the governance structure. In a recent study of board organization, the writer found many cases in which the secretaries and treasurers literally did not know whether they were responsible to the board or to the president. A single officer structure in a line relationship with the president (excepting the chairman and vice-chairman) will almost always serve better.

Even when a differentiation is made between officers of the board and officers of the university, the commonality of interests of the board and the executive officers can be made explicit by the simple device of having the principal university officers sit as full participants in all board meetings. This practice is by no means universally followed. Participation of the officers ranges from attendance by special invitation only to attendance at all meetings.[2]

Full participation is the most promising of these alternatives, for it provides the trustees with direct access to the full expertise of the management without the necessity of having all information filter through the president. Full participation brings to the college board of trustees something of the flavor of the corporate board of directors, where major officers usually sit as directors.

A common, and unfortunate, practice is to limit participation to the principal financial officer. It is far better to include the other major administrative officers—for example, the head of faculty and academic affairs, the chief student personnel officer, and the planning and development officer. Only then is the board encouraged to see all facets of the university program as having equal and related importance.

Standing Committees Standing committees are key parts of the internal organization of almost all boards of trustees. These committees are typically known by such names as executive, finance, curriculum, buildings and grounds, student life, and so on. They are supposed to implement any combination of the following purposes:

1 To accomplish more business than would be possible in meetings of the full board

2 To "educate" trustees in the problems of the institution by giving them more occasions for intimate contact

3 To utilize special skills of individual trustees more efficiently

4 To provide more occasions for direct contact between trustees and members of the staff

5 To take advantage of the availability of local trustees when the board as a whole is geographically scattered

6 To screen and prepare matters for action by the full board

Unfortunately these worthwhile purposes too often go unaccomplished, and the entire committee structure may exist for the pur-

[2] Three degrees of participation have been described: *Inner circle*—Officers sit with trustees around the meeting table. *Outer circle*—Officers attend the meetings but sit behind the trustees. *Closed circle*—Officers attend meetings upon specific invitation for the purpose of presenting data.

pose of keeping trustees busy or of giving them a sense of involvement in university affairs.

The place of the committee in the internal structure of the board cannot be specified unless the role of the board has been determined. Let us examine this statement in terms of specifics.

If the board has decided that it will make the actual decisions on selection of endowment investments, then clearly there must be a continuing group of trustees who meet regularly for this purpose. If, on the other hand, the style of the board is to delegate these decisions to an investment manager, then a standing investment committee loses its essential purpose. Indeed, its existence may dilute the responsibility delegated to the portfolio manager. Under these circumstances it would better serve the interests of the board to establish some yardstick of investment performance against which the manager will be measured. Then his performance can be periodically evaluated and the board's responsibility centers on the issue of whether to retain or replace him as their investment counselor.

In these two situations the board's internal organization is quite different. In the first case a standing committee is needed, since there are regularly recurring decisions to be made. In the second case, however, the occasions for decisions are infrequent, so a committee that meets only as needed and without a fixed schedule would be adequate.

Ad Hoc Committees   In trustee cirlces there is increasing interest in the concept of a committee that meets only upon specific occasions for specific purposes. If that idea takes hold, it is possible that most, or perhaps all, standing committees may give way to ad hoc task-oriented committees. To the extent that boards recognize that operating decisions[3] are and should be made by full-time management, the need for standing committees diminishes.

The concept of ad hoc committees as suggested here is not limited

---

[3] So much of the confusion about the trustee role lies in the misuse of the word *decision* that the term needs to be defined. When data are considered, alternative solutions are analyzed, and a course of action is determined, then it can be said that a decision has been made. Too often trustees are misled by their president into thinking that they have decided something when in fact they are merely confirming an action already taken. When trustees "decide" to raise tuition, they are in most cases confirming a decision that was made earlier by the management when they settled major issues of program and expenditures.

to groups composed only of trustees. Although a trustee-only composition would probably be best for a task such as choosing or
evaluating an investment manager, other committees might be
composed of trustees, faculty, students, and administrators in such
proportions as the nature of the problem indicates.

The ad hoc committees offer some interesting advantages over the
standing committees.

1 Time could be used more functionally and constructively without increasing
the total trustee man-hours. Problems that could not be dealt with effectively in short sessions the night before regular board meetings might be
handled in a substantive fashion in a single day-long meeting. Further, it
might be easier for a busy trustee to schedule this single larger block of time
than the more frequent shorter meetings.

2 The committee could have a composition suited to the policy issue under
consideration. For example, the question of the college's role in establishing
behavioral rules could be dealt with by a committee that would include
trustees, students, faculty, and administrative staff. Even on such matters
as filling vacancies on the board, a committee that brings together trustees,
faculty, and students might well serve to introduce a broadened view of
trustee qualifications.

3 The mere identification of the task would direct attention to the broader
issues and away from agenda-filling items. For example, instead of a finance committee considering some modification in faculty retirement benefits, the ad hoc committees might undertake a review of the entire benefit
structure for all employees.

4 The trustees would have a clearer feeling of involvement and contribution.
The experience of developing a policy position in association with active
members of the university community would be more rewarding and less
limited than the functions of merely advising, criticizing, and approving.

The concept of ad hoc committee structure need not mean that
all standing committees would be eliminated. Those that serve a
clearly identified purpose and do it well should be retained.

Executive
Committee
One of the standing committees least likely to be eliminated is the
executive committee. Its place in the board's internal organization,
however, needs to be carefully scrutinized.

A typical bylaw provides that the executive committee shall exercise all the powers of the board between meetings. The manner in
which this authority is executed varies widely. If the words are
interpreted to mean that the executive committee acts only in emer-

gencies, when a board action cannot be postponed until the next regular meeting or when it is impractical to call a special meeting, then the special powers of the executive committee have a well-defined limit. But executive committees frequently meet regularly between full board meetings. Then they begin to acquire the characteristics of an inner board. Their members have direct access to university personnel; they meet in greater privacy; and they begin to exercise power and influence not shared by the board as a whole. In some cases the increased activity of a few trustees may serve the university well, but in general it is well to keep a critical eye upon casual and inadvertent modifications to the governance system.

NONSTRUC-TURAL INFLUENCES Some factors unrelated to formal structure have a potent influence on the style of the board of trustees.

Size The size of a board may have a great deal to do with the way it operates. Small boards are more likely to become involved in management detail than large ones simply because the mechanics of interchange — both verbal and written — are easier.

Frequency of Meetings Frequency of meetings exerts a similar influence on board function. The board that meets once a month is more likely to deal with details than one that meets only three times a year. When these two factors are combined — that is, when a large board that meets infrequently is compared with a small board that meets often — then the differences in styles are more marked.

Composition of the Board The background of trustees will also influence the style of the board's operation. Businessmen and lawyers are heavily represented on most boards. Their expertise causes the board to emphasize financial, plant, and management concerns. When larger numbers of trustees are drawn from such fields as education, social service, creative arts, etc., the board tends to be concerned with broader-ranging educational issues.

Conflict of Interest Any consideration of the composition of the board leads to the specific problem of conflict of interest. Unfortunately, the term has taken on such a narrow meaning that the full importance of the issue has become lost. Conflict of interest is almost always considered in the context of monetary gain, and this preoccupation has led to some absurd results. A classic case involved one of the University of Michigan's most effective regents, who resigned when it was pointed out that his firm did business with the university. It was later established that his net gain from the relationship was of the order of $17 per year. What has been overlooked in cases like this one is that the key consideration is "conflict" and not "interest." Only when the interest affects the trustee's judgment can it be said that a conflict exists.

The most serious cases of conflict of interest are found in areas other than financial matters. The most common of these is political interest. A state officer who sits ex officio on a university board may find his political interests in serious conflict with the university's interests. And if that conflict comes from two directions, as occurred at the University of California between the governor of one party and the speaker of another, then the board of trustees loses its essential quality of objectivity.

Some conflicts of interest may be more subtle than those involving finances or politics. It is possible to find conflict between the attitudes and values of the trustees and those of the students and faculty. It cannot be asked that trustees qualify for their posts by holding those views that are congenial to the university membership. Some conflict of this sort is both tolerable and desirable. However, if these views are too far apart, then the conflict of interest can reach nonproductive extremes. For example, the views of some trustees on sexual mores are so at odds with the contemporary standard of young people that there is almost no chance that they could deal with policy issues in the area of student behavior. They would probably be happier and more useful serving as trustees of hospitals.

Students and Faculty as Trustees

It is not possible to consider the influences of board composition and conflict of interest without raising the specific issue of extending board membership to faculty and students of the institution.[4] There is a growing body of opinion that, since the board decides matters intimately affecting the academic lives of faculty and students, it ought to participate in those decisions. Considered in terms of corporate boards of directors, there is nothing very revolutionary

---

[4] In Chap. 12 (pp. 219–221), the question of faculty and student membership on the board was viewed in terms of the board's representativeness; here the emphasis is on conflict of interest.

in this concept. Employees of a corporation sit as its directors and so do individuals representing its major clientele. The similarity ceases, however, as soon as one sees the university board as an instrument of public interest. The corporate board has a narrow and self-serving purpose and, at least until very recently, its obligations to the public have been regarded as minimal. If one holds with the concept that college trustees are primarily *trustees* and not *managers,* then the introduction of special constituencies, such as students or faculty, to its membership constitutes a true conflict of interest.

A strong case can be made for the involvement of students and faculty in the decision-making process of the university. However, this kind of participation is much more effective in settings other than membership on the board of trustees.

THE FUNCTIONING OF BOARDS

Who decides what?

The modern university is an infinitely complicated set of human relationships. The seats of power are diffuse, and they change rapidly. The word *faculty* no longer describes a cohesive group with common motivation. Its members may come together under the impetus of crisis, but they will drop back into their daily routines as soon as the immediate issue is resolved or forgotten. Students may seek the scalp of the president one day and then show total apathy about the selection of his successor.[5]

The question "Who decides what?"[6] has no simple answer, and what answers there are will change with time. It is, nevertheless, a question of constant importance. The entire art of administration rests upon the capacity to make wise decisions that are broadly accepted. Many decisions are made by inaction; some of them are made better that way.[7] Most situations, however, demand clear decisions, and the failure to make them can be corrosive.

It is imperative, therefore, that the board of trustees be constantly alert to the importance of the issue of decision making. They must

[5] In the recent search for a president at Harvard, the selection committee sought the advice of 16,000 students. Only 196 responded.

[6] See Chap. 12 (pp. 221–224) for factors enhancing the quality of decisions made by the board.

[7] One recalls the intensity of the issue raised in 1967 as a result of cohabitation by a student at Barnard. It is less easy to remember how it was resolved. Inaction best suits such problems, because it is not possible for a university to legislate moral permissiveness.

be tough-minded in insisting that the whole governance process be sensible, realistic, and understandable. The response to "Power to the people" is "What power to what people?" It is not good to encourage people to think they are deciding something when in fact they are not. And perhaps the worst place of all to play such games is in the meetings of the board of trustees.

Yet that is exactly what happens at many universities, and for good reasons. In the face of conflicting claims on jurisdictions, the board's role in the decision-making process becomes more and more confused. On the one hand the board is frozen out of the process by the claims of constituency groups of faculty, students, and administrative management. On the other hand, this very competition among the constituencies tempts the board to become involved with detail, which is incompatible with its essential purpose as trustee of the total institution. The unfortunate result of this dilemma is that boards pretend to make decisions that are, in fact, predetermined.

Written rules

Some of the confusion about the decision-making process can be resolved by a set of written procedural rules. Most boards of trustees operate under a set of bylaws. These rules are only marginally useful, since they are usually too broadly stated to provide guidance when major issues of jurisdiction arise.

In a recent bath of publicity, the president of Ohio University questioned an action of his predecessor on the grounds that he had acted on a matter involving major policy without board authority; hence his action was invalid. It is difficult to imagine a president of a large university who is not constantly making "policy" decisions. Not many will have the supreme wisdom to enable them to stamp one decision "major" and another "minor." And one doubts that any set of written rules will provide that kind of judgment.

In addition to bylaws, many universities have elaborate academic statutes that attempt to codify procedure and to locate the decision-making authority. What emphasis a given board of trustees places upon these various written codes depends on the usage and customs of that university.

The president and the board

No matter how much attention is paid to the clarity of the board's internal structure, its composition, and its procedural rules, the manner in which it functions is to a large extent determined by its relationship with the president.[8]

Presidents have a way of leaping with amazing dexterity from a position of autocratic authority and professional expertise to one of boyish dependence on the ultimate authority of their boards. It is a staunch president who can consistently resist the temptation to use the board as a shield for his own unpopular decisions. And boards are likewise capable of some astonishing shifts of posture. They can move with alacrity from total support of the president to harsh criticism. We have seen this phenomenon recently in situations of campus crisis in which presidents have been called upon to deal with explosive and violent situations that are totally foreign to their experience as educators.

Boards need to remember that they have an important responsibility to the president, i.e., to shield him from public pressures. That position need not preclude criticism; friendly, consistent, and perceptive evaluation of the president's performance helps both the president and the university.[9]

Orientation of trustees

Few governing boards have any plans or programs for introducing newcomers on the board to the duties, usages, and customs of the office. Perhaps for this reason many trustees say that it takes two years before a new trustee becomes effective. The apprenticeship would not take that long were there any organized plan of orientation.

Orientation should include some or all of the following:

1   Knowledge of the essential written documents: catalogs, charter, legislation, bylaws, presidential reports, etc.

2   Familiarity with basic facts: history, size, costs, governance structure, administrative and faculty personnel, etc.

---

[8] The president's relationship to the board has also been treated in Chap. 12 (pp. 226–227).

[9] The difficulty in finding a setting suitable for such matters as discussing the president's performance suggests that boards might set brief meetings without the president as a regular procedure. Corporate directors accomplish this function on the golf course or over lunch, but such casual meetings are not usually available to university trustees.

3 Introduction to the literature of higher education: periodicals, books, educational meetings.[10]

4 Professional meetings: attendance at educational gatherings such as the Association of Governing Boards, American Association for Higher Education, etc.

"Better communications"

The prescription for curing all organizational ills these days is "better communications," but very little is said about how this prescription should be compounded. As far as trustees are concerned, one can suggest a few ingredients.

Open meetings Most boards persist in maintaining the privacy of their meetings, even though higher education has traditionally favored open deliberations. No one can possibly deny that a large measure of security goes with the cloistered atmosphere of the board room, but it does so at the price of suspicion and misunderstanding. More and more boards now recognize that meetings open to members of the academic community are not as awkward as they had imagined. It must be assumed, of course, that the privilege of deciding private matters in private is retained through the use of executive sessions.

Written material The board needs to be hard-nosed about setting the standards for the written material it receives prior to meetings. Otherwise it will suffer from glut or famine. The tendency to introduce a topic with inadequate data is not offset by excess verbiage.

The completion of the communication process takes place when the trustees read and absorb the material. If students came to class as ill prepared as some trustees come to board meetings, they would be ground up by the instructor.

Attendance It seems trivial to record that communications among the trustees themselves and between the board and other constituencies depends upon the physical presence of trustees at meetings. Yet it is surprising how reluctant boards are to set standards of attendance. In a recent trustee study, the writer found that 6 out of 30 trustees had not attended a single meeting in five years. Clearly,

---

[10] These published materials may be useful: Kelsey (1971); Rauh (1969, pp. 112–116); and Mayhew (1971).

boards need some guidelines for dealing with the ephemeral trustee.[11]

Organization for what?

The manner in which any body is organized is significant only to the extent that it contributes to the usefulness of that body. It is easy to lose sight of this essential purpose in a society surrounded by boards, investigative commissions, advisory groups, and fact finders. Therefore this chapter has stressed internal organization as an instrument for facilitating the board's function and as a structure to support its role. And so it follows that organization has meaning only when role and function are clear.

Organization is more than an array of officers, committees, and procedural rules. It is a set of human relationships that run in all directions within the complex university structure and outside it as well. Harmony and conflict develop between people; structure at its best can only foster the first and discourage the second.

It follows, therefore, that the structure must be able to accommodate change in these human relationships. The organization that is effective with one president or one era of public attitudes or one set of educational issues may not work at all with others. Boards of trustees are not immune to the volatile forces that impinge upon higher education.

---

[11] Universities have been surprisingly reluctant to adopt the corporate board's means for assuring attendance — that is, by paying fees.

Part Four
Conclusion

14. Missions and Organization: A Redefinition

by James A. Perkins

Universities have a bad case of organizational indigestion because they have swallowed multiple and conflicting missions. The remedy, assuming there is one, may be found in either of two broad approaches to reorganization—or in some combination of these two approaches.

One approach is to reduce or even eliminate one or more of the university's four major missions—teaching, research, public service, and the achievement of democratic community—stipulating those that should remain within the university and those that should be assumed by other types of institutions. The alternative is to assume that the missions will remain unchanged and that the organization will adapt itself to them.

As we review the arguments for and against the multimission university, we must bear in mind that, because of the diversity of institutions in the United States, no perfect single organizational model can be devised. The tension between competing pressures to eliminate functions or to introduce new organizational forms will doubtless continue with no final resolution. But a variety of new accommodations are possible—adjustments that will be as diverse as the institutions they serve.

Let us first examine the arguments for and against removing missions from the university in order to restore its manageability. Then we may be able to point to the most probable directions for university reorganization.

INSTRUCTION: THE INDISPENSABLE MISSION Of the university's various missions, instruction at both undergraduate and graduate levels is fundamental. Graduate and professional education added to undergraduate instruction distinguish the university from the college. A university without instruction is not a university. Thus we assume that instruction must remain the central mission of the university.

LARGE-SCALE RESEARCH: ON OR OFF CAMPUS? The cliché holds that instruction and research are reinforcing, not conflicting, functions. They can be; they sometimes are; but frequently they are not.

The conflict arises not from individual scholarship but from the requirements of large-scale research effort. For purposes of this analysis the distinction between the two endeavors is that large-scale research requires financial and administrative decisions at the college and university level, whereas scholarship decisions of this kind can be determined by the individual member of the faculty. Large-scale research generally requires outside funding and institutional commitments to external agencies, whereas individual scholarship can generally be conducted within the normal scope of faculty time and teaching commitments.

Scholarship as defined above is a necessary ingredient of good instruction. Teaching cannot remain fresh, interesting, or even relevant over any extended period of time without the discipline that comes from systematic reflection and writing—particularly if that writing can be subjected to the criticism of one's peers. However, scholarship can become an all-consuming end in itself. It can take time away from classroom instruction. And its results may not find their way into classroom lectures. Conversely, the teacher who devotes little time to scholarship because of interest in and sometimes overattention to students, particularly outside the classroom, may find the quality of his instruction degenerating.

In general, though, scholarship as we conceive it can be compatible with teaching; conflicts between teaching and scholarship can be kept in check by a department that encourages, through its hiring and promotion policies, a balance between the two activities.

The case for removal

The argument for the retention of scholarship and the transfer of large-scale research to nonuniversity bodies is strong from the point of view of instruction, particularly for the undergraduate student. The separation of research from the university would have greatest impact at the level of graduate studies. It is argued that the participation of graduate students in large-scale research projects is a learning experience of great importance. It can be. But what is it a learning experience for—instruction or research? Frequently graduate students working in a research enterprise are negatively prepared for teaching but positively conditioned for research. They are led down paths (and generally bound joyfully down these paths!) of increasing specialization and subject refinement. Since most discovery is the result of specialization, incentives toward the more general knowledge needed for undergraduate instruction are missing.

The distinction between the two modes of training graduate students is recognized in the terms *teaching assistant* and *research assistant*. The research assistant presumably divides his time between his studies and participation in a research project, while the teaching assistant presumably divides his time between graduate work and assisting the faculty with teaching chores. The research assistant belongs with the research function and therefore could presumably follow large-scale research enterprise out of the university. If such research were institutionalized off campus, the institutes might conceivably offer advanced degrees for graduate assistants. Otherwise the graduate research assistant would have to divide his time between his on-campus studies and his off-campus research project.

The university structure would be greatly simplified if large-scale research were reduced or dispensed with. On-campus research institutes with independent budgets and outside commitments could be largely eliminated. Those that remained at universities would presumably have sufficient instructional capability that they could not conveniently or logically fit into a departmental structure. Jurisdictional issues would surely remain in sufficient number to delight faculty politicians, but these issues would be framed by the mission of instruction rather than a conflict of missions. The current invidious distinction between research and teaching assistant, as well as that between the research and teaching professor, could be eliminated—at least as far as the university community is concerned.

There is also an economic argument for the transfer of large-scale research enterprise, since the full costs to the university are frequently not recovered from support agencies. And such transfer may well be argued from the point of view of achieving balance between humanistic and scientific studies.

The case against removal

There are strong counterarguments, however, to removing the

research mission from the university. As society becomes more complex and as technology continues to exert influence for change, graduate studies can easily become sterile if they are not in close touch with those who are advancing, not just transmitting, knowledge. Thus, powerful pressures exist for even closer connections between graduate study and large-scale research. The argument proceeds from the premises of the value of the product of interaction between teaching and research; the importance of graduate and postgraduate students to our advanced industrial society; and the advantage of having research administered by an established, impartial authority—thus removing, in theory at least, the taints of political purpose or partisan advantage. Today there is evidence of a temporary loss of interest and faith in research as a necessary ingredient in social and economic development. But unless we abandon our continuing dependence on technology itself, society will continue to demand that much large-scale research be conducted on campus.

There is, moreover, an economic argument for maintaining large-scale research on campus. Many research projects have more than paid their own way. The overhead on some contracts has been large enough to pay, for example, a substantial fraction of the president's salary. In some cases, support has covered the direct costs of faculty who are giving key undergraduate courses. Thus, research programs with outside funding have offered substantial financial incentives to attract and to keep competent professors. Should large-scale research be removed from the campus, the university itself might lose needed funds.

Interestingly, in research institutes that are independent of universities, professional personnel work to establish connections with university colleagues in the same profession. Separation may well lead back to attempts to bridge the efforts of independent research agencies and the university. In many continental universities, the tendencies have been in this direction. For all these reasons and more, *The Nonprofit Research Institute* (Orlans, 1972), a report prepared for the Carnegie Commission on Higher Education, concluded that much large-scale research will remain within university jurisdiction.

These in summary are the arguments pro and con the removal of large-scale research from the campus. We shall examine the most probable direction for the future of research in a later section, but first we turn to arguments concerning another of the university's major missions.

SERVICE: TO ELIMINATE OR NOT TO ELIMINATE? The university today provides a variety of social services to students and public services to society. Much of its organizational dislocation stems from the complexity of managing these service functions while simultaneously managing an academic enterprise. Thus such functions may be logical candidates for removal from the university. First we shall examine the complex of services offered to the internal university community; then we turn to public service.

Services to the Internal Community Most United States universities are complete and rounded communities. Residences, restaurants, hospitals, amusement centers, and parking spaces—all these services are provided because the university is perceived as a social community and not just as a community of scholars. But the two notions of community—social and academic—are different. Landlord-tenant relationships are just not the same as teacher-student relationships.

The case for removal
Because it is widely believed that the residential college has distinctive educational values, faculties have been concerned with housing arrangements and their contribution to education. But educational considerations have a tendency to overlap with considerations of cost and style of service. Student complaints about the quality of meals or about housing arrangements that interfere with their educational progress are likely to appear on the agenda of faculty committees. And since such problems are likely to cut across the policies of the departments of housing and dining, they usually require the attention of a vice-president, president, or board of trustees.

Similarly, almost all internal services required to support a more or less self-sufficient community—the student clinic, the bookstore, and the placement office—create organizational complications because there is a dual interest in the service qua service and the service as a contribution to the educational community.

If these services were removed from university administration and placed under independent management, there would be a drastic reduction in the number of faculty committees, an even larger reduction in the number of top administrative officers, and considerably less strain on the nervous systems of those who must settle the frequently abrasive conflicts between academic values and service efficiency.

Apparently, the university's functioning would be simplified by the removal of these functions. But aside from the difficulties of undoing present arrangements, there is a larger difficulty of dealing with the great pressures for maintaining precisely those connections that would be cut. We must be clear about what these pressures are.

The case against removal

First, whatever its disadvantages, the residential college is still presumed to make important — indeed indispensable — contributions, directly and indirectly, to education. It provides an environment that is supposed to promote interaction between student and teacher outside the classroom. Moreover, by the fact of its being a geographic community as well as a learning community, it provides an atmosphere that is presumably free of influences that interfere with the educational process.

Another factor that will contribute to the maintenance of the status quo is the negative experiences of those who have tried to remove such functions from university management. Housing and dining arrangements provided and administered by organizations outside the university are rarely salubrious. They are often expensive and they constitute a continuous source of abrasion between the university and local authorities. It is by no means clear that the hotel functions can be more easily handled outside the campus jurisdiction than within the university.

One other pressure to maintain the residential campus is the investment that has already been made — and continues to be made — in such arrangements. More university-owned housing, frequently designed to accommodate instructional activities, is being built, and the investment in dormitories and other physical facilities is so large as to preclude their early abolition. Similarly, the presence of a football stadium seating 50,000 practically guarantees the continuation of intercollegiate football. In these cases, as in other, facilities dictate policy as much as policy dictates facilities.

Services to the Public

The process of removing public service activities from the university would be complicated, to say the least. Just as teaching, scholarship, and research are part of a spectrum of activity with no sharp dividing lines, so is public service, which ranges from individual faculty consultation through special ad hoc research or training projects to the highly sophisticated interconnections developed by the land-grant institutions between the university, the private sector, and government.

The case for removal

The arguments for eliminating public service from the spectrum of university activities are based on academic and ideological values. Public service, like large-scale research, involves time, talents, and resources of the university community in many ways not directly connected to the educational process. The benefits to the university may be obscure—especially to students and faculty not directly involved in the service.

Moreover, public service has compounded organizational problems since decisions to undertake and implement these services are usually made at the top administrative level rather than at the departmental level.

The most persistent dilemma of public service, however, is that the university finds itself in the impossible position of defending its claim to neutrality while simultaneously serving some public purpose. But institutional commitment often precludes institutional neutrality. How can an institution function as a place for debate on all sides of an issue when the institution itself is committed to one or another position in the issues under debate? And in a society torn by great social issues it is no longer widely agreed that to undertake a service sponsored by government is necessarily an action in the public interest. Indeed, many today feel that to do so is to do a disservice to society at large.

Part of the university's public service would be curtailed automatically if large-scale research moved out from under the university's umbrella. Most of the faculty's consulting activity is closely intertwined with research—particularly large-scale research. Sometimes consultation, special training programs, and research projects form a network of activities that justify and support one another but have only marginal or occasional connection with instruction. Presumably, if research (not scholarship) were carved away from the university, a great deal of service activity would go with it, and only consultation on matters with a direct and demonstrable connection with instruction would remain.

It would, however, be much more difficult to unravel the carefully developed interconnections between farms, laboratories, public agencies, private associations, and county, state, and federal governments in the field of agriculture. Realistically there is no place where this chain can be broken except perhaps in laboratories clearly committed to basic research in botany, zoology, or biology generally. Such a separation admittedly would be painful, but it could be manageable once biology had been institutionalized on an interdepartmental basis. One argument for such reorganization is that biology must be freed from too great a dependence on agriculture so that it can develop increasing interconnections with chemistry, physics, the medical sciences, and engineering.

In other fields, the problem of disentanglement would not be so severe because it has not been so far advanced. Medical schools, like agricultural schools, have generally maintained a close interrelationship between research and clinical activity. But the issue of whether the current combination of activities in the medical college represents an optimum arrangement is still unresolved. There are those who argue that too close attention to patient care or even public health activities has interfered with the development of a proper research base for medical science. On the other hand, some argue that medical faculties are too preoccupied with laboratory specialization and not enough with either the whole man or the whole society. Whether the medical field should be separated into its research and public service components has hardly been examined, but such an examination would need to be made if the disentangling model of the university organization were followed.

The devolution of the public service function might ultimately require that colleges of agriculture and medicine be established as completely independent institutions. Few medical schools have really close relations with other parts of their universities, and agricultural colleges have frequently suffered from an inferiority complex induced by the attitudes of the liberal disciplines. Thus, in both cases, autonomy might have its advantages.

The case against removal
Clearly, disentanglement could be accomplished only at great cost, and the pressures against removing public service from the university are many. It may be almost impossible to turn back the clock; unraveling the government of the multiversity may be as impossible as returning city management to the form of the New England town meeting. The professoriate has become indispensable to the opera-

tions of government and business. Consequently, though students may have been neglected in the process, the content of instruction has benefited in relevance and liveliness.

Consultation and public service activities of the university are now part of the increased interdependence of our institutions that provides much of the dynamic energy that our intellectual growth brings to our society. Teachers who are involved in research or public service are needed to understand, explain, and help manage an increasingly complex society. To sever these connections might fatally damage not only the institutions concerned but also the society they support. As Lewis Mayhew has written: "When an institution is unresponsive to the fundamental demands of and needs of its society, it loses its vitality and becomes irrelevant" (1968, p. 3).

THE UNIVER-
SITY AS A
DEMOCRATIC
COMMUNITY

The newest mission of the university is to be a model of the ideal democratic community. This requirement has already had a profound effect on university organization and ways of doing business.

It has pulled the board of governors closer to the university community, exerted pressure against the idea of the self-perpetuating board and for the election of faculty and students to board membership, and has inspired the doctrine that the board should be the agent of the university community rather than the agent of society.

The democratic tenets of equality, election, and participation have also acted as a torque on the management of academic affairs. The faculty senate is giving way to the university senate, and the departmental meeting is evolving from a faculty caucus to a device for consensus making involving teacher and student.

Behind these changes is the notion that if the university is a community it must be a democratic community. A board *appointed* by outside authority sounds like colonialism. A president *appointed* by such a board sounds like the colonial governor. An administration *appointed* by such a president sounds like the colonial civil service. A faculty not accountable to the community sounds like the seventeenth-century aristocracy. And the students, the largest group in the university community, have not until recently been considered a part of the structure of the enterprise at all—rather, as Clark Kerr has said, they may feel they are the "lumpen proletariat" (1966, p. 104).

Democratic procedure has engulfed almost every aspect of the community. If the university is seen as a democratic polis, all parts of the university must be accountable to the general will as described and expressed through university structures whose members are elected by the community. But if the university is seen as a community of scholars, the faculty is not just one part of the university, it is the *chief* part; all other parts are secondary and the faculty is in no sense accountable to such others.

While the legitimacy of this new mission is subject to argument, it is hard to believe that the democratic tide can be reversed by appeals to nondemocratic requirements of the traditional faculty-student-administration relation. It may be that the organizational complexity resulting from the democratic mission can be alleviated only by a reduction in the university's role as a social community, and that the social community can be reduced in scale only by giving up residential features, pushing large-scale research off the campus, and making instruction the primary focus of attention.

THE BALANCE SHEET The alternative lines of resolution have been identified. The arguments pro and con the retention of current university missions have been stated in summary form. We now make some tentative judgments about the prospects for retention or modification of missions and then suggest the directions of organizational change.

Instruction and Scholarship We start with the mission of instruction and individual scholarship at graduate and undergraduate levels and including professional schools. Few would argue that instruction is not the central mission of the university, and we assume that it will remain so in the future.

Research In the short run, the tendency will probably be *against* expansion of the university's research commitment and *for* the transfer of large-scale research responsibility to other nonprofit or private commercial corporations or to public laboratories or institutes. Organizational arrangements for the decades ahead should acknowledge that, in addition to instruction and scholarship, there will be substantial elements of large-scale research on a slowly diminishing scale. The areas of reduction will depend largely on the tides of national interest.

Residential Campus A movement away from the residential campus and a consequent decline in the idea of the university as a geographic community are to be expected. Many forces will continue to move the university in this direction. The professions will continue to press for national or international societies based on subject matter rather than geographic propinquity. The *scientific community* will be a more meaningful term to the specialist than the *community of scholars* at Harvard or Oxford.

The independently owned and operated apartment house will replace the dormitory as the desired living arrangement for more and more students. The student of 18 has successfully asserted his right to be treated as an adult and wishes to live like one. In addition, new forms of instruction, external examination, and the granting of degrees for noncampus learning will increase and further undermine the idea of the university as a geographic community. Finally, with the relaxation of parietal rules and the student unrest of the late sixties, the notion of the residential campus as a necessary ingredient in character building is disappearing along with the doctrine of *in loco parentis.*

Whereas large-scale research will slowly gravitate to the commercial and public institution, the trappings of the campus as community or polis will probably shrink at a faster pace. Since existing facilities are a pressure for the status quo, those universities with the most complete facilities will find the adjustment most difficult and the financial consequences most serious. There is an uneasy feeling that the residential university has become too topheavy with buildings and supporting facilities that require increasingly heavy maintenance charges. *The future belongs to those instructional systems with the smallest overhead per student.*

Public Service   The public service activities of the university have an uncertain future. To the extent that research is transferred out of the university, the public service activities of the university will decrease. But there are no signs that the completely integrated public services of professional schools such as agriculture, medicine, veterinary medicine, and engineering will disappear. It would be so difficult to disentangle research, service, instruction, and consultation that it will not be attempted. Therefore those schools in land-grant institutions will probably either stay within the university *in toto* or leave *in toto.* The best guess is that they will stay within the university for the indefinite future. It may be that those public service activities that are benign in terms of new social priorities, such as environmental protection and urban redevelopment, will remain. Those that support more security-oriented aspects of the national interest may be curtailed.

Ideal Democracy The mission of the ideal democratic society will remain in full force whatever the changes in the missions of research or public service. The tenets of the democratic idea—equality, representation, and election—will continue to exert their influence on internal arrangements; courts will continue to review cases involving democratic concepts of due process; and governments will use their considerable influence to press against nondemocratic practices such as racial or sexual discrimination.

Movement toward Systems Finally, the trend from the individual autonomous campus to systems of higher education managed by quasi-public coordinating boards will have a direct influence on the organization of the university. As in all systems of coordination, there will be complex interplay between headquarters and individual institutions. For example, area studies on any individual campus will be determined by the area study coordinator at headquarters, space research by NASA (the national coordinator), etc. Important decisions will be made, therefore, with the knowledge of the campus authority but without his direction. Both the university board and its chief executive will, as a consequence, be increasingly subordinated to a web of influence and controls that involve both lower and higher authority. This development will persist, expand, and determine the direction of affairs on the campus.

Summary The changes in mission will look something like this:

1 Instruction will remain the central mission but student choice will increasingly outweigh faculty prescription.

2 Large-scale research will gradually shift to nonuniversity institutions.

3 The residential campus will give way to off-campus living systems. Nonresidential institutions such as community colleges will have a comparative cost advantage which will become increasingly attractive.

4 Service to the public will decline dramatically in some areas, such as defense and space; continue with minor modifications in agriculture, medicine, and engineering; and may substantially increase in urban affairs, ecology, race relations, and international organizations, both public and private.

5 The democratic impulse will dominate systems of governance leading to representation, election, and consensus rather than appointment and decision making by highest independent legal authority.

6 The locus of power to plan and allocate resources will continue to gravitate toward the managers of systems and from private to quasi-public and public coordinating bodies.

FUTURE DIRECTIONS With missions redefined, it will perhaps be possible to project directions for the most probable organizational change. We must repeat that the pluralism of higher education in the United States will preclude our suggesting general models of development for all institutions.

Boards of individual institutions will become less powerful. Boards are caught between two forces and are asked to serve two masters. If they maintain their position as agents of society, they will surrender their internal influence to universitywide bodies that claim authority as the only legitimate representatives of university communities. If boards become agents of the university, changing their membership and election procedures in response to campus demands, they will lose their influence as spokesmen for the state and society and their capacity to protect the university from outside pressures.

University organizations that are representative of the various internal constituencies will emerge. Their membership will be elected and their decisions will be difficult to contest. Boards of governance will therefore be reduced to ratifying institutional decisions rather than making them.

The president will become an elected official, nominated by the university senate and approved by the board, for a limited term. He will be the consensus maker, the broker between constituencies, a link—but not the only link—between the board and the senate. He will become increasingly less visible as a personality, following the course of the corporate executive, who decades ago changed from visible leader to invisible gyroscope. The president will become, in short, the organization man.

Chief administrative officers will also be selected with the participation of those who work under them. Administrative accountability will become the order of the day, and more and more officers will be elected or appointed with the participation of their own constituencies.

Administration will become more simplified as the missions of research and public service are reduced in scope and as the residential features of the university are progressively abandoned. Faculty committees now dealing with the problems of housing and other facilities will be disbanded and conflicts about service functions versus academic values will correspondingly be reduced.

The university will become less of a community in the sense of a geographic and social entity as it becomes more of a community based on professional interest. The idea of the community of scholars lost its geographic imperative decades ago. The faculty member's closest ties are no longer necessarily to colleagues in the same department or on the same campus; rather, they extend to national and international associations of professional peers. For faculty and students, too, the campus is becoming a convenience rather than a necessity.

The university will take many new forms, once freed of its geographic definition. A variety of new organizations will burst forth reflecting the new realities of greater numbers of students, increased costs, and demands for relevance. In time, technology will provide possibilities for the development of new structures. Education will increasingly come to the student, at home or at work. Classroom instruction will require less time and attention. Examinations and degrees will relate more to performance than to class attendance.

The new organizations are just beginning to emerge. TV classrooms, the open university, industry-based education, training and retraining by cassettes, degrees granted by nonuniversity authorities—all these developments foreshadow the birth, perhaps the rebirth, of a new kind of higher education.

We have purposely described these developments as tendencies. In most institutions present arrangements will continue largely intact. The form will remain even as the substance is disappearing. But the interim—while structure catches up with change—will require a new style of management, far more political in style. Votes must be sought, conflicting interests resolved, accountability of performance accepted and acted upon. And just as the city must relate to the state and federal governments, so too must the new university become not only internally accountable to its constituencies but externally accountable to society. This volume may well have provided some guideposts for this redefinition of missions and organization.

References

Accredited Institutions of Higher Education, published for the Federation of Regional Accrediting Commissions of Higher Education, by the American Council on Education, Washington, D.C., 1970.

American Council on Education: *A Fact Book on Higher Education,* Washington, D.C., 1971.

American Heritage Dictionary of the English Language, American Heritage Publishing Co., Inc., New York. © Copyright 1969, 1970, 1971 by American Heritage Publishing Co., Inc.

Arensberg, Conrad M., and Solon T. Kimball: *Culture and Community,* Harcourt, Brace and World, Inc., New York, 1965.

Assembly on University Goals and Governance: "Faculty Members and Campus Governance," a national invitational workshop sponsored by the Assembly on University Goals and Governance, Carnegie Commission on Higher Education, and Center for Research and Development in Higher Education, University of California, Berkeley, February 17–18, 1971, Houston, Tex.

Bakke, E. Wight: "Concept of the Social Organization," in Mason Haire (ed.), *Modern Organization Theory,* John Wiley & Sons, Inc., New York, 1959.

Banfield, Edward C.: *The Unheavenly City,* Little, Brown and Company, Boston, Mass., 1970.

Barnard, Chester: *The Functions of the Executive,* Harvard University Press, Cambridge, Mass., 1948.

Bell, Daniel: "By Whose Right? A Memorandum on the Governance of Universities in the 1970s," n.d.

Berdahl, Robert O.: *Statewide Coordination of Higher Education,* American Council on Education, Washington, D.C., 1971.

Bloland, H.: *Higher Education Associations in a Decentralized Education*

System, Center for Research and Development in Higher Education, University of California, Berkeley, 1969.

Bogert, George S.: "Faculty Participation in American University Government," *American Association of University Professors Bulletin,* vol. 31, no. 4, pp. 72–82, Winter 1945.

Bourricaud, François: "Plenary Sessions of the Conference on Higher Education in Industrial Societies," in *Notes on Daedalus Conference,* sponsored by *Daedalus* and the Ford Foundation, Paris, June 26–28, 1969.

Bourricaud, Francois: *Universités à la Dérive,* Stock, Paris, 1971.

Brody, Alexander: *The American State and Higher Education,* American Council on Education, Washington, D.C., 1935.

Brook, G. L.: *Modern University,* Transatlantic Arts, Inc., Levittown, N.Y., 1965.

Burnett, Howard J. (ed.): *Interinstitutional Cooperation in Higher Education,* College Center of the Finger Lakes, Corning, N.Y., 1969.

Burns, N.: "Accreditation," in *Encyclopedia of Educational Research,* The Macmillan Company, New York, 1960.

Byse, Clark: "The University and Due Process: A Somewhat Different View," *American Association of University Professors Bulletin,* vol. 54, no. 2, June 1968.

Caplow, Theodore, and Reece J. McGee: *The Academic Market Place,* Basic Books, Inc., New York, 1958.

Cartter, Allan M.: *An Assessment of Quality in Graduate Education,* American Council on Education, Washington, D.C., 1966.

Cartter, Allan M.: "All Sail and No Anchor," *The Key Reporter,* vol. 36, no. 2, pp. 2ff., Winter 1970–71.

Cheit, Earl F.: *The New Depression in Higher Education,* McGraw-Hill Book Company, New York, 1971.

Clark, Burton: "Belief and Loyalty in College Organization," *Journal of Higher Education,* vol. 42, no. 6, pp. 499–515, June 1971.

Cleveland, Harlan: "The Dean's Dilemma: Leadership of Equals," *Public Administration Review,* vol. 20, no. 1, pp. 22–27, Winter 1960.

Coleman v. Wagner College, 429 R. 2d 1120 (2nd Cir., 1970).

Columbia University: *The Role of the Trustees of Columbia University,* adopted by the trustees, November 4, 1957.

Commission on the Government of the University of Toronto: *Toward Community in University Government,* University of Toronto Press, Toronto, 1970.

Cooke, Morris L.: *Academic and Industrial Efficiency,* Carnegie Foundation for the Advancement of Teaching, Bulletin No. 5, 1910.

Corson, John J.: *The Governance of Colleges and Universities,* McGraw-Hill Book Company, New York, 1960.

Corson, John J.: "Social Change and the University," *Saturday Review,* vol. 53, no. 2, pp. 76ff., January 10, 1970.

Cowley, W. H.: *Professors, Presidents, and Trustees,* unpublished manuscript, 1964 and 1971.

Dartmouth College v. Woodward (1819), 17 U.S. 518 (4 Wheaton 518).

Davis, John P.: *Corporations,* Capricorn Books, G. P. Putnam's Sons, New York, 1961.

Dixon v. Alabama State Board of Education, 294 F. 2d 150, 157 (5th Cir., 1961), *cert.* 368 U.S. 930.

Dressel, Paul L., and Donald J. Reichard: "The University Department: Retrospect and Prospect," *Journal of Higher Education,* vol. 41, no. 5, pp. 387–402, May 1970.

Duff, Sir James F., and Robert O. Berdahl: *University Government in Canada: Report of a Commission Sponsored by the Canadian Association of Universities and Colleges of Canada,* University of Toronto Press, Toronto, 1966.

Education Commission of the States: *Higher Education in the States,* Denver, Colo., 1971.

Epstein, L.: "The State University: Who Governs," paper delivered at 66th annual meeting of the American Political Science Association, September 1970.

Esteb v. Esteb (1926), 138 Washington 174, 244, p. 264.

Fels, William C.: "College Usage," *Columbia University Forum,* vol. 2, no. 3, Spring 1959.

Forsberg, Donald G., and William E. Pearce: *Liberal Arts Departments at Syracuse University, 1873–1966,* Syracuse University, Program in Higher Education, unpublished research report, 1966.

Glenny, L., et al.: *A Guide to Statewide Coordination of Higher Education,* Center for Research and Development in Higher Education, University of California, Berkeley, 1971.

Goffman, Erving: *Asylums,* Aldine Publishing Company, Chicago, 1961.

Hamilton, Madison, and Jay: *The Federalist,* Willey Book Company, New York, 1901.

Hartnett, R.: "College and University Trustees: Their Backgrounds, Roles, and Educational Attitudes," in C. Kruytbosch and S. Messinger, *The State of the University,* Sage Publications, Beverly Hills, Calif., 1968.

Harvard Committee: *General Education in a Free Society,* Harvard University Press, Cambridge, Mass., 1946.

"Harvard Professors Rebuke Those Who Attack Magazine Author," *The Boston Globe,* November 25, 1971.

Hearn, James J., and Hugh L. Thompson: "Who Governs in Academia," *The Journal of General Education,* vol. 22, no. 2, pp. 123–137, July 1970.

Heiss, Ann M.: *Challenges to Graduate Schools,* Jossey-Bass, Inc., San Francisco, 1970.

Heyns, Roger: "Berkeley Today and Tomorrow," McEnerney Lecture, University of California, Berkeley, May 24, 1971.

Hicks, F. W.: "Constitutional Independence and the State University," unpublished doctoral dissertation, University of Michigan, Ann Arbor, 1963.

Hillery, George A., Jr.: "Definitions of Community: Areas of Agreement," *Rural Sociology,* vol. 20, no. 2, pp. 111–123, June 1955.

Hodgkinson, Harold L.: "The Next Decade," in Harold L. Hodgkinson, and L. Richard Meeth (eds.), *Power and Authority: Campus Governance in Transformation,* Jossey-Bass, Inc., San Francisco, 1971.

Hurtubise, R., and D. Rowat: *The University, Society and Governments: The Report of the Commission on the Relations Between Universities and Governments,* University of Ottawa Press, Ottawa, 1970.

Katz, D., and R. Kahn: *The Social Psychology of Organizations,* John Wiley & Sons, Inc., New York, 1966.

Kelsey, Roger R.: *AAHE Bibliography on Higher Education,* American Association for Higher Education, Washington, D.C., 1971.

Kerr, Clark: *The Uses of the University,* Harper & Row Publishers, Incorporated, New York, 1966.

Kingsbury, A. M.: *A History of Cornell,* Cornell University Press, Ithaca, N.Y., 1962.

Lee, Eugene C., and Frank M. Bowen: *The Multicampus University,* McGraw-Hill Book Company, New York, 1971.

Letwin, William: "Democracy and the English University," *The Public Interest,* no. 13, pp. 139–150, Fall 1968.

Lewis, Ewart K.: Phi Beta Kappa Address, Oberlin College, Oberlin, Ohio, 1956.

Lipset, S. M.: "The Activist: A Profile," *The Public Interest,* no. 13, pp. 39–51, Fall 1968.

Lowi, Theodore J.: *The Politics of Disorder,* Basic Books, Inc., New York, 1971.

Lunsford, T.: "University Governance by Rules: Socio-Legal Issues," in R. Schwartz and J. Skolnick (eds.), *Society and the Legal Order,* Basic Books, Inc., New York, 1970.

"The Man from Mars," *Dun's,* vol. 71, no. 41, February 1971.

McConnell, T. R.: "Faculty Participation in College and University Governance," Center for Research and Development in Higher Education, University of California, Berkeley, August 1969. (Mimeographed.)

McConnell, T. R.: *The Redistribution of Power in Higher Education,* Center for Research and Development in Higher Education, University of California, Berkeley, 1971.

McGrath, Earl J.: "The Evolution of Administrative Officers in Institutions of Higher Education in the United States from 1860 to 1933," dissertation, University of Chicago, Chicago, 1936.

McGrath, Earl J.: *Should Students Share the Power?* Temple University Press, Philadelphia, 1970.

Marjorie Webster Junior College, Inc. v. Middle States Association of Colleges and Secondary Schools, Inc., 302 F. Supp. 459 (D.D.C. 1969) Reversed 432 F. 2d 650 (D.C. Cir., 1970), *cert. denied* 39 U.S.L.W. 3272 (U.S., December 21, 1970) (No. 751).

Mayhew, Lewis (ed.): *Higher Education in the Revolutionary Decades,* McCutchan Publishing Corporation, Berkeley, Calif., 1968.

Mayhew, Lewis B.: *The Literature of Higher Education,* Jossey-Bass, Inc., San Francisco, Calif., 1971.

Meyerson, Martin: "Plenary Sessions of the Conference on Higher Education in Industrial Societies," in *Notes on Daedalus Conference,* sponsored by *Daedalus* and the Ford Foundation, Paris, June 26–28, 1969.

Meyerson, Martin: "New Paths to New Destinations," *Saturday Review,* vol. 53, no. 2, pp. 54ff., January 10, 1970.

Minar, David W., and Scott Greer: *The Concept of Community: Readings with Interpretations,* Aldine Publishing Company, Chicago, 1969.

Moore, R.: *A Guide to Higher Education Consortiums, 1965–66,* U.S. Department of Health, Education and Welfare, Office of Education, Washington, D.C., 1967.

Moos, M., and F. Rourke: *The Campus and the State,* The Johns Hopkins Press, Baltimore, Md., 1959.

Morison, S. E. (ed.): *The Development of Harvard University,* Harvard University Press, Cambridge, Mass., 1930.

Morison, S. E.: *The Founding of Harvard College,* Harvard University Press, Cambridge, Mass., 1935.

Munroe, James B.: address to the Conference of Trustees of American Colleges and Universities, reprinted in J. McKeen Cattell (ed.), *University Control,* Science Press, New York, 1913.

National Center for Educational Statistics: *Education Directory: Higher Education — 1970-71,* 1971.

National Science Foundation: *Federal Support to Universities, Colleges, and Selected Nonprofit Institutions, Fiscal Year 1969,* 1970.

Nisbet, Robert A.: *Community and Power,* Oxford University Press, New York, 1962.

O'Neil, Robert: "Higher Education as an Administrative System: Law Making and Law Enforcement by Amateurs," speech before AALS Administrative Law Round Table, December 28, 1969.

O'Neil, Robert M.: "The Eclipse of Faculty Autonomy," Assembly on University Goals and Governance, Houston, Tex., February 18, 1971.

Orlans, Harold: *The Nonprofit Research Institute: Its Origin, Operation, Problems and Prospects,* McGraw-Hill Book Company, New York, 1972.

Page's Ohio Revised Code, Section 3342.22 (effective September 6, 1970).

Parsons, Talcott: "The Strange Case of Academic Organization," *Journal of Higher Education,* vol. 42, no. 6, pp. 486–495, June 1971.

Perkins, James A.: *The University in Transition,* Princeton University Press, Princeton, N.J., 1966.

"The Place and Function of Faculties in College and University Government," *American Association of University Professors Bulletin,* vol. 39, no. 2, pp. 300–318, Summer 1953.

Quincy, Josiah: *The History of Harvard University,* 2 vols., Crosby, Nichols, Lee and Company, Boston, Mass., 1860.

Rashdall, Hastings: *Universities of Europe in the Middle Ages,* 3 vols., F. M. Powicke and A. B. Emden (eds.), Oxford University Press, London, 1936.

Rauh, Morton A.: *The Trusteeship of Colleges and Universities,* McGraw-Hill Book Company, New York, 1969.

Reeves, F. W., and J. D. Russell: *College Organization and Administration,* Board of Education, Disciples of Christ, Indianapolis, Ind., 1929.

Report of the American Bar Association Commission on Campus Government and Student Dissent, American Bar Foundation, Chicago, 1970.

Riesman, David: *Constraint & Variety in American Education,* Doubleday Anchor Books, Doubleday & Company, Inc., Garden City, N.Y., 1958.

"The Role of Faculties in College and University Government," *American Association of University Professors Bulletin,* vol. 34, no. 1, pp. 55–66, Spring 1948.

Roose, Kenneth D., and Charles J. Anderson: *A Rating of Graduate Programs,* American Council on Education, Washington, D.C., 1970.

Rudolph, Frederick: *Mark Hopkins and the Log: Williams College 1836–1872,* Yale University Press, New Haven, Conn., 1956.

Sanders, Irwin T.: *The Community: An Introduction to a Social System,* 2d ed., The Ronald Press Company, New York, 1966.

Seeley, John R.: *The University in America,* Center for the Study of Democratic Institutions, Santa Barbara, Calif., 1967.

Seller, M. Charles: "The American College Public Relations Association," dissertation, Pennsylvania State University, 1963.

Shils, Edward: "Plenary Sessions of the Conference on Higher Education in Industrial Societies," in *Notes on Daedalus Conference,* sponsored by *Daedalus* and the Ford Foundation, Paris, June 26–28, 1969.

Shils, Edward: "The Hole in the Centre: University Government in the United States," *Minerva,* vol. 8, no. 1, January 1970.

Smith, Bruce L. R., and D. C. Hague, (eds.): *The Dilemma of Accountability in Modern Government: Independence versus Control,* St. Martin's Press, Inc., New York, 1971.

State v. Chase (1928), 175 Minnesota 259, 220 N.W. 951 at 957, citing *Sterling v. Regents* (1896), 110 Michigan 369, 68 N.W. 253.

Tinker v. Des Moines Independent Community School District (1969), 393 U.S. 503, 89 S. Ct. 733.

Trow, M.: "Expansion and Transformation of Higher Education," revised and expanded version of a paper read at the annual meeting of the American Sociological Association, Washington, D.C., September 1, 1970. (Mimeographed.)

University of Utah v. Board of Examiners (1956), 4 Utah 2d 408, 295 P. 2d 348.

Veysey, Laurence R.: *The Emergence of the American University,* University of Chicago Press, Chicago, 1965.

Waldo, Dwight: "The University in Relation to the Governmental-Political," *Public Administration Review,* vol. 30, no. 2, March/April 1970.

Warren, Roland L.: *The Community in America,* Rand, McNally & Company, Chicago, 1963.

Webster's Seventh New Collegiate Dictionary, G. & C. Merriam Company, Springfield, Mass. © 1971, Publishers of the Merriam-Webster Dictionaries.

Wildermuth, Ora L.: "A University Trustee Views the Academic Profession," *American Association of University Professors Bulletin,* vol. 35, no. 2, pp. 233–239, Summer 1949.

Williams, George: *Some of My Best Friends Are Professors,* Abelard-Schuman, Limited, New York, 1958.

Witmer, David R.: *The Rise of Administration in Higher Education,* Board of Regents of State Universities, Madison, Wis., 1966.

Wright, Benjamin F.: *The Contract Clause of the Constitution,* Harvard University Press, Cambridge, Mass., 1938.

The Yale Corporation: Charter and Legislation, Yale University, New Haven, Conn., 1952.

Index

This book was set in Vladimir by University Graphics, Inc.
It was printed on acid-free, long-life paper and bound by The
Maple Press Company. The designers were Elliot Epstein and
Edward Butler. The editors were Nancy Tressel and Cheryl Allen
for McGraw-Hill Book Company and Verne A. Stadtman and Terry Y.
Allen for the Carnegie Commission on Higher Education. Joe
Campanella supervised the production.